3 1192 01436 4531

621.3916 Weave.M
Weaver, Matthew.
Small form factor PCs.

SHORT TERM
LOAN

Make: PROJECTS

Small Form Factor PCs

First Edition

Matthew Weaver & Duane Wessels

621.3916
Weave. M

EVANSTON PUBLIC LIBRARY
1703 ORRINGTON AVENUE
EVANSTON, ILLINOIS 60201

O'REILLY

BEIJING · CAMBRIDGE · FARNHAM · KÖLN · PARIS · SEBASTOPOL · TAIPEI · TOKYO

MAR 1 9 2009

Small Form Factor PCs
by Matthew Weaver & Duane Wessels

Copyright © 2008 O'Reilly Media, Inc. All rights reserved.
Printed in U.S.A.

Published by Make:Books, an imprint of Maker Media, a division of
O'Reilly Media, Inc., 1005 Gravenstein Highway North, Sebastopol, CA 95472.

O'Reilly books may be purchased for educational, business, or sales promotional
use. For more information, contact our corporate/institutional sales department:
800-998-9938 or corporate@oreilly.com.

Print History: April 2008: First Edition

Publisher: Dale Dougherty
Associate Publisher: Dan Woods
Executive Editor: Brian Jepson
Creative Director: Daniel Carter
Designer: Gerry Arrington
Production Manager: Terry Bronson
Cover Photography: Duane Wessels

The O'Reilly logo is a registered trademark of O'Reilly Media, Inc. The MAKE:
Projects series designations, *Small Form Factor PCs*, and related trade dress are
trademarks of O'Reilly Media, Inc. The trademarks of third parties used in this
work are the property of their respective owners.

Important Message to Our Readers: Your safety is your own responsibility, including proper use of equipment and safety gear, and determining whether you have
adequate skill and experience. Chemicals, electricity, and other resources used for
these projects are dangerous unless used properly and with adequate precautions,
including safety gear. Some illustrative photos do not depict safety precautions or
equipment, in order to show the project steps more clearly. These projects are not
intended for use by children.

Use of the instructions and suggestions in *Small Form Factor PCs* is at your own
risk. O'Reilly Media, Inc. and the authors disclaim all responsibility for any resulting damage, injury, or expense. It is your responsibility to make sure that your
activities comply with applicable laws, including copyright.

ISBN-10: 0-596-52076-X
ISBN-13: 978-0-596-52076-2

Make: PROJECTS

Small Form Factor PCs

First Edition

Contents

Preface

Miniaturization has been one of the great success stories of computer engineering. Most of us know that the world's first computers, such as ENIAC and the various Mark Is, were huge machines that occupied whole rooms. By the early 1980s we had more powerful computers that sat on our desks. But personal computers stopped shrinking for the next 20 years or so. Why is my Pentium 4 system from 2005 about the same size as my Apple II from 1981?

One reason, of course, is that while the size of the computer remained the same, engineers were able to pack more into that space. Both processors and memory have increased in density over the years, generally following Moore's Law. Another reason is that equipment manufacturers now build more features into the hardware. My Pentium 4 motherboard includes built-in Ethernet, video, sound, USB, and FireWire, in addition to the old-fashioned serial and parallel ports. In the good ol' days, each of those would have required an expansion card of some sort. Finally, certain physical characteristics of our computer systems have remained the same over the years in the interest of compatibility. PCI cards are the same height as ISA expansion cards so that both fit in past and future computer cases. The 200 MB hard drive from my IBM PS/2 fits in the same bay as my P4's new 250 GB hard drive.

In recent years we have seen a renewed interest in miniaturization of computer systems. Companies such as VIA Technologies and Soekris Engineering were among the first to market small, low-power, general-purpose computer systems to individual consumers. People began to realize that certain tasks and applications, such as routing and firewalling, don't require super-fast systems. Who wants a big, hot, noisy computer in their home or office when a small, silent, mini-computer works just as well?

The phrase *small form factor* (or SFF) usually refers to personal computers with a small footprint. That is, a SFF PC has most of the same features as its standard-sized ancestor: fast processor, plenty of memory, hard drive, video, sound, etc. SFF PCs usually have fewer expansion options due to their smaller size, however.

In this book we consider even smaller, and less powerful, systems as small-form-factor computers. It would be a stretch to call them PCs, since many don't have hard drives, video, or sound. For some, it may be more appropriate to think of them as *embedded devices*, although that is another vague term. Whatever you or we call them, we think you'll enjoy learning about these small computers.

How to Use This Book

Our primary goal with this book is to expose you to a variety of small-form-factor computers and devices. We want to show you how they work, how they look (inside and outside), and how you can use them. We've come up with a number of projects that demonstrate their features and capabilities. We hope that you find the projects both interesting and useful.

Even if you're not interested in putting SFF computers to the uses that we've documented, you'll still find useful information in this book. For example, we'll show you how to load an operating system onto a Compact Flash card using TFTP and NFS, and how to bootstrap the OS onto a laptop hard drive from another PC. If you have other projects or applications in mind, the information in this book will help you select an appropriate platform. Our project descriptions aim to help you understand the advantages, and disadvantages, of the computers that we've used.

Another reason to read the book (and do the projects) is to see how easily you can get Linux and BSD operating systems running on non-x86-based processors. The four largest systems in the book have Intel x86 or x86-compatible processors. The smallest computers, on the other hand, use MIPS, PowerPC, ARM, and XScale processors. For some of them we'll even show you how to cross-compile your own programs.

Who Should Read This Book

We've written this book for people who like to tinker with both computer hardware and software. Along the same lines, we expect that you have a "do it yourself" attitude, either because you simply want to understand how something works, you want some extra features, or you don't trust product manufacturers to get it right. We also assume that you already have a minor fascination with miniature computers. If you still need some convincing, check out Chapter 1 for the list of things that we especially like about SFF computers.

Most of our projects involve some hardware assembly. For the most part, however, you won't need any fancy tools. Screwdrivers and pliers will come in handy. The only time you'd need a soldering iron is to build a custom cable or two.

We devote the most space in each chapter to providing detailed instructions on how to install and configure the software components. Every project is based on an open source operating system, including Linux, OpenBSD, and FreeBSD. Previous exposure to at least one of these operating systems will be helpful. However, we try to not make too many assumptions about your experience. With a little patience and perseverance, even first-time Unix users will be able to get up and running with our instructions.

Organization of This Book

This book includes eight individual small-form-factor projects, each in its own chapter. We've chosen to place chapters roughly in order of decreasing computer size. We'll start with a couple of Mini-ITX based systems and finish with a computer the size of a stick of gum. Here is a brief description of each computer:

Chapter 1, Introduction

The introduction to the book includes a brief discussion of what "small form factor" means and why you might be interested in using SFF systems. We also introduce you to the hardware components used for each project, including where to get them and about how much they cost.

Chapter 2, Digital Audio Jukebox

Here we turn a Mini-ITX motherboard, a little memory, a laptop hard drive, and an infrared receiver into a digital jukebox. The IR receiver allows you to control the jukebox with a standard universal remote. We'll show you how to install and configure Gentoo Linux, the XMMS audio player, and a few ancillary programs. If you're so inclined, we also have a few hints for mounting the components into an antique radio cabinet.

Chapter 3, Digital Video Recorder

In this project we show you how to build your own digital video recorder. We used the toaster-sized ST62K "XPC" from Shuttle and a TV tuner card from Hauppauge. Of all the projects in the book, this one requires the most CPU processing power and storage capacity. We use Gentoo Linux as the operating system and MythTV for the actual DVR application.

Chapter 4, Home Network Gateway

We'll show you how to build your own home (or small office) network gateway from OpenBSD and a Soekris net4501. This gateway protects the systems on your network with NAT and a state-of-the-art firewall. It also provides a local DNS server and DHCP if you so desire. The Soekris box uses a Compact Flash card for storage, which allows it to be silent and use very little power.

Chapter 5, Network Monitor

In this project we'll help you build a system that can monitor the health and status of a small home or office network. We'll use Snort for passive detection of malicious traffic, Nagios for active monitoring of hosts and links, and RRDTool to store and generate traffic graphs. Our operating system of choice is FreeBSD. The hardware is Soekris' net4801, which has a faster CPU than the net4501 and accepts a laptop hard drive.

Chapter 6, Wi-Fi Extender

We feature the Access Cube from 4G Systems in this chapter, which is a low-power, cube-shaped device designed for wireless applications. It has one Ethernet port and room for two Mini PCI Wi-Fi cards. We'll use it to build a wireless network router that you can use to extend the reach of existing wireless networks. The Access Cube runs a version of Linux called OpenEmbedded.

Chapter 7, Portable Bridging Firewall

This project is based on a small computer from Japan called OpenBlockS, which has a PowerPC processor, flash memory, serial port, and two Ethernet interfaces. For storage it uses either a Compact Flash card or a laptop hard drive. The OpenBlockS runs on 5 Volts DC, which means you can power it from a USB port. The operating system is SSD/Linux.

Chapter 8, Cheap Wi-Fi SSH Client

Here, we show you how to load new firmware on the ZipIt Wireless Messenger. The ZipIt is a cheap handheld device with a thumb keyboard, LCD display, Wi-Fi interface, and very good battery life. We think it makes a good little SSH client that you can take places where you'd rather not take your laptop computer.

Chapter 9, Bluetooth LED Sign

Our final project features the smallest computer in the book. The gumstix is a modular device running a customized Linux distribution. The particular model that we've chosen has a built-in Bluetooth interface. We'll use it to add Bluetooth connectivity to a scrolling LED message sign.

Recommended Reading

While reading this book, you may want to consult some of these other O'Reilly resources for more information.

- *Wireless Hacks,* Second Edition and/or *Linux Unwired*
- *Linux in a Nutshell* or *Linux Cookbook*
- *BSD Hacks*
- *Unix Power Tools,* Third Edition

Using Code Examples

This book is here to help you get your job done. In general, you may use the code in this book in your programs and documentation. You do not need to contact us for permission unless you're reproducing a significant portion of the code. For example, writing a program that uses several chunks of code from this book does not require permission. Selling or distributing a CD-ROM of examples from O'Reilly books *does* require permission. Answering a question by citing this book and quoting example code does not require permission. Incorporating a significant amount of example code from this book into your product's documentation *does* require permission.

We appreciate, but do not require, attribution. An attribution usually includes the title, author, publisher, and ISBN. For example: "*MAKE Projects Small Form Factor PCs*, by Duane Wessels and Matthew Weaver. Copyright 2008 O'Reilly Media, Inc., 059652076X."

If you feel your use of code examples falls outside fair use or the permission given above, feel free to contact us at *permissions@oreilly.com*.

Code samples and configuration files used in this book are available from **http://sffbook.org/code**.

Conventions Used in This Book

The following typographical conventions are used in this book:

Italic
> Used to indicate new terms, filenames, file extensions, and directories. For example, a path in the filesystem will appear as */Applications/Utilities*.

`Constant Width`
> Used to indicate commands, options, classes, keys, properties, utilities, and program names, and to show the contents of files or the output from commands.

`Constant Width Bold`
> Used in examples and tables to show commands or other text that should be typed literally by the user.

`Constant Width Italic`
> Used in examples and tables to show text that should be replaced with user-supplied values.

Acknowledgments

Duane would like to thank the following people and companies:

Mini-box.com for donating power adapters, an IDE-to-CF adapter, and other toys. Plat'Home in Japan (**http://www.plathome.co.jp/**) for donating the OpenBlockS/266. Shuttle (**http://www.shuttle.com/**) for donating the Zen ST62k XPC. O'Reilly Media for the gumstix.

My sincere thanks to all the technical reviewers who took the time to read drafts of the book and provide feedback: Craig Hughes, Dave Hylands, Joel Jaeggli, Ken Keelan, Fernando Maymi, Brendan White, and N. E. Whiteford. I know myself that it takes a lot of time and effort to be a reviewer. You have earned my respect and thanks for stepping up to the task.

As usual, it's been a pleasure to work with the folks at O'Reilly Media. Our editor, Brian Jepson, didn't give up on us even after missing a few deadlines. And to all the other top-notch O'Reilly folks, thanks for turning a bunch of XML mumbo-jumbo into a beautiful-looking book.

To my wife Anne: thank you for allowing me to take on and complete this book. You have no idea how much your support means to me. To Colin, who is just now turning one year old: remind me someday to tell you how much fun it was to work on the book during your naps, and after falling asleep with you each night. Sleep well Mugs!

Matthew would like to thank the following people and companies:

Pascal Dornier (**http://pcengines.ch/**) for donating a WRAP board. Shuttle (**http://www.shuttle.com/**) for donating an SN85G4 XPC, and AMD (**http://www.amd.com/**) for donating a suitable Athlon CPU. Mikrotik (**http://www.mikrotik.com/**) for donating a RouterBOARD 230.

I owe my largest debt of gratitude to Duane. He's not only responsible for the best work in this book, he's also given me a leg up more times than I deserve one.

Everyone at O'Reilly has been extremely patient and easy to work with. Brian Jepson has been invaluable in countless ways.

Lastly, thanks to my friends and colleagues for all their help: Amy Silver, for her support and advice; Jared Spiegel, for his guidance with the occasional technical jam; David Hardy, Tanya Bokat, and Greg Willson at Nedernet for everything.

Safari® Enabled

When you see a Safari® enabled icon on the cover of your favorite technology book, that means it's available online through the O'Reilly Network Safari Bookshelf.

Safari offers a solution that's better than e-books: it's a virtual library that lets you easily search thousands of top tech books, cut and paste code samples, download chapters, and find quick answers when you need the most accurate, current information. Try it for free at **http://safari.oreilly.com**.

How to Contact Us

You can contact the authors at **wessels@packet-pushers.com** and **matt@ice-nine.org**

Please address comments and questions concerning this book to the publisher:

O'Reilly Media, Inc.
1005 Gravenstein Highway North
Sebastopol, CA 95472
(800) 998-9938 (in the United States or Canada)
(707) 829-0515 (international or local)
(707) 829-0104 (fax)

We have a web page for this book, where we list errata, examples, and any additional information. You can access this page at:

http://www.oreilly.com/catalog/smallffpfg

To comment or ask technical questions about this book, send email to:

bookquestions@oreilly.com

For more information about our books, conferences, Resource Centers, and the O'Reilly Network, see our web site at:

http://www.oreilly.com

Introduction

In this book we present eight projects based around small form factor computers. Before delving into those projects, we'll spend a little time talking about what the term *small form factor* (SFF) means to us and why we think SFF systems are interesting. We also introduce the hardware for each project in this chapter, and finish up with a list of other SFF systems that we weren't able to include in this book.

What Is Small Form Factor?

For many computer enthusiasts, the phrase *small form factor* brings to mind cube-shaped systems about the same size as a stack of books. If you visit a site such as **www.sfftech.com**, you'll see many such systems. These days they generally have a Pentium 4 or Athlon processor; a couple of hard drive bays; one or two PCI expansion slots; built-in audio, video, Ethernet, USB, FireWire; and more. They make great desktop replacements and are often used as "media center" PCs.

This book takes the small-form-factor concept a few steps further to include the very wide range of small, general-purpose computer systems now available to individual consumers. Until recently, small computers were largely considered *embedded systems* that ran custom software applications. They were available only in large quantities to commercial users and system integrators.

The largest system that we use in this book is a Shuttle XPC. Coming in a close second is a Mini-ITX motherboard from Via Technologies. Those are the only systems in the book that require fans for cooling. Next in size are two Soekris boxes, which are smaller than this book. Getting even smaller, we have a couple of computers that are about the same size as an apple or an orange. Finally, we'll talk about two computers that can fit in your pocket.

So what do these systems have in common? One answer is that they all appeal to us simply because of their size. As geeks and gadget freaks, we are always fascinated with smaller and smaller phones, cameras, music players, and computers. The trend is always toward smaller and smaller devices, or at least toward packing more performance and functionality in the same space.

Another common characteristic is that they can all run open source software, such as Linux, BSD Unix, and a myriad of additional applications. This means that these SFF systems have a certain hardware openness as well. Even though the computers are extremely small, they are still "PC compatible." For the most part, you won't have to worry about buying, finding, or writing a special driver to use any of the built-in serial, audio, Ethernet, Wi-Fi, and other interfaces. Open source is not necessarily a requirement, however. You can certainly run Microsoft Windows on the Shuttle- and Mini-ITX-sized systems. You can probably even run DOS on the smaller, x86-based computers.

Why Small Form Factor?

You may be wondering why you should choose a SFF platform for a particular task instead of simply using a full-size PC. Most people choose smaller systems because they use less power, produce less noise, generate less heat, and, of course, take up less space. Not surprisingly, these characteristics are all related as well. Let's look at each characteristic in some depth:

Size

Size is an obvious characteristic of small computer systems. You might choose to use a Mini-ITX or XPC computer on your desktop simply because it takes up less space, leaving more room for your piles of papers. If you'd like to have a PC in your entertainment center, you probably want an enclosure that looks good and blends in with your other devices (DVD player, audio amp). Small computers are often popular with gamers who bring them to LAN parties or just over to a friend's house.

Data centers usually charge for both space and bandwidth. You can fit two Mini-ITX systems in a 19-inch-wide, 1U rack-mountable enclosure.

Anyone who regularly travels with computers is strongly motivated to find the smallest one to do the job. If the computer is small enough, you can carry it with you or fit it in your luggage. If your computers must be boxed and shipped, you'll appreciate the lower shipping costs from smaller, lighter systems. Maybe you'd like to put a computer in your car, on your sailboat, or even on your bicycle.

Smaller is also better for access points and surveillance systems, as you might want to stash a computer in a closet, up in the ceiling, on a wall, or outside somewhere. Finally, the prospect of wearable computers is becoming more and more realistic.

Power

The power demands of today's high-end desktops are, in our opinion, just a little outrageous. It is not uncommon to see 500 watt power supplies these days. One company has begun selling a 1 kilowatt PSU. If you have multiple computers in your home or office, you should really think about how much power they consume, and whether you can get by with something that uses less. For example, you don't need a power-hungry AMD Athlon or Intel Pentium 4 in your office for your firewall. A low-power (4 watts) computer described in this book can do the job just as well.

Power is also important when you think about uninterruptible power supplies and battery backups. When the power goes out, a 4 watt Soekris box will stay running about 10 times longer than a 40 watt Pentium III system.

The requirements of some SFF systems are low enough that power over Ethernet (which delivers a maximum of 12.95 watts) becomes a possibility. Another nifty idea is to supply power from a solar panel.

Heat

The heat generated by a computer is directly related to the power that it consumes. In simple terms, every watt that goes in comes out of the computer as waste heat. Data centers have huge air conditioners that move the heat from inside to outside, consuming even more power in the process. Heat may be an important factor for non-data-center environments, such as your home or office. During the winter, you can sort of use a computer to help keep your house warm, but during the summer, you'll be paying a little more to keep the house cool.

Not only do SFF systems generate less heat, many of them run without any fans at all, which brings us to...

Noise

There is also a rough correlation between the noise that a computer generates and the power that it consumes. The source of noise in most computers comes from things that spin: hard drives and fans. You can certainly build quiet full-sized desktop systems by using large, low-speed fans and power supplies with gigantic passive heat sinks. However, you'll have a hard time making them truly silent.

Many SFF systems, on the other hand, have no moving parts at all. Their processors are passively cooled, and they use flash memory, instead of a hard drive, for persistent storage.

Small Form Factor Systems

We use eight different SFF systems for the projects in this book, plus various accessories, cables, and connectors. Here's a description of each hardware platform, including where you can buy your own and how much you should expect to pay.

VIA EPIA ME6000

VIA Technologies has been one of the pioneers in the SFF movement. Their small Mini-ITX motherboards (17 cm × 17 cm) seem to be especially popular with case modders and people who build media PCs. VIA's Mini-ITX motherboards are different than most because they have a built-in Cyrix CPU. Cyrix processors are, for most purposes, compatible with the Intel x86 line. They are also known for running cooler than their Intel and AMD counterparts. While Cyrix CPUs may be very energy efficient, they do not have the same levels of performance as the Intel/AMD offerings.

In Chapter 2, we'll show you how to build a digital audio jukebox based on the VIA EPIA ME6000. The processor runs at 600 MHz, which is more than enough for decoding and playing music. The ME6000 has built-in audio, video, and Ethernet, as well as a number of other standard devices. To complete the project, we also use a laptop hard drive, one stick of SDRAM, and an infrared remote-control receiver. ME6000 motherboards are available from a number of online retailers for about $150.

We also use the PW-70A power adapter from Mini-box.com (a.k.a. Ituner Networks). The PW-70A takes the place of a standard ATX power supply. It takes a 12 Volt DC input and provides various output voltages on an ATX connector. Ituner Networks was generous enough to donate the PW-70A and other items for the book. Visit their site at **http://www.mini-box.com**.

Shuttle Zen ST62K

Shuttle is another company that is largely responsible for the success and popularity of SFF systems. Their "XPCs" are roughly cube-shaped boxes designed both for looks and features. Shuttle generously sent us an ST62K for use in the book, and we felt that it would make a good digital video recorder (DVR). This project is described in Chapter 3.

The ST62K is a *bare-bones system*, which means it comes with only the motherboard, case, and power supply. The CPU, memory, and hard drive must be purchased separately. The ST62K takes an Intel Socket 478 (Celeron or Pentium 4) CPU and DDR SDRAM. We use a 2.2 GHz processor, 512 MB of memory, and a 120 GB hard drive. The motherboard has built-in video, Ethernet, and sound. The ATI Radeon 9100 IGP video processor also has a built-in TV output. Unfortunately, we had some difficulty getting the TV output to work well with the X Window System on Linux.

The ST62K is currently selling for about $250 from a number of online retailers. However, due to relatively short product life cycles in the computer industry, it may not be available by the time you read this book (however, you will be able to find comparable offerings from Shuttle).

Another key component of the DVR is a TV tuner card. We chose the relatively inexpensive WinTV-GO from Hauppauge, whose cards are well supported in Linux. In retrospect, we recommend that you get a fancier version, such as the WinTV-PVR250. The ST62K has one PCI slot, which is where the TV tuner card will go. We also use an infrared receiver and universal remote control for this project.

Soekris net4501

Soekris Engineering makes a number of small, low-power computers that are designed to be used as networking/communication devices. They are all about the size of a small textbook and run silently. They feature varying numbers of Ethernet, PCcard, and Mini-PCI interfaces. All Soekris computers can boot and run from Compact Flash memory.

We'll use a Soekris net4501 (their first product) in Chapter 4 to build a gateway for your home or office network. The gateway can be configured to provide Dynamic Host Configuration Protocol (DHCP), Domain Name System (DNS), Network Address Translation (NAT), and firewall (packet filtering) services. The net4501 is a good choice because it has three Ethernet ports. Its 486-class processor and 64 MB RAM can easily handle the amount of traffic typically found on a home network. It takes up very little space, generates very little heat, and requires very little maintenance.

The net4501 also has two PCI slots, which you can use to add a Wi-Fi interface. One of them is a Mini-PCI slot, which is commonly found in laptops. The other is a standard-sized PCI slot that accepts 3.3 volt PCI cards.

You can buy the Soekris net4501 board and case directly from Soekris Engineering at **http://www.soekris.com**. The current cost is about $170 in single quantities. You'll also need a power supply. We recommend the "mini switch mode" model from Soekris, which costs $11.

The only other item we need to complete the project is a Compact Flash card. We recommend at least 128 MB, but you really don't need more than 256 MB for this project.

Soekris net4801

Our next project (see Chapter 5) uses another Soekris computer. Compared to the net4501, the net4801 has a faster processor (266 MHz, 586-class), and more memory (256 MB). It also has two features that no other Soekris computers have: USB and a built-in 44-pin IDE interface. We won't use the USB interface, but we will add a laptop hard drive instead of using the Compact Flash slot for storage.

Our project for the net4801 is a network-monitoring system. You can use it to actively and/or passively monitor hosts and routers on your network. The entire system is built from open source software packages, including Snort, Nagios, and RRDTool. Snort is an intrusion-detection system that passively monitors network traffic. Nagios actively monitors hosts and services by periodically probing them. RRDTool is a very nice system for storing and displaying various types of measurements. We'll use it to display bandwidth usage.

The net4801 is currently priced at $240 and is available from **http://www. soekris.com**. You'll also need to buy the 2.5-inch hard drive mounting kit ($10), power supply ($11), a laptop hard drive, and a 40-to-44-pin IDE adapter. The hard drive and adapter are not available from Soekris Engineering, but you can find them from many online vendors. You'll use the IDE adapter to connect the laptop hard drive to a standard PC (with a CD-ROM drive) so you can install the operating system. The project uses less than 2 GB of disk space, so any size laptop hard drive will work. In fact, if you have an old laptop lying around, you can probably remove its hard drive and use it in the net4801 (and you could use the laptop to install the operating system, eliminating the need to use the 40-to-44 pin IDE adapter and a desktop computer). Note that older 12.5 mm laptop drives don't fit in the net4801.

4G Access Cube

4G Systems, based in Hamburg, Germany, introduced the Meshcube in mid-2004. Since then, it has been renamed to the Access Cube. The Access Cube is designed specifically for "mesh routing" and other wireless applications. The mainboard consists of a MIPS processor, 32 MB flash memory, 64 MB RAM, built-in Ethernet, and USB. An expansion card has two Mini-PCI slots, which are normally used for 802.11 Wi-Fi cards. The orange-sized case has two Wi-Fi antenna connectors.

In Chapter 6, we'll show you how to turn the Access Cube into a "Wi-Fi extender." You can use the extender to connect up with wireless networks that are too far away to provide good signal quality. If you travel often, you might take the cube with you so that you can use nearby Wi-Fi networks from your hotel room. You can also use the extender as a network address translator, providing service to multiple hosts through a network that requires authentication and gives you only one IP address.

The Access Cube is available directly from 4G Systems in Germany. Prices are not currently posted, but the cube should cost about 200 Euros. Visit their web sites, **http://www.meshcube.org/** and **http://www.4g-systems.de/en/**, or contact them at *info@4g-systems.biz*. You can also buy the Cube in the United States from Closed Networks, Inc (**http://www.closednetworks.com/**).

In addition to the Access Cube itself, you'll also need two 802.11 Mini-PCI cards and Wi-Fi antennas with RP-SMA connectors. Both of these should be available from 4G Systems or a number of other online retailers, such as **http://www.netgate.com/**. Typical prices are $50 to $70. You can also sometimes salvage an 802.11 Mini-PCI card from an old laptop that has built-in Wi-Fi.

Plat'Home OpenBlockS/266

OpenBlockS is a micro server from the Plat'Home company in Japan. It is similar in size to the Access Cube, although more brick- than cube-shaped. Plat'Home generously donated an OpenBlockS/266 to us for the book. It has one serial and two Ethernet ports, a 266 MHz PowerPC processor, 64 MB RAM, and 8 MB flash memory. One of its most interesting features is that you can fit a laptop hard drive inside the case or use a Compact Flash adapter.

Our project for the OpenBlockS, in Chapter 7, is to create a portable bridging firewall. By placing the two Ethernet ports in bridging mode, you can use the firewall on any network without any configuration changes at all. We envision this firewall to be particularly useful in situations where you need one only temporarily. For example, you probably know that an unprotected and unpatched Windows PC can become infected in less time than it takes to download and apply software updates. The next time you have to reinstall the operating system on your Mom's computer, bring this little firewall with you.

Another nice feature of the OpenBlockS is that it requires only 5 volts DC input. This means that you can power it from a USB port, which also provides 5 volts DC and a maximum of 500 mA. The OpenBlockS draws between 500 and 640 mA, so this only works if the host system provides more current than required by the USB specification.

If you'd like to order an OpenBlockS from outside of Japan, visit the Fat Gadget web site: **http://www.fatgadget.jp/english/**. The cost is about $500. Inside Japan you can probably order it directly from Plat'Home. The kit should come with a power supply and serial port cable, but does not include a Compact Flash card. For this project we recommend at least a 256 MB CF card. You'll also need a DC power plug and USB cable if you want to build a USB power cable for the OpenBlockS.

ZipIt Wireless Messenger

The ZipIt Wireless Messenger is a small and inexpensive handheld device with a QWERTY keyboard, LCD display, and built-in Wi-Fi. It runs an instant messenger (IM) application that connects to the AOL, Yahoo!, and MSN instant messenger servers. The product is really marketed to families with kids, so the kids won't tie up the family PC while chatting with their pals. Internally, the ZipIt has an ARM-based processor, 16 MB of RAM, and 2 MB of flash memory.

Although the handheld messenger gadget is a great idea, with a little software hacking, you can turn the ZipIt into a portable SSH client. In Chapter 8, we'll show you how to load a new firmware image onto the ZipIt. You can then use SSH to log into your home or office systems, read your email, and more.

The ZipIt Wireless Messenger sells for about $100 from online retailers and stores such as Target. It even comes in different colors! The only other thing you'll need is an existing Windows or Linux computer to use as a server when loading the new firmware.

gumstix waysmall

The tiniest device in the book is the gumstix "waysmall" computer by gumstix, inc. It is smaller than a cell phone and a little larger than a pack of gum. gumstix systems are modular and come in a variety of configurations and features. A *platform board* contains the processor, memory, and optional Bluetooth interface. *Expansion boards* contain additional devices, such as Compact Flash or Multi Media Card (MMC) slots, serial ports, USB, and Ethernet.

We're using a gumstix basix platform board and a waysmall STUART expansion board. The processor is a 200 MHz Intel XScale (ARM) PXA255. It has 64 MB RAM, 4 MB flash, an MMC slot, and the built-in Bluetooth module. The expansion board has two serial ports, USB, and the power connector.

In Chapter 9, we connect the gumstix to a scrolling LED message sign. We configure the gumstix to receive messages via Bluetooth and then send them to the sign to be displayed. You might use this project as a way for people to entertain themselves at a party or meeting, or in a more serious setting such as an office, manufacturing area, or Network Operations Center.

You can buy the gumstix components directly from the **gumstix.com** web site. The 200 MHz basix with Bluetooth is about $145 and includes a Bluetooth antenna. You can get the waysmall-st kit, which includes the waysmall STUART expansion board, power supply, and a little case, for $30 more. Since the gumstix uses round serial port connectors, we recommend that you purchase a null modem cable ($12) or two from the gumstix site.

For the scrolling LED sign, we recommend the Pro-Lite "Tru-Color II" signs (a.k.a. model PL-M2014R), which have a serial port interface and a known communications protocol. These are occasionally available on eBay, but you can find them other places as well, including the manufacturer's web site at **http://www.pro-lite.com/indoor-singleline.htm**. You may also be able to find the Pro-Lite signs at retailers such as Office Depot, Office Max, and Staples. Prices vary quite a bit. We paid $150 for ours through eBay. The Office Depot web site says the list price is $425. Office Max is currently selling the Tru-Color II for $200.

You'll also need to build a custom serial cable to connect the gumstix to the Pro-Lite sign. You'll need a serial cable with Mini-DIN-8 connector, an RJ11 plug, and an RJ11 crimper.

More Cool Hardware

The projects in this book represent only a subset of all the small computer systems out there. Here are some more computers and other devices that we think are interesting:

Linksys WRT54G/GS/GX

Linksys' wireless routers are perhaps one of the most well-known hackable devices. The original WRT54G has five Ethernet ports, one 802.11g Wi-Fi interface, 16 MB RAM, 4 MB flash, and a 125 MHz Broadcom/MIPS CPU. Newer models may have more and faster components. Best of all, these devices are quite inexpensive, often selling for $70 or less. **http://seattlewireless.net/index.cgi/LinksysWrt54g** has quite a bit of info about hacking the firmware on Linksys WRT54G routers, and you can download firmware images from **http://openwrt.org/**.

Nano-ITX

Hot on the heels of their Mini-ITX motherboards, VIA came out with the Nano-ITX form factor. Whereas Mini-ITX is 17 × 17 cm, Nano-ITX is 12 × 12. It seems that Nano-ITX motherboards are a little hard to find at the moment, and are much more expensive than the Minis. VIA's EPIA-N has almost all of the standard devices, connectors, and interfaces you'd expect to find on a full-sized motherboard. Two interesting differences, however, are the use of Mini-PCI instead of standard PCI, and the use of SODIMM, rather than SDRAM or DDR memory. Both Mini-PCI and SODIMM are commonly used in laptops.

Apple iPod

If you have an early (i.e., 1 GB, 2 GB, or 3 GB) Apple iPod, you can load Linux firmware onto it. In fact, you can "dual-boot" your iPod with either the Apple firmware or the iPodLinux firmware. One of the best reasons for doing so is so you can play additional file formats, such as Ogg Vorbis, or so you can record higher-quality sound with your iPod (the Apple firmware in older iPods supports only 16-bit, 8 KHz mono). See **http://ipodlinux.org** for more information.

NorhTec

NorhTec (**http://www.norhtec.com/**) offers a number of small computer systems. Some use Mini-ITX motherboards; others use custom hardware. Their smallest product, the MicroServer GP+, has VGA video, mouse/keyboard, a parallel port, Ethernet, USB, audio, and TV video input and output connectors. The case has room for a 2.5-inch hard drive as well.

PC Engines WRAP board

The PC Engines (**http://www.pcengines.ch/**) Wireless Router Application Platform boards are similar in size and features to products from Soekris Engineering. They include 1–3 Ethernet ports, 1–2 Mini-PCI slots, Compact Flash for storage, and a serial console port.

WildLab LAMB-RT-01

The LAMB-RT-01 is a very small computer designed to run Linux. It has a 66 MHz AMD processor, 16 MB RAM, a Compact Flash slot, and two Ethernet ports. The whole package is about 3 × 3 × 1 inches. If you can read Japanese, visit **http://www.wildlab.com/**. They have an English brochure at **http://www.wildlab.com/LAMB/E/LEAFLET.pdf**. Unfortunately, it seems that WildLab is no longer selling the LAMB-RT-01, although they have released schematic diagrams for anyone interested in building his own.

Sharp Zaurus SL-C3100

Sharp has produced a number of Zaurus PDAs that run Linux, although they have mostly been exclusively available in Japan. The most recent model, the SL-C3100, has a 640x480 color display, a 4 GB hard drive, Compact Flash, and Secure Digital memory slots. It uses an Intel XScale processor (similar to the gumstix), 64 MB RAM, and up to 128 MB internal flash memory.

OQO Model 01+

The OQO model 01+ is another handheld computer that packs laptop-like features into a PDA-sized package. It has a 30 GB hard drive, a Transmeta processor, 512 MB RAM, USB, FireWire, Wi-Fi, Bluetooth, sound, and an 800x480 color display. The OQO comes with Windows

XP, but a number of folks are figuring out how to make it run Linux. Unfortunately, it's more expensive than many full-sized laptops.

Mini-box M-100

The M-100 from Mini-box.com is, unfortunately, no longer available. We think it's a real shame since the M-100 was one of the most interesting and good-looking Mini-ITX systems around. The case was 1U high and only slightly larger than the motherboard. The front panel included a 2x20 character LCD display, 14-key keypad, and a Compact Flash card slot. You could also mount a laptop hard drive inside the case. See **http://www.mini-itx.com/news/10339296/**.

OpenBrick

The OpenBrick (**http://www.openbrick.org/**) is another dead product. We believe it was originally manufactured by a Taiwanese company called Lucky Star, and sold as the NET-2100. It had a 300 MHz Geode processor, 128 MB RAM, VGA, keyboard, mouse, PCMCIA, CF, USB, Ethernet, and a 2.5-inch hard drive slot.

Black Dog

Realm Systems Inc. makes The BlackDog Mobile Personal Linux Server. It looks like a large USB thumb drive but is in fact a PowerPC-based computer system. It receives power from the USB port and uses Ethernet-over-USB to communicate with the host computer. When you plug it into a Windows or Mac system, you get a virtual X desktop that allows you to run Linux applications. The manufacturer's site is **http://www.projectblackdog.com**.

Nokia 770

The Nokia 770 Internet tablet is a handheld, PDA-sized device with an ARM processor, 800x480 color touch screen, 128 MB RAM, and built-in Wi-Fi and Bluetooth. In addition, the 770 is remarkable because it is not a phone, and because Nokia is open about their use of (Debian) Linux. In fact, Nokia has open-sourced the 770's development platform, named Maemo. See the product marketing info at **http://www.nokia.com/770**.

Digital Audio Jukebox

2

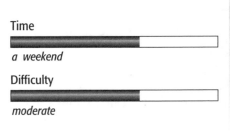

Time

a weekend

Difficulty

moderate

What You Need

- Mini-ITX motherboard with built-in audio, video, and network interface
- Memory for the Mini-ITX motherboard (at least 256 MB)
- Adapter cable for motherboard's second serial port
- Laptop (2.5-inch) hard drive
- Laptop hard drive 44-to-40 pin adapter
- Power supply or adapter, such as the PW-70A from Mini-box.com
- Irman infrared receiver
- Universal remote control
- Mini-ITX case or other enclosure
- Speakers
- Fan speed controller (optional)
- Small fan for a custom enclosure (optional)
- LCD display (optional)
- Spare CD-ROM drive for OS installation

If you're like us, you love playing music on your computer. Compressed audio file formats, such as Ogg Vorbis and MP3, mean it's easy to store huge collections of music on your computer. If you've ever wanted to build a dedicated digital audio jukebox, then this is the project for you! We'll show you how to build the system from the ground up, including a remote control, an LCD, and maybe even a custom enclosure.

Depending on how far you want to take this project, you'll spend anywhere from a few days to a few weeks on it. If you choose to create your own enclosure, you'll probably find that is the hardest part.

Introducing the VIA EPIA-M

For this project, we chose the VIA EPIA-M motherboard. It is one of their many Mini-ITX form-factor boards. As of this writing (early 2006) the EPIA-M comes with either a 1 GHz or 600 MHz CPU. We opted for the 600 MHz version (model ME6000) because it is advertised as fanless. Note the two passive heat sinks on the ME6000, shown in Figure 2-1. As we'll discuss later, that doesn't necessarily mean you can get by without any fans at all.

Figure 2-1. Rear view of the EPIA-M motherboard.

The "M" in EPIA-M might stand for multimedia. This motherboard is designed specifically for audio and video applications. That means it has more built-in hardware features than some of VIA's other Mini-ITX motherboards. For example, its CLE266 North Bridge provides both MPEG-2 acceleration and six-channel audio. The EPIA-M also has a jack for TV output (NTSC, PAL, and S-Video).

Additional EPIA-M characteristics include:

- One DDR266 184-pin memory slot, supporting up to 1 GB of RAM.
- Two parallel ATA133 (PATA) connectors and one floppy disk connector.
- Four USB2.0 ports with two jacks on the rear panel.
- Two FireWire ports in the form of 9-pin headers on the motherboard.
- Built-in fast Ethernet.
- One PCI slot.
- Two COM ports, one parallel port, mouse, and keyboard. Only one of the COM ports has a connector on the rear panel. To utilize the second, you'll need to connect a cable to a 9-pin header on the motherboard.

Of course, we won't need to use all of those for the jukebox, but some of them will come in handy during the setup and installation phase.

Additional Hardware

You'll need some additional hardware to build the jukebox. Some items, such as the power supply and memory, are mandatory. Others, like the wireless network interface and LCD display, are optional.

Power converter

The EPIA-M has a standard ATX power-supply connector. However, you probably don't want to use an actual ATX power supply because it's quite noisy and large. You can use an ATX power supply if you like, of course, although it is overkill. The EPIA-M system (with laptop hard drive) normally consumes less than 40 watts of power, while most ATX power supplies are rated for about 300 watts.

Instead, we like the power converters available from Mini-box.com (**http://www.mini-box.com**). They make a few different models, depending on power requirements and motherboard shape. For the EPIA-M, we are using the PW-70A, shown in Figures 2-2 and 2-3 (notice the ATX connector on the component board), which they were kind enough to donate for the book.

Mini-box's power converters snap directly onto the ATX connector without any cables, as shown in Figure 2-4. This eliminates the 20 or so wires that standard ATX power supplies have between the box and the motherboard connector. The PW-70A takes 12 volts DC input. In addition to the ATX connector, it also has one standard hard drive molex output, one floppy/CD-ROM-type power connector, and a general-purpose 5 volt lead.

The PW-70A manual says that the most it can power is two 5400-RPM hard drives, a floppy or CD-ROM, and 1 GB of RAM. Since 7200 RPM hard drives consume more power, you should not connect more than one of them at a time to this power converter. Our jukebox is well within these requirements, since we'll be using a single laptop hard drive. In fact, when we measured the actual power consumption with a watt meter, the peak was 23 watts, and only 19 watts when playing an Ogg file. Compare this to a standard ATX power supply, which consumed 40–47 watts during startup and shutdown, and 33 watts when playing music.

Figure 2-2. The PW-70A power converter.

Figure 2-3. Closeup of the PW-70A power converter.

BE CAREFUL:

In our personal experience, the Mini-box power converters are not as robust as standard ATX power supplies. We managed to ruin two of them by doing stupid things like plugging cables into the wrong connectors and by using home-made cables that may have been wired up incorrectly. Our best guess is that these adapters don't have any current overload protection that prevents them from burning out. We've never had any problems during normal operation—only when fiddling with something on the motherboard.

Memory

The EPIA-M takes standard 184-pin DDR SDRAM, although it has only one slot. It is rated for 266 MHz (PC2100) memory, and we're using a 256 MB stick. Future motherboard models may accept faster memory, so be sure to check the specs before you buy.

Inserting the memory is relatively simple. Notches on the bottom of the SDRAM board ensure that it fits only one way. Rest the memory on top of the slot, then push down on the ends as shown in Figure 2-5. You should hear a solid "snap" as you push down, and the little clips on the end will move to hold the board firmly in place.

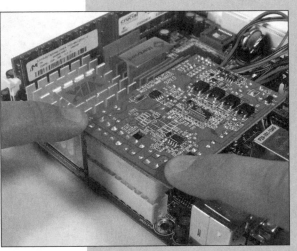

Figure 2-4. Attaching the PW-70A to the EPIA-M.

Figure 2-5. Inserting the SDRAM in the EPIA-M memory slot.

Figure 2-6. Closeup of the laptop hard drive.

Figure 2-7. The laptop hard drive with 44-to-40 pin adapter.

Hard drive

We recommend using a laptop (2.5-inch) hard drive for this project because of its small size. (Figure 2-6 shows a typical drive, in case you've never seen one before.) They also tend to be quieter and consume less power than the standard 3.5-inch drives. The downside to using a laptop drive is that they are more expensive (per GB) and come in smaller capacities. As of this writing, 80 GB Hitachi Travelstar (2.5-inch) drives are selling for about $110, while you can get a 250 GB Deskstar (3.5-inch) for $100. In other words, the larger drive gives you three times the space for about the same money.

The ME6000 Mini-ITX motherboard has a standard (40 pin) PATA connector. You'll need a 2.5-inch hard drive adapter and a 40-pin PATA cable to connect the hard drive to the motherboard. Adapters come in different shapes and sizes. The one in Figure 2-7 is flat and straight. It doesn't really matter what kind you get. One end has a 44-pin female connector for the hard drive. The other end is a 40-pin male connector for the PATA cable. The adapter also has a molex connector that supplies power to the drive.

Use caution when connecting the adapter to the 2.5-inch hard drive since the pins bend easily. Also take care to align the connectors correctly. If you are not careful, you might connect it upside down, or off by one. Pin 1 should be labeled on most hard drives and adapters. If you look at the hard drive pins straight on, you'll see two separate sets of pins. The 44-pin block is the PATA connector. Next to that is a small 4-pin jumper block. If you look closely at Figure 2-7, you should be able to see that the adapter connects only to the PATA pins and should not touch the jumper block. Pin 1 of the PATA connector is on the side closest to the jumpers. Your PATA cable should have a red stripe down one side, which also indicates pin 1.

Enclosure

You'll need to either buy or build an enclosure for your Mini-ITX system. Certainly, using a manufactured case saves time and effort. Note, however, that Mini-ITX cases tend to be more expensive than standard ATX cases. A number of nice, small cases are available from companies such as Travla, Morex, Cubid, Hoojum, and Scythe. Most of the cases should support a PCI card and CD drive, but some may not. Some of the very slim cases may require special low-profile memory.

You should also think about cooling requirements when shopping for cases. This project is based around the fanless EPIA-M motherboard. Most of the Mini-ITX cases have a case fan to provide cooling. Some of the very small cases may have a tough time keeping the system cool enough. If noise is an important factor, you may want to look at the fanless e-OTONASHI case by Scythe. It has a *heat lane* that mounts on top of the CPU and dissipates heat through the bottom of the case.

If you're up to the task, building your own case can be quite fun. We think that nonfunctioning antique radios make excellent jukebox cases. You can probably find one at a local antique store or on a site such as eBay. If you find a large-enough cabinet, you'll have no problems mounting all of the necessary components (motherboard, hard drive, power supply, and fan). Visit the **www.mini-itx.com** web site for inspiration on building your own enclosure!

On/off switch

If you'll be using an off-the-shelf Mini-ITX case, you don't need to worry about the on/off switch. On the other hand, if you plan to build your own enclosure, as we do, you'll need to fabricate a simple on/off switch.

We visited the local hardware store and purchased a push-button switch for a few dollars. The harder part is finding a cable with an appropriate connector that you can solder to the switch. The pins on the motherboard are a standard IDC header (0.10 inches apart). If you can't find an appropriate cable, search the Web for "replacement ATX power switch."

CPU/system fan

The EPIA-M is advertised as fanless, which means you can get by with a passive heat sink as long as something provides a little airflow to remove excess heat. We recommend that you put a fan in your enclosure and use something like the Zalman Fanmate controller, shown in Figure 2-8, to reduce its speed. That way, you still get some airflow while keeping the system relatively quiet. We used an old CPU fan because it is about the right size and already has the necessary two-wire connector.

Remote control

With an infrared remote control, you can control the jukebox much like a normal stereo CD player. You can change the volume, pause the music, fast forward/reverse, skip ahead, etc. We'll show you how to use the Irman infrared receiver by Evation (**http://www.evation.com/**) for this project. As you can see in Figure 2-9, the Irman is nothing more than a small box connected to a serial cable. The infrared sensor hides behind a small red window inside the box.

You'll also need a remote control. If you don't have one already lying around, any cheap universal remote control will do. We purchased a $10 universal remote from the local mega-discount store, shown in Figure 2-10.

Cable for second serial port

The VIA EPIA-M motherboard has just one serial port on the back panel. We recommend that you use it as a remote console while building the system and in case the network is down. This means you can't put the infrared receiver on that serial port.

A second serial port is available on the motherboard, but to use it you'll need to get a special cable, such as the one in Figure 2-11. To find a place where you can buy a cable like this, search the Web for "IDC10 DB9 serial" and "internal serial cable."

You may have to update the VIA EPIA-M BIOS in order to get the second serial port to work. This is apparently a common problem with these motherboards. BIOS files are available for download from http://www.viavpsd.com/.

The second serial port connector is near the rear of the motherboard, right next to the large, pinkish parallel port connector. (Refer to Figure 2-12.) It looks like two rows of five pins sticking up, except that one of the corner pins is missing. The adapter cable connector has one of the holes blocked out so that you can only attach it in one way. The cable also probably has a pink stripe down one side, marking pin 1. That stripe should be on the side closest to the rear of the motherboard.

Figure 2-9. The Irman infrared receiver.

Figure 2-10. A basic, universal remote control

Wi-Fi (optional)

The jukebox needs a network connection so you can upload new songs and perform system administration tasks. You can use the EPIA's built-in Ethernet port, although who really wants Ethernet cables running through the house? The EPIA-M has one PCI expansion slot, which you can use for a wireless network card. Unfortunately, we won't be able to give you all the details of setting up the wireless interface in this chapter. See Chapter 6 for some good hints, or grab a copy of *Linux Unwired* (O'Reilly).

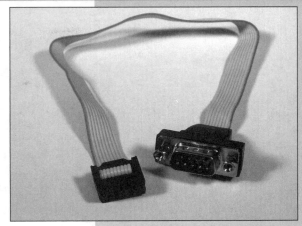

Figure 2-11. Adapter for the EPIA-M's second serial port.

LCD display (optional)

Since the jukebox isn't connected to a monitor, you might want to use an LCD display. There, you can display the artist name, song title, and other information. If you are building or modifying your own case (as we are) you'll need to find some way to integrate the LCD. See the "Extra Credit" section at the end of this chapter to learn about adding an LCD module

Step 1: Install and Configure Gentoo Linux

We chose Gentoo Linux for this particular project. If you already have a favorite Linux distribution, feel free to use that one instead. However, the remainder of this section is Gentoo-specific.

Figure 2-12. Connecting the second serial port adapter cable.

If you've never installed Gentoo Linux before, start by having a look at their online handbook. Since our platform is the VIA EPIA-M, we'll refer to the "x86" documentation at **http://www.gentoo. org/doc/en/handbook/handbook-x86.xml**. We cover the important points here, but you'll probably want to follow along in their documentation as well.

If you are new to Linux altogether, you may want to have a good reference by your side, such as *Linux Cookbook* (O'Reilly), *Linux in a Nutshell* (O'Reilly), and *Linux Administration Handbook* (Prentice Hall).

The Gentoo Live CD

The first chapter of the Gentoo handbook is an introduction to the philosophy and terminology of Gentoo. It takes only a minute or two to read. The second chapter explains your options for downloading a Gentoo Live CD and talks about the three types of installation stages. We recommend downloading the Minimal Live CD and then performing a stage3 installation. However, if you'll be performing the installation somewhere with a slow network, you may want to go ahead and download the Universal Live CD image instead.

If you don't plan on having a CD-ROM in your final jukebox, you'll need to connect one temporarily to perform the installation. Note that the Mini-box PW-70A has two power connectors. The larger one should be connected to the laptop HD adapter. The smaller connector fits floppy and slim CD-ROM drives. If you don't happen to have a slim CD-ROM, you'll need an adapter or a "Y" splitter for the larger connector. Another option is to temporarily use a standard ATX power supply during the installation.

If none of those suggestions work for you, take the laptop hard drive to another system that already has a CD-ROM. If you take this route, be aware that you may need to account for hardware differences when moving the drive back to the Mini-ITX system.

As the Gentoo CD boots, it pauses briefly and gives you a chance to load a special kernel or specify certain options:

```
ISOLINUX 3.09 2005-06-17  Copyright (C) 1994-2005 H. Peter Anvin
Gentoo Linux Installation LiveCD
http://www.gentoo.org/
Enter to boot; F1 for kernels  F2 for options.
boot:
```

Most likely you can use the default and just press Enter. We found it necessary to use a nonstandard kernel because our old VGA monitor does not support the higher resolution (probably 800x600) that the default kernel uses. At the boot prompt, we typed **gentoo-nofb** and were happy to see a good, old-fashioned VGA text screen.

When Gentoo finishes booting, you'll see a root shell prompt. During the installation, you may find it useful to switch to another (virtual) screen. While one screen is tied up with a procedure that takes a long time, you can use another screen to plan ahead or monitor its progress. To access the virtual screens, type Alt-*N* on your keyboard, where *N* is a number from 1 to 6.

Configuring the network interface

The first task after booting is to get the network working, although if you have the Universal Live CD, you may not need to. We found that the EPIA's built-in NIC is not recognized or configured by default. This can be confusing because *ifconfig* may show an *eth0* interface, but it appears to be some sort of firewire-to-Ethernet device. If you're using a VIA motherboard, load the *via-rhine* kernel module and then start the DHCP client:

```
# modprobe via-rhine
# ifconfig eth1
# dhcpcd eth1
# ifconfig eth1
```

Of course, if you don't have a DHCP server, you can manually assign the IP address, default gateway, and DNS server. Note that the real interface comes up as *eth1* because *eth0* was already assigned. The situation may be different for your particular hardware configuration.

Partitioning the hard disk

The second step is to partition your hard drive for Linux. The Gentoo Handbook covers this in some detail in Chapter 4. We suggest that you follow their recommendations and create three partitions: a small boot partition, a swap partition, and everything else on one large root filesystem. If your hard drive has been previously partitioned, you'll need to delete your existing partitions as described in the handbook. Assuming the drive is unpartitioned, here's how to create the first one:

```
# fdisk /dev/hda
Disk /dev/hda: 30.0 GB, 30005821440 bytes
255 heads, 63 sectors/track, 3648 cylinders
Units = cylinders of 16065 * 512 = 8225280 bytes

Device Boot     Start        End     Blocks   Id  System

Command (m for help): n
Command action
   e   extended
   p   primary partition (1-4) p
Partition number (1-4): 1
First cylinder (1-3876, default 1): (Hit Enter)
Using default value 1
Last cylinder or +size or +sizeM or +sizeK (1-3876, default 3876): +32M
```

Also set the bootable flag for this partition:

```
Command (m for help): a
Partition number (1-4): 1
```

The procedure is similar for adding the other two partitions. For the swap-space we generally recommend that it match the amount of RAM you have, or the maximum you expect to upgrade to. We recommend using 512 MB for swap, even if you have only 256 MB of memory:

```
Command (m for help): n
Command action
  e   extended
  p   primary partition (1-4) p
Partition number (1-4): 2
First cylinder (1-3876, default 6): (Hit Enter)
Using default value 6
Last cylinder or +size or +sizeM or +sizeK (1-3876, default 3876):
+512M
```

After adding the swap partition, be sure to change its type to Linux Swap by using the **t** command:

```
Command (m for help): t
Partition number (1-4): 2
Hex code (type L to list codes): 82
```

When adding the third and final partition, select the default value for the last cylinder to use up the rest of the disk:

```
Command (m for help): n
Command action
  e   extended
  p   primary partition (1-4) p
Partition number (1-4): 3
First cylinder (1-3876, default 69): (Hit Enter)
Using default value 69
Last cylinder or +size or +sizeM or +sizeK (1-3876, default 3876):
(Hit Enter)
```

When you're done, check the partition with the **p** command. The particular numbers for your hard drive are likely to be different than these:

```
Disk /dev/hda: 30.0 GB, 30005821440 bytes
255 heads, 63 sectors/track, 3648 cylinders
Units = cylinders of 16065 * 512 = 8225280 bytes

   Device Boot    Start      End     Blocks   Id  System
/dev/hda1   *         1        5      40131   83  Linux
/dev/hda2             6       68     506047+  82  Linux swap
/dev/hda3            69     3648   28756350   82  Linux
```

When finished, use **w** to save the new partition table and exit:

```
Command (m for help): w
The partition table has been altered!

Calling ioctl() to re-read partition table.
```

Now you can put filesystems on two of them and prepare the other for swapping:

```
# mke2fs /dev/hda1
# mke2fs /dev/hda3
# mkswap /dev/hda2
```

Next, turn on the swapspace and mount the new filesystems under */mnt/ gentoo* so you can start installing files on them:

```
# swapon /dev/hda2
# mount /dev/hda3 /mnt/gentoo
# mkdir /mnt/gentoo/boot

# mount /dev/hda1 /mnt/gentoo/boot
# mkdir /mnt/gentoo/proc
# mount -t proc none /mnt/gentoo/proc
```

Downloading an installation tarball

Now it's time to download the stage3 tarball. Start by *cd*-ing to the recently mounted filesystem; then open **http://www.gentoo.org/main/en/mirrors.xml** in a browser:

```
# cd /mnt/gentoo
# links http://www.gentoo.org/main/en/mirrors.xml
```

Select a site close to you and navigate through the subdirectories. First go to *releases*, then *x86*. Here you'll find one or two release directories. Just choose the most recent. At the time of this writing, it was the *2005.1* directory. Under that, you select the directory named *stages*.

In the *stages* directory, you'll see a list of CPU types, such as *athlon-xp*, *i686*, *pentium3*, *pentium4*, and *x86*. The CPU on VIA's EPIA-M motherboard is perhaps closest to the Pentium 3. However, as we learned the hard way, some binaries built for Pentium 3 do not work on the VIA CPU. The i686 binaries don't work either. The x86 architecture is the one that works for this system, so go into that directory.

Now you'll see large tarballs for stages 1, 2, and 3. Download the stage 3 file and save it in the */mnt/gentoo* directory. The letter **d** initiates a download in *links*.

When the download completes, exit *links* and extract the tarball into the root filesystem:

```
# pwd
/mnt/gentoo
# tar xjfp stage3-x86-2005.1.tar.bz2
```

Installing portage

Your next task is to install Gentoo's *Portage* system. This is a collection of scripts and patches similar to FreeBSD's *ports* and NetBSD's *packages*. When you install software on Gentoo Linux, Portage downloads the necessary source code, patches it if necessary, and then compiles and installs it.

The first step is to select one or more of the Gentoo mirror sites. Gentoo's *mirrorselect* program has a feature whereby it tries to automatically find the best mirror site. We found that it doesn't work all that well, however, and recommend that you select the mirror site manually. You can use this command:

```
# mirrorselect -i -o >> /mnt/gentoo/etc/make.conf
```

Look through the list and pick one or two mirror sites that you think are either topologically or geographically nearby. Afterwards you may want to look at the */mnt/gentoo/etc/make.conf* file and make sure it worked.

Until your new system is fully ready to boot from the hard drive, you'll use *chroot* to run commands from within the new filesystem. But first you must copy over the DNS configuration:

```
# cp -L /etc/resolv.conf /mnt/gentoo/etc/resolv.conf
```

Now, you can safely enter the chroot environment:

```
# chroot /mnt/gentoo /bin/bash
```

Unfortunately, for us *tcsh* lovers, *bash* is the only shell available by default. Oh well, we'll have to live with it for a while. After entering the chroot shell, the following commands update your environment variables:

```
# env-update
# source /etc/profile
```

Now you are ready to install the Portage files. It's as simple as running this command:

```
# emerge sync
```

Since Portage consists of more than 100,000 files, the transfer is likely to take quite a while. Now would be a good time to take a break or read ahead in this chapter. When it completes, you may see a message telling you that "an update to portage is available." If so, install the update with this command:

```
# emerge portage
```

You might also see a message suggesting that you run *etc-update*. This is a tool that helps keep your configuration files up to date after installing an update to an existing package. You might as well run *etc-update* if asked to, although you can probably wait and do it later if you prefer.

Before installing any additional software, you should probably take a moment to learn about Gentoo's USE flags. These are a list of preferences for optional features in certain packages. USE flags are set by adding a line to the */etc/make.conf* file. Since your jukebox won't have a display, you should minimize the amount of X-windows-related code that gets compiled. We recommend the following USE flags setting:

```
USE="-X -gtk -gtk2 -kde -gnome -qt"
```

To edit files at this point, you'll need to use a text editor named *nano*. This is GNU's version of the *pico* editor popularized by the PINE email user agent. If you've used PINE before, you should have no problems with *nano*. If you prefer another editor, such as *vi*, install it now with *emerge*.

Have a look at the Gentoo handbook for additional information on USE flags. If you find the concept too overwhelming at this point, don't worry about it. Everything should still work no matter what settings you have.

Configure your kernel

You are now ready to configure and compile a kernel for the system. The first step is to select a kernel source package and install it. Gentoo has a web page, **http://www.gentoo.org/doc/en/gentoo-kernel.xml**, which describes all of the kernel choices they provide. We suggest that you play it safe and just use the *gentoo-sources* package. This is a recent Linux-2.6 kernel with a few patches for improved security and performance. To install the sources, run this command:

```
# emerge gentoo-sources
```

After installing the sources, you need to compile and install the kernel. If you are experienced with installing Linux kernels, you may want to use the standard make menuconfig approach. However, for the sake of simplicity, we'll show you how to use Gentoo's *genkernel* utility. First, you need to install it:

```
# emerge genkernel
```

Then run it:

```
# genkernel all
```

When *genkernel* finishes, you should have a few new files in the */boot* directory, like these:

```
# ls -l /boot
total 3472
lrwxrwxrwx  1 root root        1 Sep 27 06:26 boot -> .
-rw-r--r--  1 root root  772846 Sep 28 06:56 System.map-genkernel-x86-
2.6.12-gentoo-r10
-rw-r--r--  1 root root 1780245 Sep 28 08:42 initramfs-genkernel-x86-
2.6.12-gentoo-r10
-rw-r--r--  1 root root 1874116 Sep 28 06:56 kernel-genkernel-x86-
2.6.12-gentoo-r10
```

The Gentoo Handbook recommends that you install the *hotplug* package. We found *hotplug* to be more annoying than useful because it prints lots of errors or warnings at boot, prevents the Live CD from shutting down properly, and doesn't detect any of our hardware that is not already detected by the kernel. Your experience may be different, of course, especially if you are using a different motherboard. If you don't install *hotplug* now and find that something doesn't work, you may want to install it later.

While we're thinking about the kernel, let's make sure that the *via-rhine* module is automatically loaded when the system boots:

```
# echo via-rhine >> /etc/modules.autoload.d/kernel-2.6
# modules-update
```

With the Linux-2.6.12 installation that we used, the *modules-update* command generated warnings about unresolved symbols in certain files related to SCSI and SATA. Don't worry if you see the same thing—they can be ignored.

You also need a kernel module to get the audio working, which means installing another package. Let's just worry about getting Linux up and running for now. Once you have a working system booting from the hard drive, we'll show you how to configure the sound drivers.

Configure the system

At this point in the installation, you need to set up a few files in the */etc* directory. Start with the *fstab* file first, and then tackle the networking components.

Open the */etc/fstab* file with the text editor:

```
# nano /etc/fstab
```

Initially you should see something like this:

```
# <fs>                  <mountpoint>   <type>          <opts>

# NOTE: If your BOOT partition is ReiserFS, add the notail option to
# opts.
/dev/BOOT             /boot          ext2            noauto,noatime
/dev/ROOT             /              reiserfs        noatime
/dev/SWAP             none           swap            sw
/dev/cdroms/cdrom0    /mnt/cdrom     iso9660         noauto,ro
/dev/fd0              /mnt/floppy    auto            noauto

# NOTE: The next line is critical for boot!
none                  /proc          proc            defaults
```

You'll need to change four things in this file:

1. Change */dev/BOOT* to */dev/hda1*.

2. Change */dev/ROOT* to */dev/hda3*.

3. Change */dev/SWAP* to */dev/hda2*.

4. Our earlier instructions were to use the *ext2* filesystem for the root partition. If you followed those instructions, change *reiserfs* to *ext2* for the root partition type.

You can also comment out the */dev/fd0* line if your jukebox doesn't have a floppy drive.

Now we can move on to networking. First, select a name for your system and store it in the */etc/conf.d/hostname* file:

```
HOSTNAME="jukebox"
```

Gentoo uses DHCP to configure interfaces by default, so you probably don't need to edit */etc/conf.d/net*. However, you do need to install a DHCP client with *emerge*:

```
# emerge dhcpcd
```

If you need to manually configure the network, edit */etc/conf.d/net* and add two lines based on this example, changing the numbers to match your network configuration:

```
config_eth0=( "192.168.0.2/24" );
routes_eth0=( "default via 192.168.0.1" );
```

Refer to */etc/conf.d/net.example* to learn more about how you can configure the network. Also keep in mind that if your system is like ours, the on-board Ethernet interface shows up as *eth0* later, even though it is *eth1* now. Again, it may be different for your particular hardware, so be sure to double-check after you reboot. If your Ethernet device comes up as *eth1* later, you'll need to revisit this section and change the */etc/conf.d/net* file.

To have the system automatically configure the *eth0* interface at boot, run this command:

```
# rc-update add net.eth0 default
```

The final network-configuration item to worry about is the */etc/hosts* file. If you have a home network with a DNS server, you should update your DNS configuration to reflect the addition of this new system. Otherwise, you may want to simply add a few lines to the */etc/hosts* file. For example:

```
127.0.0.1       localhost jukebox
192.168.0.1     router
```

DHCP and */etc/hosts* don't mix very well since */etc/hosts* is a static database and DHCP is, by definition, dynamic. If your network has only one or two machines on it, chances are that DHCP always assigns the same addresses to the same hosts, so you may be able to use the */etc/hosts* file to hardcode the IP addresses of computers on your network anyway. In the preceding example, we played it safe and put in two hosts we know will never change: localhost and our router.

Install a bootloader

The bootloader is a small program that is executed when the system boots from a hard disk. Gentoo offers two bootloader choices: LILO and GRUB. The Gentoo Handbook recommends GRUB, and we concur. First, use *emerge* to get the GRUB package:

```
# emerge grub
```

Then, use the *grub* program to do the initial configuration. You can save some time by starting *grub* with the --no-floppy option:

```
# grub --no-floppy
```

Now you are in the *grub* shell and need to type the following three lines:

```
grub> root (hd0,0)
grub> setup (hd0)
grub> quit
```

Now GRUB is installed on the hard drive's Master Boot Record (MBR). You still need to create a GRUB configuration file, however. That file lives at */boot/grub/grub.conf*:

```
# nano /boot/grub/grub.conf
```

We recommend that you use a symbolic link for the kernel filename. This allows you to upgrade (or downgrade) the kernel later, without re-editing *grub.conf*. Place the following lines into this file:

```
default 0
timeout 30
title=Gentoo Linux
  root (hd0,0)
  kernel /kernel root=/dev/hda3
```

Then, create the symbolic link to your kernel file. Note that the kernel pathname is relative to the root partition. For example, since (hd0,0) corresponds to the */boot* partition, GRUB loads the file named */boot/kernel*. Here are the commands:

```
# cd /boot
# ln -s kernel-genkernel-x86-2.6.12-gentoo-r10 kernel
```

If you upgrade the kernel on this system at a later date, such that the kernel filename changes, just return to the */boot* directory and change the symbolic link. If you want to be able to boot from multiple kernels, simply add more title, root, and kernel lines as necessary.

If you want to make the first serial port the system console, you simply need to add a few things to *grub.conf*. First, add these two lines to the top of the file:

```
serial --unit=0 --speed=115200 --word=8 --parity=no --stop=1
terminal serial
```

Those lines instruct GRUB to print its menu on the serial port instead of the VGA screen. Then, modify the `kernel` line by adding some options so that the kernel knows it also should use the serial port:

```
kernel /kernel root=/dev/hda3 console=tty0 console=ttyS0,115200n8
```

The `console=tty0` argument tells the kernel to send console output to the first VGA virtual terminal (i.e., the normal system console). The second one, `console=ttyS0,115200n8`, tells the kernel to also send console output to the first serial port at 115,200 bps. The kernel uses the last `console=` argument for input.

Final tasks

For some reason Gentoo does not install default *syslog* or *cron* packages for you. You must choose which particular ones you'd like to use and install them manually. We recommend using *sysklogd* and *vixie-cron*:

```
# emerge sysklogd
# rc-update add sysklogd default
# emerge vixie-cron
# rc-update add vixie-cron default
```

Have a look at Part 1, Chapter 10 of the Gentoo Handbook if you'd like to know more about the other choices.

Assign a password to the *root* account if you haven't done so already:

```
# passwd
```

You should also create one or more user accounts at this point. For example:

```
# useradd colin -m -G users,wheel,audio,tty -s /bin/bash
# passwd colin
```

We assume that eventually you'll be using the jukebox without a screen and keyboard. That means you'll need a way to log in remotely. The obvious choices are SSHD and the serial port. We recommend enabling both.

SSHD should already be installed on your system. You simply need to have the daemon start when the system boots:

```
# rc-update add sshd default
```

To log in through the serial port, you'll need a *getty* process running there. On Linux, the */etc/inittab* file contains the configuration lines for *agetty* processes. Edit */etc/inittab* and find the section with all the *agetty* lines. Then add a line like this:

```
s0:12345:respawn:/sbin/agetty 115200 tts/0 xterm
```

`115200` is the port speed, `tts/0` is the */dev* entry for the first serial port, and `xterm` is the default terminal type. After editing the file, run the following command to tell *init* to re-read its configuration:

```
# init q
```

Verify that the new *agetty* process is running on the first serial port with *ps*:

```
# ps -t tts/0
  PID TTY          TIME CMD
 1206 tts/0     00:00:00 agetty
```

You may also need to modify */etc/securetty* so that *root* can log in on the serial port. The file is just a list of TTY names, without the */dev/* part, where root is allowed to log in from. Edit the file and make sure that *tts/0* appears in it. If the line is commented out, remove the comment character.

Reboot!

It's now time to reboot the system and make sure you got everything right. First unmount the hard drive filesystems:

```
# umount /mnt/gentoo/proc
# umount /mnt/gentoo/boot
# umount /mnt/gentoo
```

Then execute the reboot command:

```
# reboot
```

If the shutdown procedure seems to stall on something related to *hotplug*, try the reboot command again.

Be sure to remove the Gentoo Live CD before the system reboots. If you've configured the serial port as a console, connect a null modem cable and open a terminal program (such as *screen* or *minicom*) on another PC so you can watch the new system boot. Pay particular attention to the network configuration.

Configuring Gentoo for sound

Getting sound to work on Gentoo is not too difficult, thanks to their documentation at **http://www.gentoo.org/doc/en/alsa-guide.xml**. The following instructions are taken from that document. Most likely your VIA motherboard has a sound chipset starting with the number 82. You can run the following command to verify the exact model number:

```
# grep -i audio /proc/pci
Multimedia audio controller: VIA Technologies, Inc. VT8233/A/8235 AC97
  Audio Controller (rev 80).
```

Tell Gentoo to build a module for this particular sound chip by adding this line to */etc/make.conf*:

```
ALSA_CARDS="via82xx"
```

Then run the following two commands to build the *via82xx* kernel module and support utilities:

```
# emerge alsa-driver
# emerge alsa-utils
```

Add the following line to the *etc/modules.d/alsa* file:

```
alias snd-card-0 snd-via82xx
```

Every time you modify one of the files in the *etc/modules.d* directory, you should run the following command:

```
# modules-update
```

If *modules-update* prints warnings about unresolved symbols, you can probably ignore them. To make your system automatically load the ALSA sound drivers when it boots, execute this command:

```
# rc-update add alsasound boot
```

To load the sound drivers immediately, without rebooting, execute the startup script manually:

```
# /etc/init.d/alsasound start
 * Loading ALSA drivers... * Using ALSA OSS emulation
 * Loading: snd-seq-oss
 * Loading: snd-pcm-oss
 * Running card-dependent scripts
 * Restoring Mixer Levels
 [ ok ]
```

Note that the audio outputs are muted and set to zero volume by default. Before you can hear anything, you'll need to unmute them and increase the levels. If you installed the *alsa-utils* package, you can use the *alsamixer* program. It has a colorful, full-screen interface for adjusting everything. Alternatively, you can use the *amixer* program, like this:

```
# amixer set Master 20 unmute
# amixer set PCM 20 unmute
```

At this point, you should be able to play and hear some sounds. You might have a hard time finding a sample sound file, at least until you install an Ogg/MP3 player and copy over some files to play. You may also want to reboot, if you haven't already, and make sure that the sound drivers are loaded correctly.

Step 2: X Windows and XMMS

XMMS is a very popular audio player for the X Window System (X Windows). It has all of the features we need for our jukebox, including good infrared remote support and plug-ins for different audio formats, such as Ogg Vorbis. The only drawback is that XMMS requires X Windows, and this project is designed to run "unattended" and without any video display.

One solution to this problem is to use a command-line player instead of XMMS. One of these, called noXMMS, is a version of XMMS with all the GUI parts stripped out. noXMMS has two drawbacks: it is not updated as often as XMMS, and a few of XMMS's neat features don't work.

Another option is to run X Windows on the built-in display. We can configure it so that X starts automatically at boot time. After everything is working, you can disconnect your monitor and keyboard and control the jukebox entirely with the infrared remote. However, if a problem arises later, you may need to reconnect the monitor and keyboard to log in and fix it.

Taking this idea one step further, we recommend that you actually install a virtual X server, also known as a VNC server. This provides a couple of advantages. First, you don't need to connect a spare monitor keyboard to the jukebox. Second, you can connect to the VNC server from one of your existing systems, including a Microsoft Windows box or even a handheld computer such as a Palm, Zaurus, or Pocket PC. One of the best features is that the X server stays running after you disconnect. When you reconnect later, the windows will still be there. We recommend that you run the VNC server as a nonprivileged user, named *colin* in our examples. If you didn't create one yet, go back to "Final Tasks."

tightvnc

Let's start by installing the VNC server. Gentoo's portage collection contains quite a few different VNC applications. We recommend using *tightvnc*, since it will perform well even over slow links (opening up the possibility that you could control your jukebox from a VNC client running on a cell phone!):

```
# emerge tightvnc
```

Installation may take a while since *emerge* probably needs to download and install all of the standard X Windows clients and libraries. When it's done, you can test it with these commands:

```
# su - colin
colin$ /usr/bin/vncserver :1 -geometry 1000x700

You will require a password to access your desktops.

Password: sekrit
Verify:   sekrit
Would you like to enter a view-only password (y/n)? n
xauth: (argv):1:  bad display name "jukebox:1" in "add" command

New 'X' desktop is jukebox:1

Creating default startup script /home/colin/.vnc/xstartup
Starting applications specified in /home/colin/.vnc/xstartup
Log file is /home/colin/.vnc/jukebox:1.log
```

The :1 argument instructs the VNC server to start itself as display number one (whereas display numbering normally starts at zero). You may want to adjust the -geometry parameters to suit your needs (if you connect from a small-screen device, VNC should allow you to either scale down a large resolution display or pan around it). *vncserver* will prompt you for a password the first time. Clients must enter this password when they connect.

To test the virtual X server, go to another computer on the network and start up a VNC client. If you've installed *tightvnc* on the other computer, the client is named *vncviewer*. For example, in our case the jukebox's IP address is 172.16.1.241, so we type:

```
# /usr/bin/vncviewer 172.16.1.241:1
```

Note that, here, :1 refers to the display number (as in the *vncserver* command), rather than a port number as you might see in a URL. The VNC client should prompt you for a password and then display a window that looks like the one shown in Figure 2-13.

The no-frills and somewhat ugly window manager that you see is called *twm*. You can use a different one if you like. In fact, if you are really gung-ho, you can install KDE or Gnome. These desktop environments are overkill for our purpose, especially since you'll be controlling the jukebox with a remote control. However, see the section "X Windows" in Chapter 3 if you would like to install Gnome or KDE.

Figure 2-13. The initial virtual X display.

While we're on the subject of *twm*, there is one little thing we should fix. By default, *twm* makes you choose the location for new windows with your mouse. The application doesn't start until the window is placed. This is trouble since, in the unattended mode, we want XMMS to start automatically. To solve this, copy the system *twmrc* to your home directory and add one line:

```
colin$ cp /etc/X11/twm/system.twmrc ~/.twmrc
colin$ chmod +w ~/.twmrc
colin$ nano ~/.twmrc
```

Somewhere near the top of that file, add the following line:

```
RandomPlacement
```

Then, the next time you start the VNC server, windows should be placed automatically on the desktop.

One final detail to take care of is starting *vncserver* automatically when the jukebox boots up. On Gentoo, */etc/conf.d/local.start* is a good place to put startup commands. We suggest that you start *vncserver* as a nonprivileged user. Here's the command you can place in *local.start*:

```
/bin/su - colin --login -c "/usr/bin/vncserver :1 -geometry 1000x700"
```

At this point, it's probably a good idea to test everything by rebooting the system. Watch the console output (if you can) as it boots and make sure that *vncserver* starts correctly. Then, connect with a VNC client and open a few xterms to make sure that the RandomPlacement option is working as well.

XMMS

Installing XMMS is easy with *emerge*:

```
# emerge xmms
```

Shortly thereafter, you should be able to test it by giving an MP3 or Ogg file as a command-line argument:

```
# xmms ~colin/music/Cabaret_Diosa/Voodoo_Pinanata/12-Mambo_Verde.ogg
```

If everything is working, you'll see the XMMS window appear and hear some music. If you've never used XMMS before, you may want to take some time and become familiar with its operation and features.

You need to install another little package, the LIRC plug-in for XMMS, to control it with the infrared remote. In Gentoo the package is named *xmms-lirc*:

```
# emerge xmms-lirc
```

After installing the plug-in, restart XMMS. Place the mouse over the XMMS window and type Ctrl-V. Select the General Plug-ins tab, and you should see a line that says "LIRC Plug-in." Highlight this line and then click the "Enable plug-in" checkbox.

We'll show you how to finish off the necessary LIRC configuration in the next section.

Step 3: Infrared Remote Control

A remote control is key to making the jukebox a standalone system. When the project is finished, you'll be able to perform almost every operation via the remote. You won't need to log in to the jukebox to start the player, adjust the volume, etc.

We're using the Irman infrared receiver from a company named Evation. The receiver costs about $35. The device is pretty small: $3 \times 2.4 \times 1$ inches or $7.6 \times 6.2 \times 2.5$ centimeters. It's a black box with an IR receiver on one side and a serial cable coming out the other.

You can also get a remote control from Evation; unfortunately, their remote is not a good choice for this project. Most importantly, it doesn't really have enough buttons. Notably missing is a numeric keypad for digits 0–9. After being disappointed by the Evation remote, we visited the local mega discount shopping store and purchased a Philips Magnavox remote with more features for less than $10. The examples in this chapter are based on this remote.

Irman technical details

Here's a little bit of info about how the Irman works that may help you debug problems if necessary. The device is powered by the serial port's RTS and/or DTR lines. Of course, serial ports were never really designed to provide power, but the Irman's power needs are so small that it can use the current flowing through these control lines.

When the Irman first receives power, it waits for a handshake from the computer before transmitting any data to it. The computer must send the two-character sequence IR. Irman then responds with OK. Both the RTS and DTR lines are normally low. When an application opens the serial port, these lines are set high, providing power to the Irman. That's the way it works on Linux, anyway. While doing some testing on FreeBSD, we found that the RTS line is always high. This confuses Irman applications. The initial handshake fails because the device is already initialized.

The Irman interprets infrared signals and converts them into groups of characters. Data transmission is fixed at 9600 bps, 8N1.

libirman

libirman is the library that other programs use to talk to the Irman. Evation provides this software for Linux and is downloadable at **http://www.evation. com/libirman/libirman.html**. For Gentoo, however, we can just use *emerge*:

```
# emerge libirman
```

After *libirman* is installed, you can perform a quick test. Connect the Irman receiver to the appropriate serial port. Here, we'll assume you are using the second port, named */dev/tts/1*. If you are using the first serial port, make sure you don't have a *getty* process running there.

Use the *test_io* program that was installed as a part of *libirman*:

```
# test_io /dev/tts/1
```

You should immediately see the following output:

```
IR
OK
```

If you you see an error message instead, the application was unable to initialize the Irman receiver. This can happen if you've connected it to the wrong serial port, or if the serial port is not working for some reason. Remember, you may need to upgrade the BIOS to get the second serial port working on an EPIA-M motherboard.

If you get the OK response, try pushing some buttons on your remote control. For each button press, you should see some numeric codes, like these:

```
[77][c0][00][00][00][00]
[75][80][00][00][00][00]
[77][d0][00][00][00][00]
[77][d0][00][00][00][00]
[75][b0][00][00][00][00]
[75][b0][00][00][00][00]
```

LIRC

The Linux Infrared Remote Control (LIRC) package is a "glue" layer that sits between hardware devices (such as the Irman receiver) and software applications. You'll use two of the LIRC programs, *lircd* and *irexec*, to remotely control the jukebox.

Before using *emerge* to install LIRC, you need to set a special *make* option in */etc/make.conf*. Add the following line so that LIRC is compiled with support for the Irman driver:

```
LIRC_OPTS="--with-driver=irman"
```

Then install LIRC:

```
# emerge lirc
# rc-update add lircd default
```

You're not quite ready to start *lircd* just yet. Note, however, that the preceding *rc-update* command means *lircd* will be started each time the system boots from now on.

lircd.conf

The next step is to create the */etc/lircd.conf* file. This file contains a bunch of magic numbers specific to your particular remote control. *lircd* uses the information in this file to map the numeric codes to button names. You can either generate */etc/lircd.conf* by running *irrecord*, or you can try to use a configuration file made by someone else.

The LIRC web site contains a number of config files submitted by users for a wide range of remote controls. To see if yours is included, visit **http://lirc. sourceforge.net/remotes/**. If you find it, copy the file to your computer and save it as */etc/lircd.conf*. Note that *universal remotes* are programmable for different brands and types of devices. Reprogramming the remote changes the codes that it emits. This means that one person's configuration file may not work for you, unless both remotes happen to be programmed for the same device.

To eliminate the uncertainty of using someone else's configuration file, we suggest that you use *irrecord* to create your own:

```
# irrecord --driver=irman --device=/dev/tts/1 /tmp/lircd.conf
```

Follow the instructions that *irrecord* gives you. One of the first things it asks you to do is hold down any button. You'll see a dot on the screen for each signal it receives. You might think that the program is not working because it just keeps printing dots. Eventually, however, it stops and reports something called the *gap length*. The output looks like this:

```
Hold down an arbitrary button.
.............................................................
..........
Found gap length: 209923
```

Then, you'll be prompted to press the buttons one at a time after typing the name for each one. For example:

```
Please enter the name for the next button (press <ENTER> to finish
recording)
POWER

Now hold down button "POWER".

Please enter the name for the next button (press <ENTER> to finish
recording)
PLAY

Now hold down button "PLAY".

Please enter the name for the next button (press <ENTER> to finish
recording)
STOP

Now hold down button "STOP".

Please enter the name for the next button (press <ENTER> to finish
recording)
```

You can make up your own button names (shown in bold above). The names that you enter will appear in the *lircd.conf*. You must use the same names later when you write the */etc/lircrc* file. The button names are not case-sensitive.

In addition to the buttons shown in the example above, you should repeat the process for "pause," "fast-forward," "rewind," "volume-up," "volume-down," "channel-up," and "channel-down." When you are finished, have a look at the */tmp/lircd.conf* file. If it looks reasonable to you (i.e., it has codes for all the buttons you want), copy or rename the file to */etc/lircd.conf*. Here's what ours looks like:

```
# Please make this file available to others
# by sending it to <lirc@bartelmus.de>
#
# this config file was automatically generated
# using lirc-0.7.0pre4(irman) on Sat Jul 10 22:31:15 2005
#
# contributed by
#
# brand:
# model no. of remote control:
# devices being controlled by this remote:
#

begin remote

  name   Philips_Magnavox_PM4B
  bits            16
  eps             30
  aeps           100

  one             0    0
  zero            0    0
  pre_data_bits   16
  pre_data        0xFFFF
  post_data_bits  32
  post_data       0x0
  gap             209915
  min_repeat      1
  toggle_bit      0

      begin codes
          POWER                         0x0000000000005590
          PLAY                          0x0000000000004200
          STOP                          0x0000000000004230
          REV                           0x0000000000004270
          FWD                           0x0000000000004210
          PAUSE                         0x00000000000043C0
          CH-UP                         0x0000000000005750
          CH-DN                         0x0000000000005740
          VOL-UP                        0x0000000000005450
          VOL-DN                        0x0000000000005440
          ZERO                          0x0000000000005550
          ONE                           0x0000000000005540
          TWO                           0x0000000000005570
```

```
            THREE                   0x0000000000005560
            FOUR                    0x0000000000005510
            FIVE                    0x0000000000005500
            SIX                     0x0000000000005530
            SEVEN                   0x0000000000005520
            EIGHT                   0x00000000000055D0
            NINE                    0x00000000000055C0
            ENTER                   0x00000000000055F0
        end codes

    end remote
```

Note that the numeric codes in *etc/lircd.conf* are a little bit different from the way they appear in *test_io* output. For example, the POWER button looks like this in */etc/lircd.conf*:

```
            POWER                   0x0000000000005590
```

But *test_io* prints it this way:

```
    [55][90][00][00][00][00]
```

This is important to know if you need to add buttons to *lircd.conf* later on.

lircd

Now that you have an *lircd* configuration file, you can start it for the first time. But first, edit */etc/conf.d/lircd* and add a command-line option that specifies the serial port where Irman is connected. This example assumes you are using the second serial port:

```
    LIRC_OPTS="-d /dev/tts/1"
```

Then, use the system startup script to start *lircd*:

```
    # /etc/init.d/lircd start
     * Starting lircd...                                [ ok ]
```

You can also check the messages in */var/log/daemon.log* to make sure *lircd* is running correctly:

```
    Jul  7 20:47:17 gentoo-jukebox lircd 0.7.0pre4[8534]: lircd(irman)
    ready
```

lircrc

LIRC clients, such as *xmms* (with the LIRC plug-in), use (yet another) configuration file that binds button names to actions or commands. The *lircrc* file contains a number of definitions like this:

```
    begin
      prog   = program-name
      button = button-name
      config = string
      repeat = digit
    end
```

Here's what they mean:

prog

Specifies the name of the client that should receive notification for this button press. In the following examples, it is set to *xmms*.

button

A remote-control button name that is listed in the */etc/lircd.conf* file.

config

A string that is passed to the client when the button press is detected. For *xmms*, config strings correspond to operations such as Play and Stop.

repeat

Specifies how quickly *lircd* acts on buttons that are held down. For example, with a value of 3, the application receives every third instance of the held-down button press.

The *lircrc* language also has `flags` and `mode` directives. Since these are kind of complicated, we won't talk about them just yet.

Here's an initial configuration file for *xmms*, which you should save as */etc/lircrc*:

```
begin xmms
  begin
    prog = xmms
    button = PLAY
    config = PLAY
  end
  begin
    prog = xmms
    button = PAUSE
    config = PAUSE
  end
  begin
    prog = xmms
    button = STOP
    config = STOP
  end
  begin
    prog = xmms
    button = CH-DN
    config = NEXT
  end
  begin
    prog = xmms
    button = CH-UP
    config = PREV
  end
  begin
    prog = xmms
    button = FWD
    config = FWD 3
```

```
      repeat = 2
    end
    begin
      prog = xmms
      button = REV
      config = BWD 3
      repeat = 2
    end
    begin
      prog = xmms
      button = VOL-UP
      config = VOL_UP 1
      repeat = 1
    end
    begin
      prog = xmms
      button = VOL-DN
      config = VOL_DOWN 1
      repeat = 1
    end
  end
```

This configuration uses the remote's "channel up" and "channel down" buttons to skip between songs. Unfortunately, our remote doesn't have any other buttons that can be used to jump to the next (or previous) song. You should be able to find a remote with the necessary buttons if that is important to you.

You may have noticed that all of the *xmms* button definitions are inside a `begin xmms ... end` block, or *mode group.* We'll refer to this as the *xmms group* and explain its purpose later in the chapter.

Now you should be able to control *xmms* with the remote. Make sure that *lircd* is running; then start *xmms*, make sure the LIRC plug-in is enabled, and try some of the buttons. If it doesn't work, try running *test_io* again to make sure the Irman is receiving signals from the remote control.

Getting fancier

The remote-control setup is pretty cool. You can start and stop songs, skip through the playlist, scan forward and backward during a song, and adjust the volume. Even so, there is still room for improvement. Here are some ways to make the remote even more useful.

Operating without a console

Since your jukebox will eventually be running without a console, you need a way to start (and stop) *xmms* without being logged in. One option is to simply start *xmms* automatically when X Windows starts and hope that it never needs to be restarted. A better approach is to use the remote control. The LIRC package comes with a client called *irexec* that can be used to execute any system command. Thus, you can tell *irexec* to execute *xmms* when the "Power" button is pressed. To make it work, add this to the end of */etc/lircrc*, outside of the begin xmms ... end section:

```
begin
  prog = irexec
  button = POWER
  config = xmms /home/colin/music/list.m3u &
  mode = xmms
  flags = once
end
```

This definition is a little more complicated than the others, so let's make sure that you understand what each line does. The prog line says that the *irexec* client will receive notification events for this button. The *button* line binds this action to the POWER button, which is defined in the */etc/lircd.conf* file. The config line is the string passed to *irexec*. This is the command that *irexec* executes when you hit the button. The playlist file */home/colin/music/list.m3u* is passed as an argument to *xmms*. Also note the ampersand on that line, so that the command runs in the background.

The mode line tells the LIRC system to enter the *xmms mode* after this button has been pressed. From then on, only the buttons defined in the *xmms* group are active. This feature, along with the once flag, ensures that *xmms* is started only once.

You can also use the Power button to stop *xmms*. The */etc/lircrc* configuration looks like this:

```
begin
  prog = xmms
  button = POWER
  config = QUIT
  flags = quit mode
end
```

This button definition goes inside the *xmms* group. The quit flag tells LIRC to stop looking through the configuration for other instances of the POWER button. The mode flag tells LIRC to leave the current mode (i.e., the *xmms* section) and return to the previous mode. This makes the other POWER button active again, so that *xmms* starts again when you press it.

You mustn't forget to actually start the *irexec* program. Otherwise, there will be no way to start *xmms* with the remote. Since *xmms* is an X Windows application, it needs to have the appropriate environment variables (e.g., DISPLAY) to start up. In other words, *irexec* should be a child process of the X server, *Xvnc*. The easiest way to accomplish this is by adding the following *irexec* command to the *$HOME/.vnc/xstartup* file:

```
/usr/bin/irexec --daemon /etc/lircrc
```

Knowing when the jukebox is ready

LIRC is now set up so that you can start *xmms* by pressing the Power button after the system boots. One little annoyance, however, is that you can't tell when the system is finished booting. If you press the Power button before all of the necessary applications are running, it has no effect. Since the system is designed to be very quiet, you might think that it is not even running. A solution to this problem is to play a sound file near the end of the boot sequence. You'll need to find an appropriate sound file that you'd like your jukebox to play when it boots. Then add these lines to */etc/conf.d/local.start*:

```
/usr/bin/amixer set Master 20 unmute
/usr/bin/amixer set PCM 20 unmute
/usr/bin/aplay /root/kill-all-humans.wav
```

Halting the system

Wouldn't it also be nice if you could shut down the system with the remote? Well, you can! You just need to select an appropriate button and make it execute the `poweroff` command. Selecting the appropriate button is the hardest part. The Power button is an obvious choice, but it already has a job: to start and stop *xmms*. Our own remote doesn't have many other buttons that aren't already being used. But we found one that works: a button labeled "Info/Select." First, you need to add the button and numeric code to /etc/lircd.conf:

```
INFOSEL 0x00000000000055A0
```

Now you have to think about where to put the button definition in */etc/lircrc*. It would be annoying if you accidentally hit the button, shutting down the system while playing music. To safeguard against such mistakes, make sure the shutdown button is active only when *xmms* is not running. First, add this button definition inside the *xmms* group:

```
begin
  button = INFOSEL
  flags = quit
end
```

Remember, the code for your remote is probably different. Use the *test_io* command to find the code for your particular remote.

Then, lower in the file, add this definition outside the xmms section:

```
begin
  prog = irexec
  button = INFOSEL
  config = /sbin/poweroff &
end
```

With these two definitions, the shutdown button (e.g., INFOSEL) is disabled when *xmms* is running. If you stop *xmms*, the second definition becomes active, and you can halt the system with the remote control.

Since you're running *vncserver* as a nonprivileged user, the poweroff will fail unless you do something to make it run as *root*. An easy solution to this problem is to enable the setuid bit for */sbin/halt*:

```
# chmod 4755 /sbin/halt
```

This change may be undone later, however, when you upgrade Gentoo. A more complicated solution is to install *sudo* and configure it to allow the nonprivileged user to run poweroff without supplying a password.

> If the poweroff command halts your system but doesn't actually turn off the power, check the power-management settings in the BIOS and make sure that APM and/or APCI are enabled in your kernel.

Managing playlists

Recall that *irexec* passes a playlist file to *xmms*. This is simply a list of audio files, which you can easily generate with a command like this:

```
colin$ find music -type f > music/list.m3u
```

Most people find it boring to listen to their music collection in the same order each time. We have a few ideas for adding some variety to the order of songs:

- The simplest technique is to use *xmms*'s built-in randomize feature. Simply click the RAND button on the main window. *xmms* remembers your settings, and even where it left off in the playlist.

- Another option is to randomize the order of the playlist file, perhaps each time the system boots. For example, you might add these commands to */etc/conf.d/local.start*:

```
su - colin -c "find music -type f \
| perl -e 'print sort {1-int(rand(3))} <>;' \
> music/list.m3u"
```

- Or, you could choose an unused button on your remote control. Use an *irexec* definition to execute the preceding command. As with the system startup sequence, you may want to have it play a little tune when this command has finished doing its thing.

- The *xmms-lirc* plug-in has a neat feature that allows you to select songs in the playlist with the numeric keypad. To make it work, you'll need to add definitions to */etc/lircrc* for the numbers and the ENTER button:

```
begin
  prog = xmms
  button = ONE
  config = ONE
end
begin
  prog = xmms
  button = TWO
  config = TWO
end
...
begin
  prog = xmms
  button = ENTER
  config = SETPOS
end
```

To use this feature, simply enter the song number on the remote and press "Enter."

- The *xmms-lirc* plug-in has another advanced feature that allows you to search for song titles with a technique similar to the way we enter text messages on our mobile phones. However, we feel that this mode is too awkward to use reliably, especially since it brings up a pop-up window to help make the selection. If you want to research this on your own, look for the word "SELECT" in the sample *lircrc* included in the *xmms-lirc* distribution.

- You may prefer to organize your music by genre (folk, jazz, rock, etc). If you take the time to organize your music in this way, you can assign numeric buttons to different genres. To do it, you can use the PLAYLIST_ SET feature of *lirc-xmms*, like this:

```
begin
  prog = xmms
  button = ONE
  config = PLAYLIST_SET /home/colin/music/folk.m3u
end
begin
  prog = xmms
  button = TWO
  config = PLAYLIST_SET /home/colin/music/jazz.m3u
end
begin
  prog = xmms
  button = ONE
  config = PLAYLIST_SET /home/colin/music/rock.m3u
end
...
```

Case Modding

The Mini-ITX motherboard provides a perfect opportunity to attempt a "casemod." Rather than put the system into a boring, or maybe even ugly, computer case, why not stuff it into something unique that you won't be ashamed to have on display in your house? Case modding is quite popular, and you should have no trouble finding numerous pages describing what others have done. Be sure to check out **http://www.mini-itx.com/** if you haven't already!

Since each casemod project is unique, we won't be able to give you specific instructions or advice for your project. Instead, we'll describe how we turned a nonworking antique radio into an enclosure for our jukebox.

Figure 2-14. The antique radio that we'll convert to a digital jukebox.

Preparing the cabinet

One of us purchased an old radio from an antique store some years ago with plans to repair and restore it—a Silvertone-brand tube-type radio manufactured in 1954. Of course, it just sat in the bottom of the closet since then with no progress whatsoever toward making it work again. This particular radio looks pretty good on the outside and seems to have all of its original components on the inside. It has a nice dial; four knobs for volume, tuning and such; and five preset station buttons (see Figure 2-14).

The first step in preparing the cabinet was simply to clean it out and decide what to keep and what to toss. This radio had accumulated quite a bit of dust and dirt over the years. After removing the tuner/amplifier assembly, we used a wet sponge and can of compressed air to clean out the inside. We found that the speaker no longer works, so we removed that as well (which is a good idea in general, since you don't want an unshielded mag-

Figure 2-15. Inside the radio cabinet.

net next to your hard drive!). The tuner/amplifier assembly no longer works, and takes up about half of the cabinet. The tuner dial and all of the knobs are attached to this assembly. We decided to keep it for that reason—to make the cabinet look authentic on the outside. The cabinet is pretty big overall (11 × 19 × 11 inches), so we still had plenty of room for the Mini-ITX motherboard and other parts.

With the cabinet cleaned out, we started to think about where all the new parts should go and how to attach them. Our jukebox consists of a motherboard, laptop hard drive, Irman receiver, and a fan; Figure 2-15 shows how we placed the components inside the cabinet.

The motherboard

We decided to mount the motherboard to the bottom (inside) of the cabinet. It would also fit mounted to one of the sides, but since we were drilling holes in the wood, we preferred to do that to the bottom where it is less visible. We used the same sort of hex mounting screws that you'll find in most computer cases. Unfortunately this is not an item you can find at the local hardware store. We found some at a specialty electronics store and also by searching the Web for various combinations of the terms *hex motherboard standoff screws*.

The Mini-ITX form factor has four holes near each corner of the motherboard for mounting. Our radio cabinet was too short to allow us to drill from the inside, so we drilled four holes from the bottom of the cabinet. This was a relatively tricky procedure for two reasons. First, it was hard to translate an inside position to an outside position because of the way the cabinet is built. Fortunately, we had plenty of wiggle room and made a good approximation. The harder part was marking the holes for drilling on the bottom of the cabinet. We lay the motherboard on the cabinet in the same orientation that it would be mounted. That meant the bottom of the motherboard was more than an inch away from the wood because of the heat sinks and other components. We eyeballed the drill holes by standing above the motherboard and looking down through the existing holes. After marking, we verified their relative positions by measuring both the motherboard holes and the pencil marks.

We drilled the four holes with a 3/32-inch drill bit and then inserted the four hex standoffs. It turns out our eyeballing was good for only three out of the four holes. One of them was off by about 5 millimeters. We drilled a second hole for this one, but missed a little and overcompensated. Rather than put yet another drill hole in such a small area, we decided to just leave it as is. We placed a small piece of insulating material between the motherboard and the standoff to make sure that it didn't touch any exposed solder.

CPU/case fan

Even though our motherboard is "fanless," we thought it should have some airflow inside the cabinet to provide at least a little cooling. The advantage of a fanless system, of course, is that it's much quieter. We didn't want our fan to turn this into a noisy system, so we used two tricks to keep the fan noise to a minimum.

First, we used a fan speed controller, such as the Zalman Fan Mate-1. It has a small knob that controls fan speed (by adjusting the voltage). Once installed, the knob is accessible only from the inside. We planned to leave ours on the slowest and quietest setting, at which it still provides decent airflow and cools the heat sinks.

Figure 2-16. We use sticky pads designed for cable ties to hang things from the top of the cabinet.

Figure 2-17. A fan hangs just above the CPU to provide some cooling.

Our second trick was to suspend the fan above the heat sinks with thin wires. Vibrations are a common source of noise in standard enclosures. When fans are firmly attached to the heat sink and motherboard, vibrations travel throughout the case and may become amplified. Suspending the fan is a great way to eliminate vibration noise. You may be able to use thread or string instead of wire.

We considered inserting small eye screws into the roof of the cabinet. However, it was hard to get them started without being able to drill some pilot holes. Instead we used two square cable-tie attachments that were sticky on one side. These applied to the cabinet quite easily and had a strong adhesive. Then we ran a loop of wire through each one and shaped them into tall triangles, as shown in Figure 2-16.

For the fan we used a spare CPU fan that came with a boxed Pentium 4 CPU. It's about three inches in diameter and its outer plastic has notches that allow it to easily rest on our wires. Although it may not be clear from Figure 2-17, the fan hangs about an inch above the two heat sinks.

Hard drive

We used a 30 GB laptop hard drive and a 44-pin-to-40-pin PATA adapter. As with fans, hard drives are another common source of computer noise for the same reason: the spinning platter.

We used the same suspension trick to reduce noise from the hard drive. Two more sticky cable-tie attachments and a loop of wire kept the hard drive in mid-air, away from the sides of the cabinet. We fed the wire through the holes in the hard drive where you might normally insert screws. See Figure 2-18.

Another way to reduce hard drive noise is to enable power-management features that allow the drive to spin down after some period of inactivity. This is normally a setting in the motherboard's or hard drive's BIOS (if it's in the hard drive, you'll need to get a utility from the hard drive manufacturer that will probably need to run under some form of DOS). We've also noticed that newer hard drives are much quieter than older ones. This might be because manufacturers are paying more attention to noise, but more likely it's simply because drives become noisy after a few years of use.

Irman receiver

The Irman receiver presented a small challenge. The receiver needed to be exposed so that it can receive the infrared signals. However, we didn't want to cut any holes in the cabinet, and we didn't really want the Irman sitting outside the case. Fortunately, we found that the receiver worked quiet well behind the speaker grille cloth. We used sticky cable-tie attachments and wire to suspend it behind the cloth so that the small receiver window is right up against the cloth. Problem solved! You can see the Irman located behind the cloth in Figure 2-18.

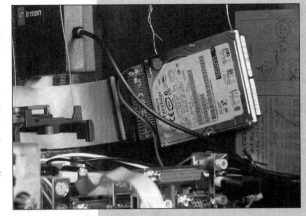

Figure 2-18. Closeup of the hanging hard drive.

On/off switch

As we mentioned earlier, we haven't yet thought of a way to actually turn on the jukebox with the remote control. This meant we needed a power-button switch somewhere. Our preference was to avoid cutting new holes in the cabinet if possible. That left only a couple of options.

We considered mounting our switch on the rear of the cabinet. For example, we might take a small square of scrap wood and mount the switch into it, then attach the scrap wood to the cabinet with glue or screws. While this technique keeps the switch out of view, it also makes it hard to reach.

Another idea was to use one of the existing knobs as an on/off switch. Unlike today's computers that use "soft" switches, old radios use "hard" switches. A computer power button keeps the circuit closed only as long as you hold it down. The radio's on/off switch stays closed (on) once you set it there. To make this work, we'd have needed to replace one of the radio controls with a momentary switch that fits in the same place. We didn't try that.

Instead, we noticed that the station preset buttons behave much like a momentary switch. They even have a little piece of metal that protrudes from the back when a button is pressed. We considered trying to rig up some metal contacts that would make a closed circuit but instead settled on placing the new push button behind the protruding preset slider. Thus, when the preset button is pressed, the slider comes out and touches the modern push-button switch. This was kind of an ugly hack, but since it was inside the case, we didn't really care.

One thing missing from our custom case is an indicator of whether or not the system is running. Standard cases have at least one LED that lights up when you turn on the computer. And even if you can't see the light, you can usually tell when a computer is running because of the noise it makes. Since the jukebox is designed to be silent (when not playing music!), we sometimes have a hard time telling if it is on or off. It's a strange feeling

Figure 2-19. Close-up of the ATX power adapter.

Figure 2-20. The power jack, semi-securely attached to the cabinet.

to press the power button and not receive any feedback that you've actually turned it on. For now we have no plans to add a power indicator to our jukebox, but you might consider using an LED to illuminate the radio dial.

Power supply

We used the Mini-box PW-70A and a spare laptop power supply. Figure 2-19 shows the adapter in place on the motherboard. We considered mounting the AC/DC transformer inside the radio cabinet as well, but opted to leave it out so that our power cord was three feet longer. The power jack has two holes for screws. We attached the jack to the wooden cabinet with just one screw, shown in Figure 2-20.

Speakers

We considered a number of speaker alternatives for our jukebox. An obvious choice is to simply use a standard set of computer speakers. They are trivial to connect and should sound very good if you get a nice set. We used a couple of these while designing the jukebox and found they picked up a significant amount of AM radio interference, most likely from the large antenna that was less than a mile away.

We also considered placing a speaker inside the antique radio cabinet. However, our cabinet only had an opening for one speaker. We would rather enjoy the stereo aspects of the music played on the jukebox.

While visiting the local thrift store, we found a nice pair of used, wall-mounted speakers for $3. They look like something you might find in a junior high school from the 1970s. We were pleasantly surprised to discover that the EPIA-M can drive the speakers to a decent volume without any additional amplifiers. They're not loud enough for a dance, but more than loud enough for use around the house or office.

Extra Credit

In this section, we'd like to give you some ideas and hints for making the jukebox even better.

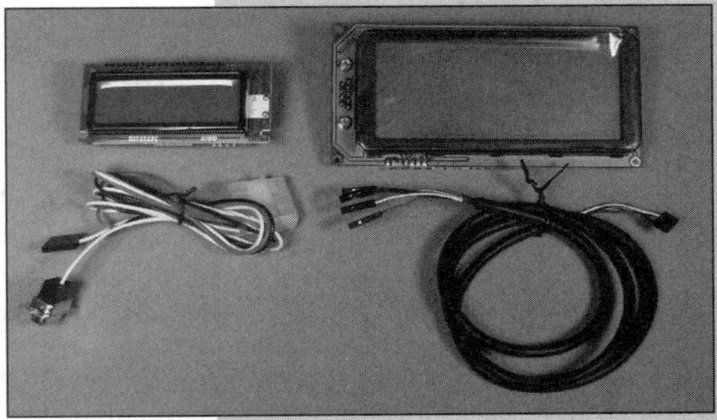

A better sound card

The VIA EPIA-M has a built-in sound chip that seems to be pretty good. However, audio snobs may feel that it lacks certain features. If VIA's sound chip doesn't meet your requirements, you can always use the PCI slot for a fancier sound card.

Figure 2-21. The Seetron SGX-120L (left) and the Crystalfontz CFA634 (right).

A CD-RW drive

We haven't said much about putting a CD reader in the jukebox. Chances are that you already have a CD drive on an existing system. That means you'll do the ripping on one box and copy the files over to the jukebox. Instead, you might prefer to have a CD reader (and writer) on the jukebox itself. The 12-volt-to-ATX power converter should have more than enough power for a CD drive. If you decide to build your own case, the CD drive may present a bit of a challenge. You might also consider using an external CD drive with a USB interface.

Streaming

If you already have a computer that stores your entire music collection, you might want to use a streaming setup. Instead of copying all the music files to the jukebox, transfer them over the network as they are played. XMMS has good support for streaming, and a number of other streaming clients are also available.

If you take this approach, you can probably even build a Compact Flash–based jukebox and avoid the heat and noise that comes from most hard drives. You can also use the PCI slot for a wireless network interface. Then you won't have an Ethernet cable running across your floor.

LCD display

An LCD display is a very cool addition to the jukebox. Not only can it show you the name and artist of the current song, but you can also use it for feedback when the system is starting up and shutting down.

LCDproc (**http://lcdproc.omnipotent.net/**) is the most popular LCD software for Linux and BSD systems. It uses a client/server model to control an LCD display. The server (*LCDd*) communicates with an LCD display over a serial, parallel, or USB port. It accepts connections and commands from clients. When multiple clients are connected to the server, each client's screen is displayed in a round-robin fashion.

Make sure that the LCD display you purchase is supported by LCDproc. Fortunately, it supports quite a few so you have many to choose from. Displays made by Crystal Fontz (**http://www.crystalfontz.com**) and Matrix Orbital (**http://www.matrixorbital.com**) are very popular, and most should be supported. You can expect to spend $50 to $100 on a decent display.

LCD displays come in a variety of sizes (and colors). Two popular sizes are 2×16 and 4×20 characters. We recommend that you get a 4×20 display if you can, since that is the size assumed by one of the XMMS plug-ins we'll talk about shortly. You'll want to consider the display's physical size if you plan to mount it into a drive bay or custom enclosure. Both of the LCD displays shown in have 4×20 characters.

We chose the Crystal Fontz CFA634-TFB-KU, which has 4×20 characters and a USB connection. One of the reasons we recommend USB is that the jukebox's two serial ports are already tied up: one for the system console, the other for the Irman receiver. You'll need to load the following kernel modules to activate and use a USB interface to the LCD:

```
# modprobe uhci-hcd
# modprobe usbserial
# modprobe ftdi_sio
```

You should then see messages like this in */var/log/messages*:

```
usbcore: registered new driver usbserial
usbcore: registered new driver usbserial_generic
ftdi_sio 2-1:1.0: FTDI 8U232AM Compatible converter detected
usb 2-1: FTDI 8U232AM Compatible converter now attached to ttyUSB0
usbcore: registered new driver ftdi_sio
```

Next, install LCDproc on Gentoo with emerge:

```
# emerge lcdproc
```

The current version, *lcdproc-0.4.5*, does not compile due to a bug in its Irman driver. If this happens to you, try installing it manually by running configure without any driver options:

```
# cd /tmp
# tar xjvf /usr/portage/distfiles/lcdproc-0.4.5.tar.bz2
# cd lcdproc-0.4.5
# ./configure --prefix=/usr
# make && make install
```

Next, configure *LCDd* by editing */etc/LCDd.conf*. Find the section that starts with [server]. Comment out the none driver and uncomment the driver line for your particular LCD. For example, we have a Crystal Fontz CFA-634, so we uncomment the CFontz driver:

```
[server]
DriverPath=/usr/local/lib/lcdproc/
#Driver=none
#Driver=curses
#Driver=HD44780
#Driver=lcdm001
#Driver=MtxOrb
Driver=CFontz
#Driver=CwLnx
#Driver=Wirz-sli
#Driver=SGX120
```

Then, search for the [CFontz] section later in the file. There, you can set various parameters such as the serial port device, speed, and display size:

```
[CFontz]
# CrystalFontz driver
Device=/dev/tts/USB0
Size=20x4
Contrast=140
Speed=19200
NewFirmware=yes
Reboot=no
USB=yes
```

After saving *LCDd.conf*, run *LCDd* with this command:

```
# /usr/local/sbin/LCDd -s &
```

You should probably also add this command to */etc/conf.d/local.start*.

You can test out the display with this simple LCDproc client command:

```
# lcdproc T
```

XMMS has a number of LCD-related plug-ins. The best one is called *lcdraptor*. You can download it from **http://www. retechnologies.org/**. To install it, run these commands:

```
# tar xzvf lcdraptor-0.3.tar.gz
# cd lcdraptor-0.3/
# make
# make install
```

Then, start or restart *xmms*. Type Ctrl-V to see the list of available visualization plug-ins. You should see "LCD Raptor vis-plugin v0.3" in the list. Highlight it and then click on the "Enable plugin" checkbox. You should immediately see the song title, time remaining, and dancing bars on your LCD, as shown in Figure 2-22.

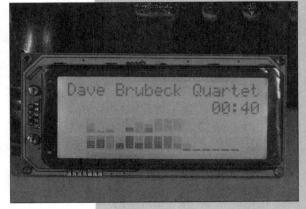

Figure 2-22. Close-up of the LCD display when playing a song

Digital Video Recorder with MythTV

3

Time

three days

Difficulty

difficult

What You Need

- Shuttle Zen ST62K XPC (or similar)
- Processor, memory, and hard drive for PC
- Hauppauge TV tuner card
- CD/DVD drive (optional)
- Irman infrared receiver
- Universal remote control
- Spare screen and keyboard to use during setup

Digital Video Recorders (DVRs) have added a new dimension to watching television. Many people like being able to pause live TV for a short amount of time. Another great feature is the ability to store hours and hours of recorded programs. With a 160 GB hard drive, you can store between 50 and 100 hours of video, depending on your encoder settings. That's an order of magnitude more than you can get on a VHS tape. Recording programs is very easy with a DVR. Instead of going to your VCR and programming in a channel and a start and stop time, you can simply select a menu option that says "record The Simpsons every time it is on."

You can turn almost any PC into a DVR with a little extra hardware and software. The most important component is a TV tuner card—a PCI device that converts your analog cable/satellite television signal into a digital format. You'll also want a large hard drive to store recordings and other things. If you want to use the DVR with your television, you should also get an infrared remote control. Finally, you might also want a DVD/CD drive in your DVR.

For software we'll be using Linux, XOrg, MythTV, LIRC, and numerous other behind-the-scenes packages. Installing and configuring the software may take quite a while, especially if you've never used these programs before. You might spend a week or so if you work on this project during your free time.

XOrg? MythTV? LIRC?

XOrg is one of two popular X Window System implementations for Unix. The other is XFree86, which is now becoming less popular after adding an advertising clause to its license in early 2004. See http://en.wikipedia.org/wiki/Xfree86 and http://www.x.org* for more information.

MythTV refers to a number of programs that work together to turn your TV into a media center. You can use MythTV to record and watch television programs, listen to music, get the weather forecast, and more. Its homepage is http://www.mythtv.org/.

LIRC is the Linux Infrared Remote Control project. It allows a number of applications, such as MythTV, to be controlled by a remote control. See http://www.lirc.org/.

*Who did XOrg sleep with to get a single-letter domain name?

Figure 3-1. Front view of the Shuttle ST62K.

If you're planning to purchase new hardware for this project, you'll probably spend between $750 and $1,000. Combine this with the time requirement, and you might be wondering if you shouldn't just go out and get a TiVo or ReplayTV. Certainly, those products will get you on the DVR bandwagon quickly and easily. They are also cheaper up front, although they are subsidized by your monthly subscription fees. So why build your own?

Of course, the standard do-it-yourself reasons apply (see Preface). Building your own DVR gives you control over its use and operation. Don't like the color scheme? Change it! Want the DVR to work with your existing remote control? It can! Want to put the DVR on your wireless network? No problem!

Privacy concerns are another good reason for taking on this project. Maybe you don't want ReplayTV and their affiliates to know that you can't get enough of the *Powerpuff Girls* and *Saved by the Bell*. Perhaps you are insulted when TiVo automatically records episodes of *The Golden Girls* because it thinks you would really like to watch them.

Another great reason to build a MythTV box is all of the extra features you get. For example, you can use multiple tuner cards and separate systems for recording and playback. MythTV comes with a number of great plug-ins too. With these, you can get the weather forecast, listen to music, give someone a slideshow of your vacation pictures, catch the latest news, and even make a video and voice-over-IP phone call to a friend.

Whatever your reasons, we think that you'll really enjoy using MythTV to record and watch television programs.

Introducing the Shuttle ST62K XPC

Unlike some of our other projects in this book, a digital video recorder requires substantial processing power and a large hard drive. We'd like to have a P4-class processor and a 100 GB or larger disk. A few companies now make Pentium 4 Mini-ITX systems, so we could build our own. However, for this project, Shuttle was kind enough to send us a very nice bare-bones system: the Zen ST62K XPC.

The ST62K looks a lot like most of Shuttle's XPC products. It is more or less cube-shaped (7.5 × 7 × 11 inches) and made of brushed aluminum. The front has a 5.25-inch drive bay, a 3.5-inch drive bay, three audio jacks, and two USB ports. It also has the standard power button, reset button, power indicator, and disk activity light. See Figure 3-1.

The rear panel has pretty much everything else you'd need on a computer: video, Ethernet, serial, parallel, mouse, keyboard, FireWire, additional

USB, S-Video output, and S/PDIF ports, as shown in Figure 3-2. The ST62K has one PCI slot for expansion.

One thing that makes this box unique is its power supply. The ST62K uses a rather large external, brick-type, 180 watt power supply. Figure 3-3 shows the power supply sitting next to the computer. Like most external power supplies, this one uses passive cooling, which probably explains why it is so large and heavy. Taking the power supply out of the case leaves more room for other components and reduces fan noise. SilentPCReview.com reports that this external supply is very efficient. Still, the ST62K draws about 40 watts during normal operation.

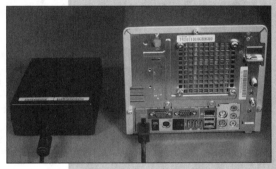

Figure 3-2. Rear view of the Shuttle ST62K.

Looking inside the ST62K, you'll find another 3.5-inch hard drive bay, and two SDRAM DIMM memory slots. The designers paid particular attention to keeping the case free of cable clutter. The internal hard drive is mounted just over the motherboard parallel ATA (PATA) connector. Shuttle provides a 2-inch-long PATA cable to connect the two. You'll also find another PATA and power cable running along the frame to the rear of the CD/DVD drive bay.

The ST62K's CPU fan is interesting as well. Unlike older systems, there is no fan on top of the CPU heat sink. Instead you'll find heat pipes that transfer heat from the CPU to the rear of the case. You can see the heat sink, pipes, and rear-facing fan in Figure 3-4. This is nice because the system has only one fan. It cools the CPU and removes hot air from the case.

Figure 3-3. The ST62K and its power supply.

Assembling the system

Obviously, the first step in building your digital video recorder is to assemble the hardware components. In addition to the bare-bones system (i.e., motherboard and case), you'll need a CPU, memory, hard drive, and TV tuner card. You may also want to use a CD/DVD-ROM drive. We're using a 2.2 GHz Pentium 4, a 512 MB SDRAM DIMM, a 120 GB hard drive, a Hauppauge WinTV-GO, and a Sony CD/DVD drive.

You can start by installing the CPU. Remove the four thumbscrews that secure the fan to the back of the case. Find and disconnect the three-wire fan connector near the motherboard's PCI slot. Remove the heat-sink clip by pressing down until it unlatches. At this point, you should be able to carefully remove the whole heat-pipe assembly. Prepare the CPU socket by pulling the lever to a vertical position. Note that the CPU fits into the socket in only one orientation. You can tell by looking at the pins on the CPU and the holes in the socket. One of the corners has a pin/hole missing. These must line up, or else the CPU will not easily drop into the socket.

Figure 3-4. Top-down view of the CPU cooler assembly.

Figure 3-5. Inserting the hard drive.

Figure 3-6. Inserting the DVD/CD drive.

Once the CPU is in place, push the lever back down to the horizontal position and lock it in place.

Your bare-bones system should include a small heat-sink compound packet. This is some gooey white or gray stuff that goes between the CPU and the heat sink to improve heat transfer between them. First, make sure the surface of your CPU is clean and free of dust (polish it with a lint-free paper towel or soft cloth). Cut open the packet and place a small bead in the middle of the CPU. Note that you need very little because it will be squished and spread out over the whole surface. Use about as much as would fit on the head of a small screw. Next, make sure the surface of the heat pipe that presses down on the CPU is clean and free of dust. Then, re-insert the heat-pipe assembly. Press down on the heat sink to spread the compound around. Replace the clip that secures the heat sink to the motherboard. Remember to plug the fan cable back into the motherboard. Finally, secure the fan to the rear of the case with the thumbscrews. Double-check your work before turning on the system, since a mistake here could cause the CPU to overheat, resulting in permanent damage.

To install the memory, select one of the two banks. Make sure that the two end latches are opened outward. Also note that the DIMMs and slots have a notch so that you cannot install them backwards. When they are lined up correctly, the DIMM should drop in easily. Then, press down firmly until it snaps into place. The two end latches should automatically flip inward when the board is properly installed.

The ST62K has a nifty hard drive mounting system. You must first remove a screw to free the drive carrier. The carrier slides out diagonally from underneath the 3.5-inch drive bay, as shown in Figure 3-5.

Insert the drive into the carrier such that the power and PATA connectors will be on the correct side of the case when you slide it back in. Secure the drive to the carrier with three small screws. Then, slide the drive into position and secure it again with the thumbscrew. Attach the power cable to the drive and connect the short PATA cable to both the drive and the motherboard. The power cable doesn't have much slack so it might be difficult to attach. If so, loosen the carrier and pull it out a little, then attach the cable and slide it back in.

If you're adding a CD/DVD drive, remove the cover for the large drive bay. Slide the drive into the bay as shown in Figure 3-6 and secure it with four screws, making sure that the front of the drive lines up nicely with the front of the case. Attach the power and PATA cables to the drive.

Finally, install the TV tuner card in the PCI slot, as shown in Figure 3-7. The ST62K has a small bracket on the rear of the case, just above the PCI slot opening. Remove the screw and lift up this bracket as you insert the TV tuner card. When the card is fully inserted, place the screw back into the bracket and tighten it. Our WinTV-GO card came with a short audio cable designed to connect the TV tuner card audio output to the sound card input. The shuttle ST62K has two audio inputs (line and microphone) on the front of the case—too far away for the short cable to reach. We purchased a longer cable to connect the TV tuner audio output to the line input. You don't need this audio cable if you get the PVR250/350 because the card encodes audio directly into the MPEG stream.

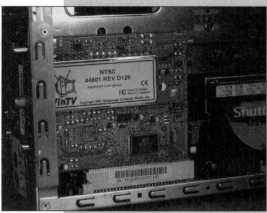

Figure 3-7. The PCI TV tuner card.

Test the system after you have all the components installed, but before you put the cover back on. Connect a keyboard, mouse, and the power supply. When you turn on the system, you should see some Power On Self Test (POST) messages from the system BIOS. You may want to enter the BIOS menu and poke around. Make sure that it sees your hard drive and CD/DVD drive if you have one. If the system doesn't start up correctly, try removing components one at a time until you isolate the problem.

You'll need to make an important BIOS change if you plan to eventually use the system without a keyboard. On the Standard CMOS Features BIOS page, you'll see an option labeled "Halt On" with three settings. We recommend that you set it to either "None" or "All, But Keyboard." If you forget to set this and try to boot the system without a keyboard connected, you'll get a paradoxical message that says *No keyboard present: press F1.*

ST62K quirks

A number of ST62K users report that the system fan stops turning after some time. Since the box is normally very quiet, they don't hear a change when the fan stops working. They may notice the problem when the CPU overheats, however. In fact, that is how we noticed that our fan had stopped. The problem is not with the fan itself but with the fan controller on the motherboard. Fortunately, the motherboard has two fan connectors (FAN1 and FAN3). Most users are able to continue using their systems after moving the fan to the FAN3 connector.

Some users also report problems with using inexpensive memory in the system. If you experience random crashes or other problems, you may want to reduce the memory speed in the system BIOS.

We also recommend updating the system BIOS if you can. Visit the support pages on Shuttle's web site and download the current BIOS and installer. Our own ST62K was hanging every few days until we upgraded the BIOS to version FT62S00Z.

Notes on Noise

The ST62K is a relatively quiet system—much better than most XPCs. The external power supply is a big help. The system's only fan starts off loud when you turn the system on but quickly reduces in speed and quiets down. For us, the noisiest part is the hard drive, which may be because the hard drive had been used previously. Newer hard drives tend to be quieter. If you are purchasing a new drive for your MythTV system, you may want to seek out drives designed to be quieter than most, such as the Seagate Barracuda 7200 series.

You may hear some vibrational noise that sounds like buzzing if the case is not on tight, or if something is not quite right. You may be able to eliminate that noise by adjusting the thumbscrews. If that doesn't make the buzzing go away, try placing something heavy, like a textbook, on top of the computer. An even better idea is to hang the hard drive from the mounting bracket using wire, string, or shock cord as shown at http://www.silentpcreview.com/article109-page1.html.

Were money not an issue, we would like to try out a very quiet hard drive in a system from Hush Technologies or Tranquil.

Operating System: Gentoo Linux

As with the audio jukebox project in Chapter 2, we recommend that you use Gentoo Linux for the DVR system as well. The installation procedure is almost the same, so we will be somewhat brief in this chapter. One important difference here is that the DVR uses X Windows, which means there is more software to install.

One of the first steps in installing Gentoo is to configure the network interface so that you can download software packages from the Internet. Our Shuttle ST62K uses a RealTek RTL8139 Ethernet controller. The kernel doesn't see the interface until you load the *8139too* module:

```
# modprobe 8139too
# dhcpdc eth1
```

You're probably using a much larger hard drive for this project than for the jukebox, since the ST62K holds a standard 3.5-inch disk. We recommend that you create a separate filesystem partition to store recorded programs and other media. For example, you may want to have four partitions: 32 MB for */boot*, 512 MB for *swap*, 5120 MB for */*, and the remainder for */media*. When you are finished adding all the partitions with *fdisk*, they should look something like this:

```
Disk /dev/hda: 123.5 GB, 123522416640 bytes
16 heads, 63 sectors/track, 239340 cylinders
Units = cylinders of 1008 * 512 = 516096 bytes

   Device Boot    Start      End     Blocks   Id  System
/dev/hda1    *        1       63      31720+   83  Linux
/dev/hda2            64     1056     500472    82  Linux swap
/dev/hda3          1057    10978    5000688    82  Linux
/dev/hda4         10979   239340  115094448    82  Linux
```

Continue with the installation by running *mke2fs* on the new partitions; then mount the new filesystems. Visit the Gentoo *mirrors.xml* page (see Chapter 2) and download the *stage3* tarball for your processor. The Shuttle ST62K has a Pentium 4, so you should download *stage3-pentium4-2005.1.tar.bz2* (or a later version). Extract the tarball when the download is complete.

The next step in the installation process is to chroot to the new filesystem root and install a bunch of things with *emerge*:

```
# chroot /mnt/gentoo /bin/bash
# env-update
# source /etc/profile
# emerge sync
# emerge portage
# emerge gentoo-sources
# emerge genkernel
```

Now it is time to configure the kernel. Unlike in Chapter 2, you'll need to enable two nondefault options in the new kernel. One adds support for the

ATI IXP chip in the Shuttle ST62K. The IXP chip does many things, including interfacing with PATA hard drives. We had poor disk performance on the ST62K before enabling ATI IXP support in the kernel. The other configuration change adds support for the TV tuner card. Bring up the kernel configuration menu with this command:

```
# genkernel --menuconfig all
```

The ATI IXP option is under the following menu options:

```
Device Drivers  --->
    ATA/ATAPI/MFM/RLL support  --->
        <Y> ATI IXP chipset IDE support
```

Your TV tuner card (such as our Hauppauge WinTV-Go) most likely uses the popular Brooktree 848 (or compatible) chip. That chip corresponds to the *bttv* driver/module in the kernel. Menuconfig doesn't show the *bttv* driver as an option until you enable "I2C bit banging interfaces":

```
Device Drivers  --->
    I2C support  --->
        <M> I2C support
            I2C Algorithms  --->
                --- I2C bit-banging interfaces
```

Then go back up the configuration menu and find the *bttv* driver under the following menus:

```
Device Drivers  --->
    Multimedia devices  --->
        <M> Video For Linux
            Video For Linux  --->
                <M> BT848 Video For Linux
```

Exit the kernel configuration menu and let *genkernel* work its magic. While *genkernel* is running, you can switch to another screen (Alt-F2) and take care of the following tasks:

- Fix up */etc/fstab*. For example:

```
/dev/hda1   /boot       ext2    noauto,noatime   1 1
/dev/hda3   /           ext3    noatime          0 0
/dev/hda2   none        swap    sw               0 0
/dev/hda4   /media      ext3    noatime          1 2
none        /dev/shm    tmpfs   defaults         0 0
none        /tmp        tmpfs   defaults         0 0
```

- Install a boot loader, such as GRUB.

- emerge dhcpcd

- emerge sysklogd.

- emerge vixie-cron.

- Set the *root* password.

Hauppauge PVR Products

Although we used the WinTV-GO, in retrospect we would recommend that you get a WinTV-PVR250 or WinTV-PVR350 instead. Both of these models include a hardware MPEG encoder, which takes a significant burden off the CPU. The PVR350 also has its own frame buffer with built-in MPEG decoder and television output. Both packages also include an infrared remote control and receiver.

Retail, OEM, and Warranties

When buying a processor, you have two choices: retail or OEM. Retail packages come with a heat sink/fan unit and have a warranty. OEM packages do not include a heat sink and often have no warranty at all. Not surprisingly, OEM packages are usually (but not always!) cheaper than retail.

Another thing to consider is that the retail package warranty is only good as long as you use the fan that comes with the processor. A standard Pentium 4 heat sink won't really fit in the ST62K, so you're forced to use the Shuttle heat sink, which, technically, violates the warranty anyway.

Note that you compiled the *bttv* driver as a kernel module. When *genkernel* is finished, add the following line to */etc/modules.autoload.d/kernel-2.6*:

```
bttv
```

As always, run *modules-update* after modifying one of the module configuration files:

```
# modules-update
```

We recommend rebooting the system at this point, mostly so you can take advantage of the ATI IXP driver. If you're not using the Shuttle ST62K (or some other system with the ATI IXP chip), you may prefer to just continue configuring Gentoo as described in the following subsections.

When you reboot, make sure that your TV tuner card is recognized. Check the */var/log/messages* file for lines containing bttv:

```
bttv: driver version 0.7.108 loaded
bttv: using 4 buffers with 2080k (8320k total) for capture
bttv: Bt8xx card found (0).
bttv0: Bt878 (rev 17) at 02:07.0, irq: 5, latency: 64, mmio: 0xec200000
bttv0: detected: Hauppauge WinTV [card=10], PCI subsystem ID is
0070:13eb
bttv0: using: Hauppauge (bt878) [card=10,autodetected]
bttv0: Hauppauge/Voodoo msp34xx: reset line init [5]
bttv0: Hauppauge eeprom: model=44801, tuner=Temic 4036FY5 (8), radio=no
bttv0: using tuner=8
bttv0: i2c: checking for MSP34xx @ 0x80... not found
bttv0: i2c: checking for TDA9875 @ 0xb0... not found
bttv0: i2c: checking for TDA7432 @ 0x8a... not found
tvaudio: TV audio decoder + audio/video mux driver
tvaudio: known chips: tda9840,tda9873h,tda9874h/a,tda9850,tda9855,tea6
300, tea6420,tda8425,pic16c54 (PV951),ta8874z
tuner: chip found @ 0xc2
tuner: type set to 8 (Temic NTSC (4036 FY5))
bttv0: PLL: 28636363 => 35468950 .. ok
bttv0: registered device video0
bttv0: registered device vbi0
bttv0: PLL can sleep, using XTAL (28636363).
```

If you are happy with the system so far, proceed with the remaining setup tasks.

Misc setup

You should configure your system to use NTP so that its clock is synchronized to an accurate source. This is especially important if you want to record television broadcasts:

```
# emerge ntp
# ntpdate us.pool.ntp.org
# echo driftfile /var/lib/ntp/ntp.drift > /etc/ntp.conf
# echo server us.pool.ntp.org >> /etc/ntp.conf
# /etc/init.d/ntpd start
# rc-update add ntpd default
```

If you have a local NTP server, use it instead of us.pool.ntp.org. Also, if you are located outside the United States, you should probably replace us with your own country code. See **http://www.pool.ntp.org/** for more information.

If you are using DHCP, you'll probably want to place this line in */etc/conf.d/net* so that *dhcpcd* doesn't clobber your */etc/ntp.conf* file:

```
dhcpcd_eth0="-N"
```

You should also set the local time zone. Replace America/Denver with your own time zone filename:

```
# cd /etc
# rm localtime
# ln -s /usr/share/zoneinfo/America/Denver localtime
```

Now, when you type date, you should see the correct local time:

```
# date
Mon Sep  6 14:41:18 MDT 2005
```

Gentoo installs the *nano* editor by default. If you are more comfortable with *vi* you can install it now:

```
# emerge nvi
```

If you plan to use the DVR without its own keyboard and display, you should enable the SSH daemon for remote access. Run the following command so that *sshd* starts automatically when your system boots:

```
# rc-update add sshd default
```

Finally, set the hostname to something meaningful in */etc/conf.d/hostname*:

```
HOSTNAME="dvr"
```

You may also want to add the hostname to the localhost line in */etc/hosts*:

```
127.0.0.1       localhost dvr
```

Don't forget to configure the startup scripts to automatically bring up the interface each time the system boots:

```
# vi /etc/conf.d/net
# rc-update add net.eth0 default
```

Finally, you may want to set the following USE flags in */etc/make.conf*:

```
USE="X kde qt mysql jpeg dvd"
```

Audio configuration

We explained how to configure the sound system for Gentoo in Chapter 2. The procedure here is essentially the same, although the driver name is different. Our jukebox motherboard had a VIA sound chip, but the ST62K uses the ATI IXP for sound. To begin, add this line to */etc/make.conf*:

```
ALSA_CARDS="atiixp"
```

Then run:

```
# emerge alsa-driver
# emerge alsa-utils
```

Next, add the kernel module to */etc/modules.d/alsa*:

```
alias snd-card-0 snd-atiixp
```

Then run:

```
# modules-update
# rc-update add alsasound boot
# /etc/init.d/alsasound start
# amixer set Master 20 unmute
# amixer set PCM 20 unmute
```

You can look at */proc/asound/cards* to make sure that the kernel recognizes your sound card or chip:

```
# cat /proc/asound/cards
0 [IXP          ]: ATIIXP - ATI IXP
                        ATI IXP rev 0 at 0xec305000, irq 11
```

X Windows

Now it's time to install X Windows and associated applications. It takes only a few *emerge* commands, but quite a long time, to install everything. You may want to chain all of these commands together and go on a day hike while your system downloads, compiles, and installs all the necessary software. First, install the main X Windows package:

```
# emerge xorg-x11
```

Since *xorg-x11* doesn't include *xterm*, which we recommend over the KDE/ Gnome versions, you'll have to install it separately:

```
# emerge xterm
```

At this point, you should have enough X Windows components installed to give it a test. Before launching anything, however, you must either reboot or manually update your environment variables so they pick up the newly installed *bin* directories:

```
# env-update
# source /etc/profile
```

Historically, one of the most difficult parts of installing X Windows was writing the X server configuration file. Fortunately, XOrg provides two utilities that make it pretty easy. The first one you should try is:

```
# Xorg -configure
```

It leaves a file called *xorg.conf.new* in your current directory. You can quickly test the configuration file with this command:

```
# startx -- -config xorg.conf.new
```

If it works, you should see a few windows (xterms) with bland colors. Test that your mouse and keyboard work by moving the cursor and typing a few things. You can exit this session by typing **exit** in all the xterms or by pressing the Ctrl, Alt, and Backspace keys simultaneously. If you are happy with this configuration file, move it to the default location:

```
# mv xorg.conf.new /etc/X11/xorg.conf
```

If that configuration file doesn't work on your system, you can edit the file and tweak some of the settings. See **http://www.gentoo.org/doc/en/xorg-config. xml** for some suggestions. Alternatively, you can try using *xorgconfig* to generate the *xorg.conf* file. With this approach, you need to know a little about your hardware. In particular, you should know the name and model number of your video card/chip, how much memory it has, and the vertical and horizontal sync frequencies for your monitor. In many cases, you can make conservative guesses and come out with a working system.

Now that you have a working X server, you might want to install one of the popular integrated desktop environments: KDE or Gnome. Both provide a window manager, a web browser, and many other applications. Later, when we get to running MythTV on your television, we'll recommend not using any window manager or desktop environment at all. However, KDE or Gnome may prove useful while you are getting all this stuff up and running. The downside is that these are large collections of software. You may have to wait a long time while Gentoo compiles everything. If you are impatient, you can get by with a nice, but not-too-big, standalone window manager such as FVWM.

The following sections explain how to install FVWM (a lightweight window manager that's much quicker to install than KDE or Gnome), KDE, or Gnome.

FVWM

To install FVWM, simply type:

```
# emerge fvwm
```

To use FVWM, place these lines into your ~/.xinitrc file:

```
#!/bin/sh
xterm &
fvwm &
wait
```

Then, start X Windows from the command line:

```
# startx
```

Since FVWM is a window manager only, you'll probably want to install a web browser such as Opera and/or Mozilla:

```
# emerge opera
# emerge mozilla-firefox
```

KDE

The entire KDE collection takes a long time to install. You may want to let it run overnight, or while you go watch a couple of movies. To start the installation, run:

```
# emerge kde
```

When it finishes, you'll have a new directory named something like */usr/kde/3.4*. To update your environment variables, run env-update and then source /etc/profile. To try out KDE, place these lines into your ~/.xinitrc file:

```
#!/bin/sh
xterm &
startkde
```

Then, start X Windows:

```
# startx
```

Gnome

Installing Gnome is very similar to installing KDE. To install:

```
# emerge gnome
```

Gnome installs binaries and libraries into */usr* so you don't need to worry about the env-update command. Here is a minimalist ~/.xinitrc file:

```
#!/bin/sh
xterm &
gnome-session
```

Then, start X Windows:

```
# startx
```

xdm

Some people prefer to use an X Display Manager with X Windows. The display manager starts the X server and then presents the user with a place to enter a username and password. The display manager is usually started when the system boots, and it eliminates the need to run startx. If you want to go this route, add these lines to /etc/rc.conf:

```
DISPLAYMANAGER="kdm"
XSESSION="kde-3.4"
```

Or, for Gnome fans:

```
DISPLAYMANAGER="gdm"
XSESSION="Gnome"
```

Then, configure the display manager to start each time your system boots and start it manually now:

```
# rc-update add xdm default
# /etc/init.d/xdm start
```

Note that later we'll suggest that you use startx to automatically start X Windows, so you'll need to delete *xdm* from the default startup sequence.

MythTV

By now you have the operating system, X Windows, and maybe even a desktop environment. Finally it's time to install MythTV! During this part, you may also want to refer to **http://gentoo-wiki.com/HOWTO_Setup_MythTV** as we go along.

Installation

Installing MythTV on Gentoo is simple. The only tricky part is that we are now dealing with *masked packages*.

In Gentoo-speak, a package is masked when the developers feel it is unstable or suspect there might be bugs or problems on a particular system architecture. Note that Gentoo portage often knows about different versions of a given package. An older version may be unmasked (stable), while a newer version is masked (possibly unstable). This is the case with many of the MythTV packages. We recommend that you create the file named /etc/portage/package.keywords:

```
# mkdir /etc/portage
# vi /etc/portage/package.keywords
```

Masked what?

If this masking stuff seems confusing, have a look at http://gentoo-wiki.com/Masked.

This file contains package names, one per line. By adding a package name to this file, you are telling Gentoo to give you the most recent version of a package, even if it is unstable. For MythTV, add these lines to the file:

```
dev-perl/Tk-TableMatrix
media-tv/mythfrontend
media-tv/mythtv
x11-themes/mythtv-themes
```

Then, install MythTV and associated packages:

```
# emerge mythtv mythfrontend mythtv-themes
```

Setting up: mythbackend

mythbackend is the heart of MythTV. It controls the TV tuner hardware, encodes audio and video streams, and records them on disk. It knows the names and numbers of your TV channels and has access to the program listings. *mythbackend* is responsible for recording your favorite shows while you are away. It can even manage multiple TV tuner cards connected to multiple television inputs.

MythTV stores various things in a MySQL database. MySQL was automatically installed when you ran emerge mythtv. The MySQL daemon (*mysqld*) must be configured and running before you can run MythTV. Run the following commands to initialize the database now, and to make it start each time your system boots:

```
# /usr/bin/mysql_install_db
# /etc/init.d/mysql start
# rc-update add mysql default
```

Then create the MySQL *mythtv* user with this command:

```
# mysql < /usr/share/mythtv/database/mc.sql
```

The next task is to populate the database with the appropriate channel listings. The procedure for doing so varies from country to country. For those of us located in North America, it's pretty simple. You can get the listings from **zap2it.com**, through their DataDirect service. The catch is that you must register and answer their long-ish survey to get a password.

Start the registration procedure by visiting **http://labs.zap2it.com**. You'll need to enter a valid "certificate code" during the process. These are, apparently, assigned to various projects such as MythTV and others so that **zap2it.com** can track their popularity. These codes are not too hard to find (e.g., Google for "zap2it certificate code"). The MythTV documentation instructs people to use the code ZIYN-DQZO-SBUT.

DataDirect subscriptions are currently valid for only three months. To maintain the subscription, you'll need to go through another short survey each time it expires.

To begin the MythTV configuration process, start *mythsetup*:

```
# mythsetup
```

You should see a screen similar to the one in Figure 3-8. Note that MythTV hides the mouse cursor in its windows. Navigating the menus with the keyboard is relatively simple. Use the arrow keys to highlight the menu option that you are interested in. Press the spacebar to select that option. On pages that look like forms, always use the up/down arrow keys to move between items and use the left/right arrow keys to select among choices associated with an item. The Escape key takes you back to the previous menu.

Select the General option from the main page. It has five sub-pages, but you only need to make changes on two of them. The first page (Host Address Backend Setup) shouldn't require any changes. On the second page, titled Host-specific Backend Setup, you'll probably need to change the two directories at the top. As you can see in Figure 3-9, we suggest storing your recordings in */media/mythtv*.

On the next page, titled Global Backend Setup, you may need to change a couple of things, such as the "TV format" and "Channel frequency table" settings. See Figure 3-10 for an example from our configuration. The defaults on the fourth (Shutdown/Wakeup Options) and fifth pages (WakeOnLan settings) should be fine.

When you find yourself back at the main menu, select "Capture cards" next. Then, select "(New capture card)," and you should see the screen shown in Figure 3-11. You probably won't need to change any of the settings. Make sure, however, that the video and audio device names are set. If the fields are blank, you need to exit and make sure the kernel modules are loaded properly.

Return to the main *mythsetup* screen and choose "Video sources." Then select "(New video source)," and you should see the screen shown in Figure 3-12. Supply a name for this video source and select the appropriate TV listings grabber for your region. If you are using DataDirect, enter your username and password.

So far, you've told MythTV about your tuner card and about your television service provider. Now it's time to connect them to each other. Return again to the main *mythsetup* screen and then go to the "Input connections" page. You should see a screen like Figure 3-13. The "Input connections" screen is where you tell MythTV which of the TV tuner card's inputs is connected to the television signal. Select the appropriate input connector, such as Television.

Figure 3-8. The main mythsetup menu.

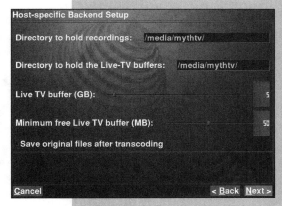

Figure 3-9. The Host-specific Backend Setup screen allows you to change the directory where MythTV stores recorded programs.

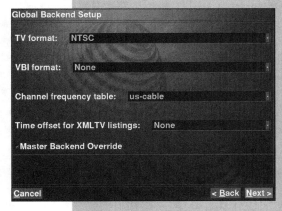

Figure 3-10. The Global Backend Setup screen has settings for your video format and channel frequencies.

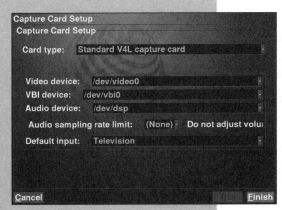

Figure 3-11. Check the device settings on the "Capture Card Setup" screen.

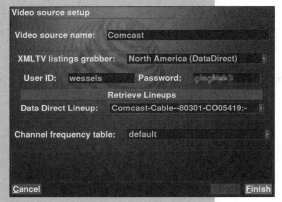

Figure 3-12. The "Video Source Setup" screen is where you configure the TV listings grabber.

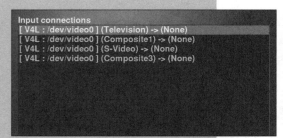

Figure 3-13. The mythsetup Input connections screen.

Then, on the "Connect source to input" screen, select the corresponding video source for the input, as shown in Figure 3-14.

You probably don't need to worry about the final *mythsetup* screen, the Channel editor. Simply exit *mythsetup* by pressing Escape.

We suggest that you run *mythbackend* as a nonprivileged user. You can create a new user with this command:

```
# useradd -m -G audio,video,cdrom mythtv
```

Note that it is important to place the *mythtv* user into the *audio*, *video*, and *cdrom* groups so that it can access those devices. After creating the user, edit */etc/conf.d/mythbackend* and set the MYTH_USER variable:

```
MYTH_USER=mythtv
```

You won't be able to watch or record TV until you populate the database (i.e., channel listings) by running *mythfilldatabase*. You can run it as *mythtv* with this command:

```
# su - mythtv -c mythfilldatabase
```

This utility downloads channel listings for the next week or so. You should run *mythfilldatabase* daily from a *cron* job. Use **crontab -e mythtv** to edit *mythtv*'s crontab and add this line:

```
07 11 * * * /usr/bin/mythfilldatabase
```

Now you can start the backend processes. To start it manually now, and each time the system boots, run these commands:

```
# /etc/init.d/mythbackend start
# rc-update add mythbackend default
```

Check */var/log/mythtv/backend.log* for error messages and make sure the backend daemon actually starts. If it doesn't start, fix the problem and then run:

```
# /etc/init.d/mythbackend zap
# /etc/init.d/mythbackend start
```

We highly recommend that you keep tail -f /var/log/mythtv/backend.log running in an xterm window as you explore how MythTV works.

Running: mythfrontend

By now you've probably put many hours into this project. Finally you should be able to actually *use* MythTV to watch television! Start by running *mythfrontend*:

```
# mythfrontend
```

Then simply select Watch TV. If everything works, you should see something resembling a television broadcast on your screen. You can change channels with the Up and Down arrow keys, or by typing the channel number followed by Enter. Don't worry if you are disappointed by the quality of the audio or video. You can probably improve them by configuring the audio and video encoders, which we'll go through shortly.

If your experience is similar to ours, you'll spend some time tinkering with the audio before it works very well. The first time we heard any sound, it was very choppy, out of sync with the video, and it stopped entirely after 10–15 seconds. Here are some things you can try to improve the sound quality:

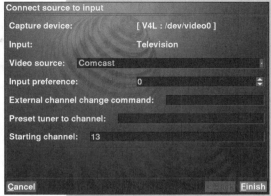

Figure 3-14. The "Connect source to input" screen.

- KDE's audio daemon, *artsd*, sometimes interferes with other programs that access the sound device. You may want to permanently disable it by selecting the following sequence of menu items:

  1. KDE "start" menu
  2. Settings
  3. Control Center
  4. Sound & Multimedia
  5. Sound System
  6. Uncheck "enable the sound system"

- Make sure the TV tuner card's audio output is connected to the sound card's line input if using the WinTV-GO or similar.

- Fiddle with the mixer settings. We recommend that you mute all the unused inputs and outputs. The Master and PCM outputs should be unmuted and have nonzero volume. The Line input should be selected for capture, but it should also be muted. The Capture input should be selected and unmuted. These settings are summarized in Table 3-1 and correspond to the following *amixer* commands:

```
# amixer set Master,0 81%,81% unmute
# amixer set PCM,0 71%,71% unmute
# amixer set Line,0 0%,0% mute captur
# amixer set Capture,0 87%,87% captur
```

Table 3-1. Sound Card Settings.

Control	Muted?	Level
Master	Unmute	81%
PCM	Unmute	71%
Line	Mute	0%
Capture	N/A	87%

You might find it easier to use a GUI interface, such as kmix. The settings that work for us are shown in Figures 3-15 and 3-16.

Try btaudio

Some TV tuner cards also have a built-in audio device. You may be able to use the btaudio driver to get sound directly from the TV tuner card.

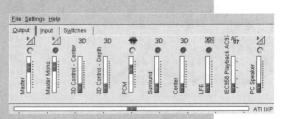

Figure 3-15. Audio mixer output settings that work for us.

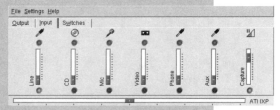

Figure 3-16. Audio mixer input settings that work for us.

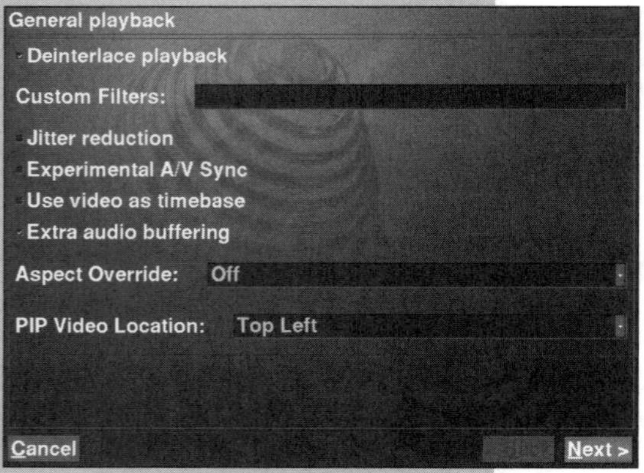

Figure 3-17. You may want to enable extra audio buffering on the "General Playback" screen.

- Visit the General Playback settings page. Start at the main *mythfrontend* menu, then select Utilities/Setup→Setup→TV Settings→Playback. The first page is titled General Playback and looks like the one in Figure 3-17. Check the box next to "Extra audio buffering."

Once you have the sound settings just right, save them with this command:

```
# /usr/sbin/alsactl -f /etc/asound.state.mythtv \
    store
```

Note that we're suggesting you save the sound card settings to a non-standard file. This is because Gentoo calls alsactl when it shuts down, and that would overwrite the settings you saved. Shortly, we'll show you how to restore the settings from asound.state.mythtv each time the system boots.

If you take a look at */var/log/mythtv/mythbackend.log* while watching TV, you may see this message:

```
Unknown video codec
Please go into the TV Settings, Recording Profiles and setup the
four 'Software Encoders' profiles.
Assuming RTjpeg for now.

Unknown audio codec
```

To fix this little problem, you need to go to the main MythTV menu. From there, select Utilities/Setup→Setup→TV Settings→ Recording Profiles, and then the line that says "Software Encoders (v4l based)." You should now have a screen that looks like the one in Figure 3-18. It shows four profiles: Default, Live TV, High Quality, and Low Quality. These profiles determine the encoding parameters that MythTV uses when recording broadcasts. You should update at least the Default and Live TV profiles.

For each profile, you need to go through a sequence of four screens. You probably don't need to change anything on the first ("Profile") or second ("Image Size") screens. The third screen, shown in Figure 3-19, has the settings for the video encoder. You can choose between RTjpeg and MPEG-4. We think that RTjpeg looks better, but it requires more CPU power. For example, compiling some software while watching TV caused jitter with the RTjpeg encoder, while MPEG-4 was unaffected. If you go with the MPEG-4 encoder, we recommend enabling the "Enable interlaced DCT encoding" and "Enable interlaced motion" options.

On the final screen, shown in Figure 3-20, you can set the audio encoding options. We recommend Uncompressed over MP3. You can also change the sampling rate to 32,000, 44,100, or 48,000 bits per second. In our subjective tests, changing the sampling rate did not make any noticeable difference.

Adding a Remote Control

The best way to use MythTV is with a remote control. You really shouldn't have to use a mouse and keyboard while lying on the couch watching TV. If you built the Digital Audio Jukebox (Chapter 2), then you already know how to do this. If not, here is a quick recap. You'll need a remote control and an Irman infrared-to-serial adapter.

If you plan to buy a remote control for this project, we highly recommend that you get one with up, down, left, and right buttons that are separate from the volume and channel controls, such as the one shown in Figure 3-21. This is primarily because you'll want to use the direction keys for traversing the MythTV menus. Alternatively you can use two different modes of the remote (e.g., TV and VCR) to separate the volume controls at least.

Install the Irman interface library (*libirman*) with this command:

```
# emerge libirman
```

Next, install the LIRC software. Before running *emerge*, tell LIRC that you'll be using the Irman driver:

```
# echo 'LIRC_OPTS="--with-driver=irman"' >> \
/etc/make.conf
# emerge lirc
```

After the software is installed, you can connect the Irman to a serial port, as shown in Figure 3-22 and test everything with the *test_io* command. You should see numeric codes when you press buttons on your remote control:

```
# test_io /dev/tts/0
IR
OK
[77][c0][00][00][00][00]
[75][80][00][00][00][00]
```

You'll need an */etc/lircd.conf* file that corresponds to your particular remote control. You might be able to find one at **http://lirc. sourceforge.net/remotes/**. Alternatively, it's almost just as easy to make one yourself with *irrecord*:

```
# irrecord -d /dev/tts/0 /etc/lircd.conf
```

We decided to use the VCR mode of our multi-function remote to control MythTV. Here's the */etc/lircd.conf* file we got after running *irrecord*:

```
begin remote

  name  foo
  bits        64
```

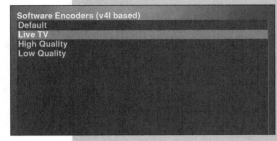

Figure 3-18. The "Software Encoders (v4l based)" screen.

Figure 3-19. Choose between MPEG-4 and RTjpeg on the Video Compression screen.

Figure 3-20. We recommend uncompressed audio at any available bitrate.

Figure 3-21. A remote control for the DVR with a separate navigation keypad.

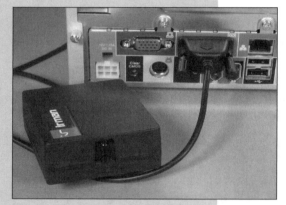

Figure 3-22. Connecting the Irman receiver.

```
eps           30
aeps         100

one            0      0
zero           0      0
gap       209963
toggle_bit     0

    begin codes
        POWER             0xFFFF419000000000
        CH+               0xFFFF435000000000
        CH-               0xFFFF434000000000
        VOL-              0xFFFFC0F800000000
        VOL+              0xFFFFC07800000000
        MUTE              0xFFFFC03800000000
        1                 0xFFFF414000000000
        2                 0xFFFF417000000000
        3                 0xFFFF416000000000
        4                 0xFFFF411000000000
        5                 0xFFFF410000000000
        6                 0xFFFF413000000000
        7                 0xFFFF412000000000
        8                 0xFFFF41D000000000
        9                 0xFFFF41C000000000
        0                 0xFFFF415000000000
        ENT               0xFFFF43D000000000
        MENU              0xFFFF43E000000000
        CHAP-             0xFFFF434000000000
        CHAP+             0xFFFF435000000000
        QUIT              0xFFFF432000000000
        SCAN-             0xFFFF427000000000
        PLAY              0xFFFF420000000000
        SCAN+             0xFFFF421000000000
        REC               0xFFFF422000000000
        STOP              0xFFFF423000000000
        PAUSE             0xFFFF43C000000000
        RETURN            0xFFFF408000000000
        UP                0xFFFF439000000000
        DOWN              0xFFFF41B000000000
        RIGHT             0xFFFF41A000000000
        LEFT              0xFFFF418000000000
    end codes
```

Before starting *lircd*, you need to edit */etc/conf.d/lircd* and tell it to use the Irman driver by adding this line:

```
LIRCD_OPTS="-d /dev/tts/0"
```

Now you can start *lircd* immediately, and each time the system boots:

```
# /etc/init.d/lircd start
# rc-update add lircd default
```

At this point, we have the LIRC daemon configured and running. The next step is to write a LIRC client configuration file. You'll use two LIRC clients: *irexec* and *irxevent*. Most of the functionality is handled by *irxevent*. Note that they share a single configuration file.

The *irxevent* program sends fake events (keypresses and button clicks) to an X Window. You'll use it to send the keystrokes that control MythTV. The MythTV documentation has a full list at **http://www.mythtv.org/docs/mythtv-HOWTO-11.html**. You'll implement only a subset of those commands with the remote control. The following */etc/lircrc* file maps remote control buttons to *irexec* and *irxevent* instructions:

```
begin
    prog = irxevent
    button = QUIT
    repeat = 1
    config = Key Escape CurrentWindow
end
begin
    prog = irxevent
    button = CH+
    repeat = 1
    config = Key Up CurrentWindow
end
begin
    prog = irxevent
    button = CH-
    repeat = 1
    config = Key Down CurrentWindow
end
begin
    prog = irxevent
    button = ENT
    repeat = 1
    config = Key Return CurrentWindow
end
begin
    prog = irxevent
    button = SCAN+
    repeat = 1
    config = Key Right CurrentWindow
end
begin
    prog = irxevent
    button = SCAN-
    repeat = 1
    config = Key Left CurrentWindow
end
begin
    prog = irxevent
    button = PLAY
    repeat = 1
    config = Key P CurrentWindow
end
begin
    prog = irxevent
    button = PAUSE
    repeat = 1
    config = Key P CurrentWindow
end
```

```
begin
    prog = irxevent
    button = MENU
    repeat = 1
    config = Key M CurrentWindow
end
begin
    prog = irxevent
    button = 0
    config = Key 0 CurrentWindow
end
begin
    prog = irxevent
    button = 1
    config = Key 1 CurrentWindow
end
begin
    prog = irxevent
    button = 2
    config = Key 2 CurrentWindow
end
begin
    prog = irxevent
    button = 3
    config = Key 3 CurrentWindow
end
begin
    prog = irxevent
    button = 4
    config = Key 4 CurrentWindow
end
begin
    prog = irxevent
    button = 5
    config = Key 5 CurrentWindow
end
begin
    prog = irxevent
    button = 6
    config = Key 6 CurrentWindow
end
begin
    prog = irxevent
    button = 7
    config = Key 7 CurrentWindow
end
begin
    prog = irxevent
    button = 8
    config = Key 8 CurrentWindow
end
begin
    prog = irxevent
    button = 9
    config = Key 9 CurrentWindow
end
begin
    prog = irxevent
```

```
        button = UP
        repeat = 1
        config = Key Up CurrentWindow
end
begin
        prog = irxevent
        button = DOWN
        repeat = 1
        config = Key Down CurrentWindow
end
begin
        prog = irxevent
        button = LEFT
        repeat = 1
        config = Key Left CurrentWindow
end
begin
        prog = irxevent
        button = RIGHT
        repeat = 1
        config = Key Right CurrentWindow
end
begin
        prog = irexec
        button = POWER
        config = /usr/local/bin/start-myth.sh
end
#begin
#       prog = irexec
#       button = VOL-
#       repeat = 1
#       config = amixer -q set Master 1-
#end
#begin
#       prog = irexec
#       button = VOL+
#       repeat = 1
#       config = amixer -q set Master 1+
#end
#begin
#       prog = irexec
#       button = M
#       config = amixer -q set PCM mute
#end
```

Note that you're telling *irexec* to run a shell script when the POWER button gets pressed. This provides a way to restart both *mythbackend* and *mythfrontend* in case either one crashes or if you unintentionally exit the application. The script reads the process ID file for *mythbackend*. If the PID file is not found, or if the process is not running, the script starts it up again. For the frontend, it just kills the entire X session and starts it up again. Here's the *start-myth.sh* script:

```
#!/bin/sh
start_backend() {
        # zap the state back to stop in case mythbackend
```

```
        # crashed
        /etc/init.d/mythbackend zap
        /etc/init.d/mythbackend start
}

if test -f /var/run/mythtv/mythbackend.pid ; then
        PID=`cat /var/run/mythtv/mythbackend.pid`
        if kill -0 $PID ; then
                echo "mythbackend is already running"
        else
                start_backend
        fi
else
        start_backend
fi

# just kill the X server, wait for X clients to die, then start it
again
killall X
sleep 3
count=0
while test $count -lt 10 ; do
        $HOME/startx.sh
        sleep 1
        count=`expr $count + 1`
done
```

The *start-myth.sh* script calls *startx.sh*. We decided to separate out the commands for starting X Windows so that you can also call that script when the system boots. Here is the *startx.sh* script:

```
#!/bin/sh
exec > $HOME/xsession.log
exec 2>&1
exec startx
```

Note that the last few lines of the */etc/lircrc* file are commented out. We commented out the button definitions for VOL-, VOL+, and Mute because of an interesting feature of our universal remote. When the remote is in the VCR mode, which we use for MythTV, the volume buttons work the same as they do when the remote is in the TV mode. That is, the volume buttons automatically change the TV volume. Of course, this only works if you've also programmed the universal remote for your particular TV. If your remote control does not work this way, you may want to uncomment the volume-related buttons in */etc/lircrc* so you can control the volume with *amixer*.

Starting MythTV Automatically

In our quest to build a keyboard-less, remote-controlled digital video recorder, we now need to talk about automatically starting MythTV when the system boots. We initially planned on suggesting that you use KDE's auto-login and auto-start features. However, we feel that KDE (or Gnome) is an unnecessary complication for the task. They spawn too many extra processes that we don't need, and they also like to fiddle with the sound settings. So instead, we suggest a very simple startup scheme with no window manager at all.

Start by editing */etc/conf.d/local.start* and adding these two lines:

```
/bin/su - mythtv --login -c /usr/bin/irexec /etc/lircrc &
/bin/su - mythtv --login -c /home/mythtv/startx.sh &
```

The first runs *irexec*, which acts on some of your remote control buttons. The second line runs the *startx.sh* script (listed in the previous section), which starts X Windows.

startx.sh, of course, just runs *startx* after redirecting stdout and stderr. The rest of the programs are started after X is running. If you've already written a *~/.xinitrc* file, replace its contents with these few lines (as promised, we're restoring the sound settings from the file we created earlier):

```
#!/bin/sh
irxevent /etc/lircrc &
alsactl -f /etc/asound.state.mythtv restore
mythfrontend
```

Note that since *mythfrontend* is the last command in the *.xinitrc* file, X Windows shuts down if/when *mythfrontend* exits. If that happens to you, simply press the remote's Power button to restart X Windows and *mythfrontend*.

Using Your TV as the Display

Many Mini-ITX–sized motherboards, such as the Shuttle ST62K, come with built-in TV outputs. We were really looking forward to using that feature on this project. Unfortunately, it didn't "just work."

The first few times we tried to run X Windows on the TV, the display was scrambled, as though either the horizontal or vertical sync settings were wrong. Even though the text-display mode worked just fine, the graphics mode did not. We tried numerous horizontal and vertical sync settings, different screen resolutions, but nothing worked.

The Shuttle ST62K uses an ATI Radeon 9100 IGP chip for its display. ATI releases proprietary drivers for Linux and XFree86, but getting them to work is a little bit tricky. For Gentoo, you may want to refer to **http://gentoo-wiki.com/HOWTO_ATI_Drivers** as you go along. Begin by installing the ATI drivers:

```
# emerge ati-drivers
```

Then, execute this command:

```
# opengl-update ati
```

The Gentoo documentation instructs you to run *fglrxconfig* next. But this program will ask you a bunch of technical questions that you (and we) probably don't know the answer to. Instead, we suggest that you try the following *xorg.conf* file:

```
Section "dri"
    Mode 0666
EndSection

Section "Module"
    Load        "dbe"
    SubSection  "extmod"
      Option    "omit xfree86-dga"
    EndSubSection
    Load        "type1"
    Load        "freetype"
    Load        "glx"
    Load        "dri"
EndSection

Section "Files"
    RgbPath     "/usr/X11R6/lib/X11/rgb"
    FontPath    "/usr/X11R6/lib/X11/fonts/misc/"
    FontPath    "/usr/X11R6/lib/X11/fonts/75dpi/:unscaled"
    FontPath    "/usr/X11R6/lib/X11/fonts/100dpi/:unscaled"
    FontPath    "/usr/X11R6/lib/X11/fonts/Type1/"
    FontPath    "/usr/X11R6/lib/X11/fonts/75dpi/"
    FontPath    "/usr/X11R6/lib/X11/fonts/100dpi/"
EndSection
```

```
Section "InputDevice"
        Identifier    "Keyboard0"
        Driver        "kbd"
EndSection

Section "InputDevice"
        Identifier    "Mouse0"
        Driver        "mouse"
        Option        "Protocol" "auto"
        Option        "Device" "/dev/input/mouse0"
EndSection

Section "Monitor"
        Identifier    "TV"
        VendorName    "SomeVendor"
        ModelName     "SomeModel"
        DisplaySize   160 120
EndSection

Section "Device"
    Identifier                      "ATI Graphics Adapter"
    Driver                          "fglrx"
    Option "no_accel"               "no"
    Option "no_dri"                 "no"
    Option "mtrr"                   "off"
    Option "DesktopSetup"           "0x00000000"
    Option "MonitorLayout"          "CTV,NONE"
    Option "IgnoreEDID"             "off"
    Option "HSync2"                 "unspecified"
    Option "VRefresh2"              "unspecified"
    Option "ScreenOverlap"          "0"
    Option "NoTV"                   "no"
    Option "TVStandard"             "NTSC-M"
    Option "TVHSizeAdj"             "0"
    Option "TVVSizeAdj"             "0"
    Option "TVHPosAdj"              "0"
    Option "TVVPosAdj"              "0"
    Option "TVHStartAdj"            "0"
    Option "TVColorAdj"             "0"
    Option "GammaCorrectionI"       "0x00000000"
    Option "GammaCorrectionII"      "0x00000000"
    Option "Capabilities"           "0x00000800"
    Option "VideoOverlay"           "on"
    Option "OpenGLOverlay"          "off"
    Option "CenterMode"             "off"
    Option "PseudoColorVisuals"     "off"
    Option "Stereo"                 "off"
    Option "StereoSyncEnable"       "1"
    Option "FSAAEnable"             "no"
    Option "FSAAScale"              "1"
    Option "FSAADisableGamma"       "no"
    Option "FSAACustomizeMSPos"     "no"
    Option "FSAAMSPosX0"            "0.000000"
    Option "FSAAMSPosY0"            "0.000000"
    Option "FSAAMSPosX1"            "0.000000"
    Option "FSAAMSPosY1"            "0.000000"
    Option "FSAAMSPosX2"            "0.000000"
```

```
            Option "FSAAMSPosY2"              "0.000000"
            Option "FSAAMSPosX3"              "0.000000"
            Option "FSAAMSPosY3"              "0.000000"
            Option "FSAAMSPosX4"              "0.000000"
            Option "FSAAMSPosY4"              "0.000000"
            Option "FSAAMSPosX5"              "0.000000"
            Option "FSAAMSPosY5"              "0.000000"
            Option "UseFastTLS"               "0"
            Option "BlockSignalsOnLock"       "on"
            Option "UseInternalAGPGART"       "yes"
            Option "ForceGenericCPU"          "no"
            Screen 0
    EndSection

    Section "Screen"
        Identifier   "Screen0"
        Device       "ATI Graphics Adapter"
        Monitor      "TV"
        DefaultDepth 24
        SubSection "Display"
            Depth        24
            #Modes       "640x480"
            Modes        "800x600"
        EndSubSection
    EndSection
```

The `DisplaySize` line in the monitor definition is not strictly necessary. However, it affects the size of MythTV's fonts. We found that the fonts were too small by default, so we added the `DisplaySize` line. The ratio of these two numbers should match your TV's aspect ratio. For example, 160/120 equals 4/3. If you have a wide-screen TV then you should use numbers that correspond to 16/9.

Using the VESA driver

If you can't get the ATI (*fglrx*) drivers working, you can always fall back on the VESA driver. The ST62K's TV output works well with the VESA driver, and the configuration is much simpler. First, make sure you change the OpenGL settings back to the default:

```
# opengl-update xorg-x11
```

Then, try using these *xorg.conf* section definitions:

```
    Section "Module"
            Load   "extmod"
            Load   "dbe"
            Load   "record"
            Load   "xtrap"
            Load   "type1"
            Load   "freetype"
    EndSection

    Section "Monitor"
            Identifier   "TV"
            VendorName   "SomeVendor"
```

```
        ModelName      "SomeModel"
        DisplaySize  160 120
EndSection


Section "Device"
        Identifier  "VESA Device"
        Driver      "vesa"
        VendorName  "All"
        BoardName   "All"
EndSection

Section "Screen"
        Identifier "Screen0"
        Device     "VESA Device"
        Monitor    "TV"
        DefaultColorDepth 24
        SubSection "Display"
                Depth     24
                Modes "640x480"
                #Modes "800x600"
        EndSubSection
EndSection
```

Note that the VESA driver does not support the X-video extension, also
known as *XVideo*. That extension takes advantage of the video hardware
to perform certain operations such as scaling and contrast/brightness
adjustments. Without XVideo support, these operations are performed in
software, placing considerable load on the CPU.

The problem is especially noticeable when watching live TV because the
system is encoding and decoding the video stream at the same time. When
the CPU is working too hard, the decoder skips some frames. The previous
version of MythTV would occasionally lose audio/video synchronization
and even stop playing audio altogether. This is why we've commented out
the 800x600 mode line and are using 640x480 instead. It looks the same on
our TV screen, while using a little less of the CPU.

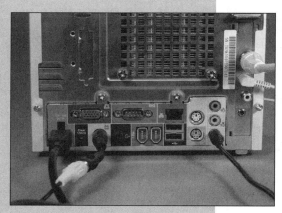

Figure 3-23. Connecting cables to the rear panel.

Figure 3-24. Our digital video recorder in place.

Working without a mouse

Even though MythTV is an X Windows application, it doesn't use a mouse. You navigate the menus with a remote control or standard keyboard. One little problem is that X doesn't normally start if it fails to detect a mouse. Fortunately, that's easy to fix with a special *xorg.conf* option:

```
Section "ServerFlags"
        Option "AllowMouseOpenFail"  "true"
EndSection
```

Putting it all together

Figure 3-23 shows what the back of the ST62K looks like with all of the cables (except the Irman) connected (note that the audio output from the TV tuner card connects to the Line input on the front of the case). The left-most cable on the bottom goes to the external power supply. Next to that is the video output, which connects to your television. On the bottom right is the audio output, which also connects to your television, or perhaps to a separate home theater audio system. On the far right, you can see two white cables connecting to the TV tuner card. One is the coaxial cable carrying the TV signal. Below that is the tuner card's audio output, which connects to the PC's sound input on the front of the system. Figure 3-24 shows how the ST62K looks sitting next to a 27-inch television.

Extra Credit

Here are a few ideas for improvements that you can explore on your own.

Additional Myth components

MythTV can do much more than record and play TV programs. It has quite a few additional components, or plug-ins, that we haven't covered. When installing a MythTV plug-in on Gentoo, don't forget to add the package name to */etc/portage/package.keywords*, as we did for *mythtv* and *mythfrontend*.

Our favorite plug-in is MythWeather. From the Setup menu you enter your Zip Code. MythWeather retrieves weather data from msnbc.com and weather.com. It rotates through four different screens that display current weather conditions, the forecast, and an animated doppler radar image. Very cool!

MythDVD is the component that plays movies from the DVD drive. It uses *mplayer* to play DVDs by default, which works well. If you plan to really use MythDVD, you'll need to add more lines to */etc/lircrc* so you can control *mplayer* with the remote. Search the Web for "mplayer lircrc" to get started.

MythMusic is the plug-in for playing music. You can rip CDs or import previously encoded music files. MythMusic supports playlists, ratings for individual songs, cool visualizations, and more. After you install MythMusic, be sure to visit the Music Settings menus and set the directory where music files are stored. If MythTV runs as a non-root user, make sure that user has write permission to the music directory.

MythNews is an RSS news feed client. You can select from numerous sources and then browse the news items. We think it would be nice if MythNews automatically displayed the news items like a "ticker," rather than forcing us to browse.

MythGallery is a very nice, no-frills plug-in for displaying images. It recognizes JPEG, PNG, TIFF, BMP, GIF, and PPM image file formats. You can browse image directories, rotate, zoom in/out, and display images as a slideshow. You can also use MythGallery to import new images from CD-ROM, over the network, or directly from your camera.

MythGame is a frontend for the X Windows version of the Multiple Arcade Machine Emulator (MAME). Xmame is a program that emulates the hardware of many older, arcade-style, coin-operated games, such as Pac Man and Donkey Kong. While Xmame is Free Software, most of the game ROMs are not. Game ROMs are difficult to find because they are copyrighted and you can't distribute them without permission. However, **pdroms.de** offers a few public domain and freeware ROMs that work with MAME. If you plan to use MythGame, you'll probably want to have a joystick connected to your computer.

MythBrowser is a KDE-based web browser for MythTV. It looks like the konqueror browser, but without the top menu bar. We feel that it is a little too difficult to use with a TV and without a keyboard/mouse.

MythPhone is a plug-in that allows you to make video phone calls using a simple webcam and microphone. Calls are established with the Session Initiation Protocol (SIP), which is used by most voice-over-IP applications and devices. It currently interoperates with Windows Messenger 4.7 and, of course, other MythPhone users.

Add a wireless keyboard

Some MythTV components and features are really difficult to use with a remote control. For example, the Setup screens often require you to type pathnames and other options. Using the arrow keys to search for names in the program guide can take a long time as well. You might enjoy MythTV a little more with a wireless keyboard. Either an infrared (IR) or radio frequency (RF) model should just work without any Linux configuration changes.

Alternatively, if you find yourself frequently sitting in front of the TV with a notebook computer, you could use an application such as x2x (**http://x2x. dottedmag.net/**) or Synergy (**http://synergy2.sourceforge.net/**) to control your MythTV system using your notebook's keyboard and mouse.

Multiple tuners

MythTV supports multiple tuner cards, which allow you to record more than one show at a time or to record one show while watching another. You might also need more than one tuner if you have more than one video feed entering your house. To add additional tuners, run *mythsetup*, select "Capture cards," and then configure the corresponding Video source. However, since the Shuttle ST62K has only one PCI slot, you'd need to use a case/motherboard combo or a bare-bones system with more slots.

Client/server

Another neat thing about MythTV is that you can run the frontend and backend on different machines. This means, for example, that you can have a single backend server (perhaps hidden in your closet) with multiple frontend boxes scattered around the house. If you take this approach, it also makes sense to have multiple tuners, although it's not required.

Using the Hauppauge PVR350

If you have the WinTV-PVR350, you need to install some additional drivers and make some adjustments to the system configuration. The best reason to use the PVR350 or PVR250 is the hardware MPEG encoder.

Note that the PVR350 is a little bit difficult to install in the ST62K because the PCI card is relatively large. The back of the card has two threaded coax connectors. It is difficult to get the top connector into the opening in the back of the case. It takes a little patience and maneuvering, but the card does fit.

The PVR350 uses a driver called *ivtv* rather than *bttv*. You can install it with *emerge*:

```
# emerge media-tv/ivtv
```

Then add it to */etc/modules.autoload.d/kernel-2.6*:

```
# echo ivtv >> /etc/modules.autoload.d/kernel-2.6
# modules-update
```

Also create a file named */etc/modules.d/ivtv* with these contents:

```
alias char-major-81      videodev
alias char-major-81-0    ivtv
alias char-major-81-1    ivtv
```

As you go through *mythsetup*, certain configuration options will be different. For example, on the Capture Card Setup screen, select "MPEG-2 Encoder card (PVR-250, PVR-350)" and set the default input to Tuner 0. On the Input Connections screen, connect your video source to Tuner 0 as well.

If you have trouble, play around with *ivtvctl* and *ivtv-tune*. You can also install and use *tvtime* and *xawtv* to make sure the tuner is working correctly.

External tuners

The examples in this chapter assume that the television source is a standard analog cable signal. If you have digital cable or a satellite-based service such as DISH network or DirecTV, you'll need to do a little extra work to use MythTV. At issue is whether or not MythTV can control the tuner for your particular television service.

You should probably start by reading the (short) section titled "Adding support for an external tuner" in the MythTV HOWTO document (currently at **http://www.mythtv.org/docs/mythtv-HOWTO-11.html#ss11.5**).

Unfortunately, that section tells you only that you need a *changechannel* program, which does not come with MythTV. You'll probably need to spend a bit of time searching the Web for phrases that include "mythtv" and your particular television tuner.

If you have a DirecTV tuner, you can use a serial cable and the *directv.pl* script to make MythTV change the channel. You can buy a premade cable from **http://www.dtvcontrol.com/.** You can currently find the *directv.pl* script at **http://www.pdp8.net/directv/directv.shtml**.

If you have DISH network service, you probably can't use a serial cable to control the tuner. Instead you'll need to build or buy an infrared transmitter, affectionately called the IR Blaster, which connects to your serial port. The IR Blaster uses LIRC to transmit the same codes as your tuner's remote control. See the IR Blaster HOWTO at **http://www.mythtv.org/wiki/index.php/Using_an_ IR_Blaster_with_MythTV.** You can purchase an IR Blaster from **http://www.irblaster. info/.**

Note that the DataDirect (**zap2it.com**) listing service also contains channel lineups for DirecTV, DISH network, and other noncable services.

Conserving power

Leaving the MythTV box on all day is equivalent to leaving a 40–60 watt light bulb on. Certainly a MythTV box uses much more power than a VCR or DVD player. If you're like us, you already have one or two computers in your house that stay on most of the time. We feel strongly that everyone should use energy responsibly and conserve it whenever possible. MythTV has some interesting power-saving features, although we did not have time to try them out.

The MythTV box can shut itself down when it is idle and knows there are no upcoming shows to record. But how can it be automatically started again? One way is to use the Wake-On-LAN feature of some network cards. While the computer sleeps, the network card looks for a packet that contains a certain sequence of bytes. If found, the network card instructs the computer to wake up. In order to use this approach, you need another computer on your network that can send the Wake-On-LAN packet.

The other technique takes advantage of BIOS wake-up features found on certain motherboards. This works only if your motherboard has that BIOS feature and is supported by one of the Linux applications that try to set the wake-up time.

For more information on these techniques, see **http://www.mythtv.org/docs/ mythtv-HOWTO-11.html** and **http://gsd.di.uminho.pt/jpo/software/wakeonlan/ mini-howto/.**

Home Network Gateway

4

Time

a day

Difficulty

easy

What You Need

- Soekris net4501 with case and power supply
- Compact Flash Card, 128–256 MB
- PC to be temporarily configured as DHCP and TFTP server
- DB9-to-DB9 null modem serial cable
- Ethernet crossover cable

In this chapter, we'll show you how to build a nifty little OpenBSD-powered gateway for a home or small office network. This gateway provides four important services: network address translation (NAT), DHCP, DNS, and a stateful packet filtering firewall. NAT is the technology that allows multiple computers to share a single IP address. DHCP is a service that automatically assigns IP addresses to systems on your network. The gateway also provides a local DNS server for your network, which reduces lookup latencies and also frees you from having to manage *hosts* files across multiple machines. The most important component, the firewall, protects your systems from malicious network attacks and scans. Figure 4-1 shows how the gateway fits into your home or office network.

The stateful firewall is one of OpenBSD's best features. It works by remembering the addresses and port numbers for packets at the beginning of a connection. Then, subsequent packets with the same addresses are recognized and allowed as a part of an existing conversation. The stateful firewall is particularly useful with UDP and other so-called stateless protocols. For example, your gateway may receive an unsolicited, and potentially malicious, DNS reply from a random host on the Internet. A traditional, stateless firewall, would allow this packet through because it doesn't know the reply is unsolicited. A stateful packet filter, on the other hand, remembers the

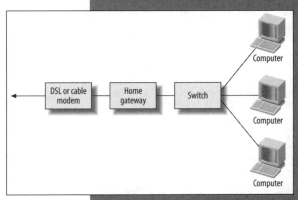

Figure 4-1. The gateway's place in your home network.

89

Linksys and NetGear Vulnerabilities

According to http://www.securityfocus.com/bid/10441, certain versions of the Linksys WRT54G router firmware allowed anyone, anywhere, access to the device's web-based administration interface. Less than a week later, someone reported a backdoor administrative account in certain versions of the Netgear WG602 access point firmware (http://www.securityfocus.com/bid/10459).

addresses of outgoing DNS queries. The DNS reply is allowed to pass only if a state entry was created by a previous outgoing query.

For most people this is a one-day project. If you are new to Unix, it may take a little longer as you learn about the intricacies of DHCP and TFTP. You should also be somewhat familiar with FTP, SSH, the Unix shell, and the *vi* text editor.

Your DSL/cable modem must have an Ethernet port to connect to this home network gateway. Some of the devices sold today use a USB interface with drivers available only for Microsoft Windows. The net4501 does not have any USB interfaces, and the operating system (OpenBSD) we're using does not support USB DSL/cable modems, anyway.

You may be wondering, "Why should I build one of these when I can just go buy a router from Linksys or NetGear for under $100?" Certainly, if price is the most important factor, this project may not suit your needs. However, many of us hackers are not willing to leave the security of our networks in the hands of the equipment manufacturer. Recent security advisories (see sidebar), show that companies like Linksys and NetGear have bugs or design flaws that leave your network very vulnerable to attacks. At the time of this writing, OpenBSD had only experienced one remotely exploitable security hole in its default configuration in eight years. Another reason to build your own security gateway is simply to have more features and more control.

Introducing the Soekris net4501

The net4501 was the first system introduced by Soekris Engineering (**http://www.soekris.com/**). Small and lightweight, this box takes up less space than most consumer-grade routers.

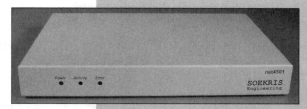

Figure 4-2. The net4501 case.

On the outside, the net4501 is a pleasant light-green box measuring roughly 8.5 × 6 × 1 in (21.5 × 15 × 2.5 cm). The front of the case (Figure 4-2) has three LEDs, labeled Power, Activity, and Error. The activity light blinks each time the box sends or receives a network packet. The error LED can be controlled from software after the operating system boots.

On the back (Figure 4-3) you can see three Fast Ethernet (100Base-TX) ports, a DB-9 serial connector, and a small power plug that accepts between 6 and 20 volts DC. The net4501 consumes no more than 7 watts by itself. Power requirements may go up to 10 watts if you add expansion (PCI) devices.

Figure 4-3. The rear of the net4501 with the top off.

Taking the cover off, you can see the small mainboard (Figure 4-4). A full-size PCI connector dominates one side of the board. With such a thin case, the PCI card must be mounted parallel to the mainboard. The net4501's PCI slot is for 3.3V cards only. The PCI slots on larger motherboards accept either 3.3V or 5V cards. This means that many of the available PCI cards cannot work in the net4501. Be sure to check the card's specifications before making a purchase.

On the other side of the board, you'll see a white Mini-PCI connector and a black Compact Flash (CF) slot. Next to the Mini-PCI connector is a number of general purpose I/O (GPIO) pins and the header for a second serial port. Hardware hackers use the GPIO pins to communicate with a wide range of devices, including digital thermometers and GPS receivers, and to control circuit components like relays.

Figure 4-4. The net4501 mainboard.

Designed for network and communications applications, the net4501 is based on AMD's "Elan" platform. It has a 486-class embedded processor that uses very little power. This version of the net4501 runs at 133 MHz and has 64 MB of RAM soldered onto the mainboard.

The net4501 comes with a small 12 volt universal power supply ("wall wart"). Any power supply that outputs between 6 and 16 volts and is capable of 10 watts will do the trick. The power connector is wired such that positive is on the center pin. It is protected against reverse polarity so

Figure 4-5. Inserting a CF card..

Figure 4-6. Close-up of the net4501 CF card stopper.

that you won't fry the board if you try connecting something with reversed polarity. Instead, it just won't power up.

The net4501 doesn't generate enough waste heat to require active cooling. It does not have any fans and operates in total silence. Our measurements show that it consumes between 4 and 7 watts during normal operation. The board uses so little power that it hardly even warms up.

Additional Hardware

The net4501's only storage option is the CF slot. To the operating system, the CF looks just like an ATA/IDE hard drive. Note, however, that not all CF cards are created equal. Some perform badly (or not at all) when asked to emulate an ATA disk. We have always had good luck with the SanDisk brand of CF cards.

These days, CF cards are pretty cheap, so you shouldn't buy the smallest possible card for this application. An absolute minimum for the project is a 128 MB card. A 256 MB card allows for luxuries like manual pages. If you are using a previously used CF card, you should make sure to make a copy of anything you want to keep and erase the card completely before inserting it into the case.

As shown in Figure 4-5, installing the CF card is straightforward. Remove the outer case from the 4501 if you haven't already. To do so, unscrew the four small black Phillips screws on the bottom of the case.

Inside you'll see a tall Phillips screw with a plastic sheath standing up from the case next to the board itself. This screw holds the CF card in the slot, as indicated in Figure 4-6. Remove it, slide the CF card in (label up), and replace the screw to secure the CF card.

Installing OpenBSD

This project is based on OpenBSD (**http://www.openbsd.org/**), which many people consider to be the most secure operating system money can't buy. OpenBSD's security and networking focus make it well suited for a firewall, gateway, and router. However, installing OpenBSD is a bit grungier than Linux or Windows.

Netboot, the OpenBSD installer

The easiest way to install OpenBSD on the net4501 is to do so over the network using the Pre-eXecution Environment (PXE) network boot protocol. The net4501 first makes a DHCP request to get an IP address. Then it downloads a boot image via TFTP (Trivial FTP) and executes it. To make all this work you'll need another PC where you can run DHCP and TFTP servers. We'll describe how to set up DHCP and TFTP for Linux and BSD. Mac users can follow the BSD instructions. If you'd like to use Windows, you can grab a free TFTP server, such Tftpd32 from **http://tftpd32.jounin.net/** or PumpKIN from **http://kin.klever.net/pumpkin/**.

Use an Ethernet crossover cable to connect the net4501 directly to the other PC. Plug the cable into the first Ethernet port on the net4501— the one closest to the serial console. When the net4501 is turned on, the lights on your network interface cards should light up, indicating that the two systems are connected. If not, you are probably using a standard Ethernet cable, rather than a crossover.

You'll need to create a little IP network for the two systems. We recommend that you use a network from the RFC1918 "private address space." We'll use the 192.168.23.0/24 network in the following examples. Begin by assigning the PC's interface an address from this network. For example, you can use this command on Linux:

```
# ifconfig eth0 inet 192.168.23.1 netmask 255.255.255.0
```

You can use almost the same command on a BSD system. The only difference is that the interface will be named something like fxp0 or em0, rather than eth0.

The next step is to get a DHCP server up and running on the PC. In Unix-land, ISC's DHCP server seems to be the most popular. You should be able to find it in all of the BSD ports collections, and various packages are available for Linux. You can also get the source code from **http://www. isc.org/sw/dhcp/** and install it that way. The configuration file is usually */etc/dhcpd.conf*. Here's how ours looks:

```
# The IP address of the PC
server-identifier 192.168.23.1;

# subnet declaration
subnet 192.168.23.0 netmask 255.255.255.0 {
        filename "pxeboot";           # boot image
        option routers 192.168.23.1; # PC's IP address

        # The net4501 will be assigned an address in this range
        range 192.168.23.191 192.168.23.200;
}
```

Don't Have a Crossover?

You can always use an Ethernet switch or hub in place of a crossover cable. If you do, make sure that the PC and net4501 are the only devices connected.

Making an Ethernet crossover cable is simple, if you have an RJ45 crimper. You can cut the plug off a perfectly good cable, swap pins 1 & 3 and 2 & 6, and stick a new plug back on.

If you don't have a crimpers, you can probably cut an existing cable in half, strip the ends off the bare wires, cross the pairs, and twist the fine copper strands back together. Search the web for "Ethernet crossover" to find a proper wiring diagram.

You can start the DHCP server with a command like this, possibly replacing fxp0 with a different interface name:

```
# dhcpd fxp0
```

Now it's time to configure the TFTP server, which is normally started by the *inetd* process. Edit */etc/inetd.conf* and look for a line that contains tftp. It should look something like this:

```
tftp dgram udp wait root /usr/libexec/tftpd tftpd -s /tftpboot
```

If you don't see such a line, go ahead and add one. The files that *tftpd* serves go in the */tftpboot* directory. If you want to use a different directory, change the last argument of the tftpd command. After saving *inetd. conf*, restart the *inetd* process. The following commands should work:

```
# killall -HUP inetd
```

You need to download two files from an OpenBSD mirror site and place them in the */tftpboot* directory: *pxeroot* and *bsd.rd*. Have a look at OpenBSD's list of mirror sites (**http://openbsd.org/ftp.html**) and pick one that is close to you. The files you want are in the */pub/OpenBSD/n.n/i386/* directory. The PXE boot loader is named *pxeboot*, and the RAM disk installation kernel is named *bsd.rd*. Download these and place them in the */tftpboot* directory. Make sure they are world-readable (i.e., chmod a+r).

Before booting OpenBSD, you must create a *boot.conf*. Since the net4501 doesn't have a normal video interface, you'll be doing everything over the serial port. You need to tell OpenBSD that the serial port is the console. The boot loader looks for instructions like this in a file named *etc/boot. conf*. To force the boot loader to use the serial console, create */tftpboot/ etc/boot.conf* on the PC and put these two lines in the file:

```
set tty com0
boot tftp:bsd.rd
```

Now you're almost ready to try booting the net4501 for the first time. First, you need to configure the serial console.

Configure the net4501 serial console

Before powering up the net4501, connect a "null-modem" cable between the serial port on the net4501 and the serial port on the PC as shown in Figure 4-7. If your PC doesn't have a serial port, you can probably use a USB-to-serial adapter. Start a terminal emulation program on the PC (e.g., *hyperterm*, *minicom*, *cu*, or *tip*) and set it for 19,200 bps, 8 data bits, no parity, and 1 stop bit (8N1). For example, if your PC is running FreeBSD, you can use:

```
# cu -s 19200 -l cuaa0
```

Figure 4-7. net4501 connected to PC with crossover cable and null modem.

Or, if you have the excellent GNU *screen* program installed, simply type:

```
% screen /dev/tts/0 19200
```

Note that */dev/tts/0* is the name of the first serial port on Linux. Different operating systems use different device names, unfortunately. When you supply power to the net4501, you should see some output like this almost immediately:

```
comBIOS ver. 1.26a  20040819  Copyright (C) 2000-2004 Soekris
Engineering.

Soekris Engineering net4501

0064 Mbyte Memory                       CPU 80486 133 Mhz

Pri Mas  SanDisk SDCFB-128              LBA 980-8-32   125 Mbyte

Slot   Vend Dev  ClassRev Cmd  Stat CL LT HT Base1     Base2     Int
---------------------------------------------------------------------
0:00:0 1022 3000 06000000 0006 2280 00 00 00 00000000 00000000
0:18:0 100B 0020 02000000 0107 0290 00 3F 00 0000E001 A0000000 10
0:19:0 100B 0020 02000000 0107 0290 00 3F 00 0000E101 A0001000 11
0:20:0 100B 0020 02000000 0107 0290 00 3F 00 0000E201 A0002000 05

 5 Seconds to automatic boot.   Press Ctrl-P for entering Monitor.
```

If you don't see any output, double check your null-modem cable connections and software settings. Also, your PC may have more than one serial port. You can either try using */dev/cuaa1* (FreeBSD) or */dev/ttys/1* (Linux), or move the cable from one port to the other.

Now you have to deal with a minor net4501 annoyance. Its BIOS comes factory-set with a serial port speed of 19,200 bps. However, after OpenBSD is installed, the default console speed will be 9,600 bps. Since you want to be able to read both the BIOS boot messages and log in to the OpenBSD console, you should change the BIOS console speed now to avoid any future headaches. To change settings in the BIOS, hit Ctrl-P before the countdown reaches zero. Then, you'll find yourself in the comBIOS Monitor. A simple command changes the serial port speed:

```
comBIOS Monitor.   Press ? for help.
```

```
> set ConSpeed 9600
```

The change is saved immediately. Reconfigure your terminal program (*cu*, *screen*, *kermit*, etc.) settings for 9,600 and power-cycle the net4501. You should see the same boot screen as before. If you see gibberish, try going back to 19,200 and changing the serial port speed again.

No PXE?

The net4501 BIOS may not attempt a PXE boot if it thinks the CF card contains a filesystem. If you see an error such as "No OS" or a generic "Disk error," you'll need take the CF card out, erase it, and put it back into the net4501.

The best way to erase the CF card is to attach it to your PC with a USB or IDE CF card adapter, and then use the *dd* utility to fill it with zeroes. For example:

```
# dd if=/dev/zero of=/dev/da0
```

Make absolutely sure that you use the correct device name for the CF card. It should appear in your *dmesg* output and/or *syslogd* messages. If you use the wrong device name you may overwrite another filesystem!

Boot the OpenBSD installer

With DHCP, TFTP, and the serial console ready to go, the net4501 should boot into the OpenBSD install kernel. The PXE boot process outputs some indicators as it moves along. It should get an address with DHCP and fetch the boot loader with TFTP. Then it executes the boot loader, sets the console to *com0*, and loads the *bsd.rd* kernel:

```
BootManage UNDI, PXE-2.0 (build 082)
BootManage PXE-2.0 PROM 1.0, NATSEC 1.0, SDK 3.0/082 (OEM52)
Copyright (C) 1989,2000 bootix Technology GmbH, D-41466 Neuss.
PXE Software Copyright (C) 1997, 1998, 1999, 2000 Intel Corporation.
Licensed to National Semiconductor

CLIENT MAC ADDR: 00 00 24 C0 0C A8
CLIENT IP: 192.168.23.191  MASK: 255.255.255.0  DHCP IP:
192.168.23.1
GATEWAY IP: 192.168.23.1
probing: pc0 com0 com1 pci pxe![2.1] mem[577K 63M a20=on]
disk: hd0+*
net: mac 00:00:24:c0:0c:a8, ip 192.168.23.191, server 192.168.23.1
>> OpenBSD/i386 PXEBOOT 1.02
switching console to com0
>> OpenBSD/i386 PXEBOOT 1.02
booting tftp:bsd.rd: 4302596+825452 [52+147936+134838]=0x5291b0
entry point at 0x100120

Copyright (c) 1982, 1986, 1989, 1991, 1993
    The Regents of the University of California.  All rights
reserved.
Copyright (c) 1995-2005 OpenBSD. All rights reserved.
http://www.OpenBSD.org
```

Don't worry if you don't get this far the first time. Configuring DHCP, and especially TFTP, can be difficult. You'll probably be able to figure out what's working and what's broken by looking at the console output. If you get stuck, double-check the DHCP configuration and make sure that *dhcpd* was restarted after any configuration changes. Check the system logs on the server for errors or warnings from *dhcpd* and *tftpd*. Filename permissions are a common problem with TFTP. Make sure that the *pxe-boot* and *bsd.rd* files are readable by the *tftpd* process owner. You may also want to run *tcpdump* on the server while all this happens.

As the kernel boots, it outputs various messages about the processor, memory, buses, controllers, and devices. Once the kernel has booted, the installation script runs and you'll see a prompt like this:

```
(I)nstall, (U)pgrade or (S)hell?
```

Enter **I** to start the installation process. You'll get two questions about your terminal type and keyboard encoding. Simply hit Enter to accept the defaults, since they should be fine:

```
Terminal type? [vt220]
Do you wish to select a keyboard encoding table? [no]
```

Next, you'll receive a stern warning about backups, and the script asks if you are sure that you want to continue installing OpenBSD. Answer **yes**. Since there is no data on the CF card yet, you have nothing to lose!

```
IS YOUR DATA BACKED UP? As with anything that modifies disk
contents, this program can cause SIGNIFICANT data loss.

It is often helpful to have the installation notes handy. For
complex disk configurations, relevant disk hardware manuals and a
calculator are useful.

Proceed with install? [no] yes
```

Partition the CF card

The next step is to select and partition the disk for OpenBSD. The only disk is the CF card, which shows up as *wd0* to OpenBSD:

```
You will now initialize the disk(s) that OpenBSD will use. To enable
all available security features you should configure the disk(s) to
allow the creation of separate filesystems for /, /tmp, /var, /usr,
and /home.

Available disks are: wd0.
```

Again, the installation script has the right idea, so just hit Enter to use *wd0*:

```
Which one is the root disk? (or 'done') [wd0]
```

The installation script then asks if the entire disk should be used for OpenBSD. Answer **yes** to this question:

```
Do you want to use *all* of wd0 for OpenBSD? [no] yes
Putting all of wd0 into an active OpenBSD MBR partition (type
'Ad6')...0: no dl
done.
```

Next you'll find yourself in OpenBSD's disk-label editor:

```
# using MBR partition 3: type A6 off 32 (0x20) size 250848 (0x3d3e0)

Treating sectors 32-250880 as the OpenBSD portion of the disk.
You can use the 'b' command to change this.

Initial label editor (enter '?' for help at any prompt)
```

Partitioning the disk with a disk label is straightforward. First, delete any existing partitions with the **d** command (CF cards often come with an MS-DOS filesystem):

```
> d
partition to delete: [] a
```

Then, create one large partition (or "slice") for the root filesystem. Don't use the whole CF card, however. You'll create a small swap partition of 1,024 blocks after this. Take the default size value (250,848 in the following example) and subtract 1,024. Use that value for the size of the "a" partition:

```
> a
partition: [a]
offset: [32]
size: [250848] 249824
FS type: [4.2BSD]
mount point: [none] /
```

And finally, create a small swap partition for reasons we'll explain later:

```
> a
partition: [b]
offset: [249856]
size: [1024]
FS type: [swap]
```

Save the new partition and exit with the **q** command:

```
> q
Write new label?: [y] y
No more disks to initialize.

OpenBSD filesystems:
wd0a /
```

After creating the disk label, allow the installer to create a filesystem on the first partition:

```
The next step *DESTROYS* all existing data on these partitions!
Are you really sure that you're ready to proceed? [no] yes
/dev/rwd0a:     249824 sectors in 976 cylinders of 8 tracks, 32
sectors
        122.0MB in 2 cyl groups (952 c/g, 119.00MB/g, 15232 i/g)
/dev/wd0a on /mnt type ffs (rw, asynchronous, local, ctime=Thu Oct
13 21:43:07 2005)
```

The filesystem is now ready. Before you can fill it up, however, you have to configure the network interface.

Configure the network

The next thing you should see is a prompt for the new system's hostname. We named ours "enki":

```
System hostname? (short form, e.g. 'foo') enki
```

After assigning the hostname, you'll enter the network configuration phase of the installation process. For now, configure only the *sis0* interface and leave the other two (*sis1* and *sis2*) alone.

At this point, you'll probably just want to configure *sis0* to get an address via DHCP. You know it already works, or else you wouldn't have gotten this far. For many of the prompts, you can hit Enter to accept the default values. Be sure to enter **dhcp** when asked about the IP address for *sis0*:

```
Configure the network? [yes]
Available interfaces are: sis0 sis1 sis2.
Which one do you wish to initialize? (or 'done') [sis0]
Symbolic (host) name for sis0? [enki]
The media options for sis0 are currently
        media: Ethernet autoselect

Do you want to change the media options? [no]
IPv4 address for sis0? (or 'none' or 'dhcp') dhcp
Issuing hostname-associated DHCP request for sis0.
DHCPDISCOVER on sis0 to 255.255.255.255 port 67 interval 1
DHCPDISCOVER on sis0 to 255.255.255.255 port 67 interval 1
ip length 328 disagrees with bytes received 332.
accepting packet with data after udp payload.
DHCPOFFER from 192.168.23.1
DHCPREQUEST on sis0 to 255.255.255.255 port 67
ip length 328 disagrees with bytes received 332.
accepting packet with data after udp payload.
DHCPACK from 192.168.23.1
bound to 192.168.23.191 -- renewal in 43200 seconds.
Available interfaces are: sis1 sis2.
Which one do you wish to initialize? (or 'done') [sis1] done
DNS domain name? (e.g. 'bar.com') [life-gone-hazy.com]
DNS nameserver? (IP address or 'none') [192.168.23.1]
Use the nameserver now? [yes]
Default IPv4 route? (IPv4 address, 'dhcp' or 'none') [dhcp]
Edit hosts with ed? [no]
Do you want to do any manual network configuration? [no]
Password for root account? (will not echo) sekrit
Password for root account? (again) sekrit
```

Don't worry if you see some errors from the DHCP client about "accepting packet with data after udp payload." You should be able to get a DHCP lease anyway.

Install software sets

Now that you have the network configured, you need to tell the installer how to obtain the installation sets. These are *.tgz* files that contain the OpenBSD operating system. We recommend that you download these files from an OpenBSD mirror site and serve them up locally with Apache or *ftpd*. You can also copy the files from an OpenBSD CD-ROM, if you have one.

Got Internet?

If the net4501 can communicate with hosts on the Internet, you can just use one of the OpenBSD mirror sites (in order for it to do so, the PC that is acting as DHCP and TFTP server must have supplied a router address and DNS server addresses when it offered a DHCP lease). If not, you'll need to copy some of the files onto a server on your local network.

At the time of this writing, the latest OpenBSD version was 3.7. We'll use this version in the remaining example instructions. To download the installation sets, visit a mirror site and go to the */pub/OpenBSD/3.7/i386* directory. On the CD-ROM it is just *3.7/i386*. Download or copy the following files:

- *index.txt*

- *bsd*

- *base37.tgz*

- *etc37.tgz*

If you have a 256 MB CF card, you can also get these sets:

- *misc37.tgz*

- *man37.tgz*

- *game37.tgz*

- *comp37.tgz*

It's probably easiest to stick these files in a directory to be served by Apache. You may need to install Apache if it is not already on your PC. We suggest that you create an *openbsd* directory under Apache's DocumentRoot and place the installation sets there. For example:

```
# mkdir /usr/local/www/data/openbsd
# mv index.txt bsd *.tgz /usr/local/www/data/openbsd
```

Make sure that the *openbsd* directory and the files in it are readable by the Apache process user ID.

Now, getting back to the installation procedure, the media-selection prompt looks like this:

```
You will now specify the location and names of the install sets you
want to load. You will be able to repeat this step until all of your
sets have been successfully loaded. If you are not sure what sets to
install, refer to the installation notes for details on the contents
of each.

Sets can be located on a (m)ounted filesystem; a (c)drom, (d)isk or
(t)ape device; or a (f)tp, (n)fs or (h)ttp server.
```

Select **h** for HTTP, nothing for the proxy URL, and **no** when asked if you want to see the list of known servers:

```
Where are the install sets? h
HTTP/FTP proxy URL? (e.g. 'http://proxy:8080', or 'none') [none]
Display the list of known http servers? [yes] no
```

Enter a URL that corresponds to your local HTTP server and directory where you put OpenBSD software sets. For example:

```
Server? (IP address, hostname or 'done') http://192.168.23.1/
openbsd/
```

Once the installer connects to Apache, it obtains a list of files available on that server. You'll see a menu like this:

```
The following sets are available. Type a filename, 'all' to select
all the sets, or 'done'. You may de-select a set by prepending a '-'
to its name.

        [X] bsd
        [X] bsd.rd
        [ ] bsd.mp
        [X] base37.tgz
        [X] etc37.tgz
        [X] misc37.tgz
        [X] comp37.tgz
        [X] man37.tgz
        [X] game37.tgz
        [ ] xbase37.tgz
        [ ] xetc37.tgz
        [ ] xshare37.tgz
        [ ] xfont37.tgz
        [ ] xserv37.tgz

File name? (or 'done') [bsd.mp]
```

You'll at least need *bsd*, *base37.tgz*, and *etc37.tgz*. These should barely fit onto a 128 MB CF card. If you have a 256 MB (or larger) CF card, you may want to include the manual pages (*man37.tgz*) as well. Compiler tools and a build infrastructure are in *comp37.tgz*, while *game37.tgz* contains frivolous things like *fortune* and *pom*. We recommend de-selecting *comp37.tgz* and *game37.tgz*, although they will fit on a 256 MB CF card.

Once you've selected the file sets you want, type **done**. The installer then fetches, verifies, and unpacks each file set. Since writing to the CF card is relatively slow, this process may take a while. After all the sets have been unpacked, the installer returns to the prompt asking where to find installation sets. Here you can enter **done** to continue:

```
Where are the install sets? (or 'done') done
```

The installer now asks a few configuration questions. The first is about *sshd*, which you should enable:

```
Start sshd(8) by default? [yes]
```

We recommend that you also enable the Network Time Protocol daemon. If you have an NTP server on your network, you can edit */etc/ntpd. conf* later:

```
Start ntpd(8) by default? [no] yes
```

It also asks about X Windows, which you definitely do not want:

```
Do you expect to run the X Window System? [yes] no
```

Finally, OpenBSD asks if you want to make *com0* the console. You must answer **yes** here:

```
Change the default console to com0? [no] yes
Available speeds are: 9600 19200 38400 57600 115200.
Which one should com0 use? (or 'done') [9600]
Saving configuration files...done.
Generating initial host.random file...done.
```

Then you'll be prompted to choose a time zone. Enter **?** to list the available choices:

```
What timezone are you in? ('?' for list) [US/Pacific] ?
Africa/      Chile/       GB-Eire      Israel       NZ-CHAT    Turkey
America/     Cuba         GMT          Jamaica      Navajo     UCT
Antarctica/  EET          GMT+0        Japan        PRC        US/
Arctic/      EST          GMT-0        Kwajalein    PST8PDT    UTC
Asia/        EST5EDT      GMT0         Libya        Pacific/   Universal
Atlantic/    Egypt        Greenwich    MET          Poland     W-SU
Australia/   Eire         HST          MST          Portugal   WET
Brazil/      Etc/         Hongkong     MST7MDT      ROC        Zulu
CET          Europe/      Iceland      Mexico/      ROK        posix/
CST6CDT      Factory      Indian/      Mideast/     Singapore  posixrules
Canada/      GB           Iran         NZ           SystemV/     right/
What timezone are you in? ('?' for list) [US/Pacific] US
What sub-timezone of 'US' are you in? ('?' for list) ?
Alaska          Central       Hawaii          Mountain    Samoa
Aleutian        East-Indiana  Indiana-Starke  Pacific
Arizona         Eastern       Michigan        Pacific-New
Select a sub-timezone of 'US' ('?' for list): Mountain
Setting local timezone to 'US/Mountain'...done.
```

Following time zone selection, the installer populates the */dev* directory on the new filesystem. This takes a while because of slow write speeds on the CF card.

Configure some /etc files

At this point, the installer has done all it can do. It shows you an uplifting message of congratulations and leaves you at a shell prompt. Before rebooting, as the installer's message suggests, you must take care of a few more things. By default, this system attaches its console to the video device and the PC keyboard port, neither of which exists on the net4501. You'll need to tell OpenBSD to use the serial port instead and make sure it starts a *getty* process on that port so you can log in.

The installer leaves the recently installed filesystem mounted under */mnt*. You can use the *chroot* utility to run a shell "inside" this new filesystem (it will be as if you booted into the operating system):

```
# /mnt/usr/sbin/chroot /mnt sh
```

Now, what used to be */mnt* is actually */* from this shell's perspective. This allows you to easily modify some of the files in */etc* using *vi* and other standard tools that aren't present in the installer RAM disk.

We suggest that you disable the *getty* processes that are normally started for VGA consoles. In OpenBSD, the */etc/ttys* file controls how and where to start the *getty* processes. Use *vi* to edit this file:

```
# export TERM=vt100
# vi /etc/ttys
```

The format of */etc/ttys* might seem confusing at first, but is actually quite simple. If you want the complete rundown, see the *ttys(5)* manual page. Looking at the file, you'll see a number of lines for *ttyC0* through *ttyCb*. These are for the video console, which does not exist. Change the status to off for each of them.

You should also make sure that *getty* is enabled for *tty00*. The installer should have done this for you, but it is a good idea to double-check. Otherwise, you won't be able to log in on the serial port. The *tty00* line in */etc/ttys* should look like this:

```
tty00   "/usr/libexec/getty std.9600"   xterm   on  secure
```

The next order of business is to fix up the */etc/fstab* file. As you may have heard, Compact Flash memory has a weakness: a single sector can only sustain a finite number of writes before it burns out and becomes unusable. To extend the CF card's lifetime, you can put parts of the filesystem that see a lot of write activity in memory (RAM, not flash). This is easier than it sounds. Simply edit the */etc/fstab* file and add two mfs lines for the memory filesystems:

```
/dev/wd0a /        ffs rw,noatime 1 1
/dev/wd0b /var/run mfs rw,-s1024  0 0
/dev/wd0b /tmp     mfs rw,-s8192  0 0
```

This is why you created a small swap partition earlier. OpenBSD uses the swap partition as a virtual mount point for memory filesystems, even if you don't use that partition for swapping. The -s option dictates the size of the memory filesystem in 512 byte blocks. The sizes just shown (512 KB for */var/run* and 4 MB for */tmp*) work well for us, but you many need to adjust them for your environment. Note that we've also added the noatime option to the root filesystem, which prevents the kernel from storing a "last accessed" time for files on that filesystem. Otherwise, the kernel constantly updates the filesystem each time you open a file for reading. By disabling these updates, you can extend the lifetime of the CF card.

If you have a 128 MB CF card, you may find that it is almost out of space:

```
# df
Filesystem 1K-blocks    Used    Avail Capacity Mounted on
/dev/wd0a    121022    117174    -2202   102%    /
```

Negative Available Space?

Don't be alarmed if you see a negative number under Avail and a Capacity greater than 100%. Unix filesystems typically subtract some percentage of disk space from those calculations. Only *root* can create new files when the capacity reaches 100%.

You can free up some space by removing binaries that you'll probably never use. Here's a good way to find candidates:

```
# du -a /bin/* /usr/bin/* /sbin/* /usr/sbin/* | sort -n | tail
1008    /usr/sbin/dnssec-signzone
1024    /usr/sbin/nsupdate
1040    /usr/sbin/host
1040    /usr/sbin/named-checkconf
1040    /usr/sbin/nslookup
1056    /usr/sbin/dig
1072    /sbin/isakmpd
1088    /usr/bin/lynx
1328    /usr/sbin/named
2144    /usr/bin/gdbtui
```

For example, you can probably do without *gdbtui*, *named-checkconf*, *dnssec-signzone*, *nslookup*, and *lynx*. If you need to free up a lot more space, consider getting rid of Perl. The */usr/libdata/perl* directory takes up about 35 MB.

Reboot!

With all these details taken care of, you are ready to reboot the net4501 into OpenBSD from the CF card:

```
# exit
# reboot
```

On reboot, you should see the OpenBSD boot loader messages and then the kernel itself:

```
Using drive 0, partition 3.
Loading...
probing: pc0 com0 com1 pci mem[639K 63M a20=on]
disk: hd0+
>> OpenBSD/i386 BOOT 2.06
com0: 9600 baud
switching console to com0
>> OpenBSD/i386 BOOT 2.06
boot>
booting hd0a:/bsd: 4686240+945680 [52+241328+223324]=0x5d0864
```

After the kernel loads and prints lots of information about the devices available on the system, the serial console should have a login prompt:

```
OpenBSD/i386 (enki.life-gone-hazy.com) (tty00)
login:
```

Congratulations! You've successfully installed OpenBSD on your net4501.

From Installation to Gateway

Now that you have the operating system installed, the next task is to configure the services necessary to make the box function as a gateway and firewall. In particular, you need a Dynamic Host Configuration Protocol (DHCP) server, Network Address Translation (NAT), and a packet filter. You'll also need to set up a DNS cache and an FTP proxy. Before that, however, you need to configure the net4501's network interfaces.

Configuring network interfaces

The net4501 has three Fast Ethernet interfaces. On the outside, these are labeled Net 0, Net 1, and Net 2. On the inside (i.e., in OpenBSD), they are named *sis0*, *sis1*, and *sis2*. For this project, you need only two: you'll use *sis0* as the upstream interface (connected to your DSL or cable modem) and *sis1* as the internal interface (connected to your home network). In OpenBSD, files named */etc/hostname.sis0*, */etc/hostname.sis1*, and */etc/hostname.sis2* determine the IP address for each interface. See the *hostname.if(5)* manual page for more information.

Chances are good that your ISP uses DHCP to assign the IP address for your Internet connection. This makes configuring the *sis0* interface very simple. If you followed the previous instructions, *sis0* is already configured to use DHCP. The */etc/hostname.sis0* file should already contain this line:

```
dhcp NONE NONE NONE
```

If you had a computer or router plugged directly into your cable or DSL modem before you installed your home network gateway, you may need to power-cycle the modem before it gives you an IP address. Some cable and DSL modems lock themselves to the first device they see when they are turned on.

If you need to give *sis0* a static IP address, you'll need to edit */etc/hostname.sis0*. The format is fairly simple. The file should contain a single line with four fields:

```
[address family] [address] [netmask] [broadcast]
```

Here is an example:

```
inet 192.168.23.32 255.255.255.128 192.168.23.127
```

When using a static IP address, you also need to manually configure the upstream default gateway. On OpenBSD, this bit of information goes in the */etc/mygate* file:

```
192.168.23.1
```

You'll use *sis1* as the internal network (your LAN) interface. Your other computers will either connect directly to this port or be connected to it through a switch. For the *sis1* interface, use a subnet from the private address space as described in RFC1918 (**http://www.faqs.org/rfcs/rfc1918. html**). The following examples are based on using the 10.0.23.0/24 subnet. Your */etc/hostname.sis1* file might look like this:

```
inet 10.0.23.1 255.255.255.0 10.0.23.255
```

Reboot after you make your changes to the */etc/hostname.** files to be sure that the settings take effect correctly on their own. Check that the addresses are assigned correctly by pinging both local interfaces, as well as a server on the Internet (if you are connected).

Name services (DNS)

We recommend running a caching DNS server on your net4501. This improves the response time for certain transactions because lookups are cached locally. You might also find it is more reliable than the servers operated by your ISP.

OpenBSD comes with a customized version of ISC's BIND. The executable is called *named*. To enable it, simply edit */etc/rc.conf* and change the `named_flags` line so that it looks like this:

```
named_flags=""           # for normal use: ""
```

The next time your system boots, *named* will start automatically.

Even if your ISP has unreliable nameservers, you can leverage them to reduce overall DNS query times. Since your ISP's DNS servers likely have a large amount of cached responses and are presumably close (network-wise) to your gateway, it makes sense for the DNS server to query them first before initiating its own recursive query.

You can tell *named* to use your ISP's DNS servers as forwarders. Edit */var/named/etc/named.conf* and look for the `options` section. Add these two lines inside the `options` section, replacing *10.1.2.3* with your ISP's nameserver address:

```
forward first;
forwarders { 10.1.2.3; };
```

Note that your ISP's DNS server may move to a different address at some time in the future. You should periodically make sure your *named.conf* is up to date, or write a *cron* script to check it for you. See "Monitoring your ISP's Nameserver" at the end of this chapter for an example.

You can start *named* now by running **named**. You'll probably see some syslog messages on the console when it starts. You may also want to check the tail of */var/log/messages* for errors with **tail -f /var/log/messages**.

Since *named* is (or will be) running on the gateway, you probably want the gateway's local */etc/resolv.conf* to point to the gateway's DNS server, rather than your ISP's. Note, however, that *dhclient* usually overwrites *resolv.conf* with values received from the DHCP server each time the system boots. You need to tell *dhclient* that it should ignore the nameservers received from DHCP and put localhost into *resolv.conf* instead. The way to do so is to add this line to */etc/dhclient.conf*:

```
supersede domain-name-servers 127.0.0.1;
```

The DHCP server

The DHCP daemon, *dhcpd*, listens for address assignment requests from machines on your internal network. OpenBSD comes with a customized version of ISC's DHCP server installed by default. To enable *dhcpd*, edit */etc/rc.conf* again and change the line that starts with dhcpd_flags to look like this:

```
dhcpd_flags=""          # for normal use: ""
```

The next step is a little harder. You have to write a DHCP configuration file that matches the subnet and addresses you've chosen for *sis1*. Here's how it looks for the 10.0.23.0/24 subnet:

```
shared-network LOCAL-NET {
        # Specify your DNS server(s) here
        option  domain-name-servers 10.0.23.1;

        # Declaration for your subnet
        subnet 10.0.23.0 netmask 255.255.255.0 {
                # Specify your router here
                option routers 10.0.23.1;
                # Specify the range of address to dish out
                range 10.0.23.33 10.0.23.254;
        }
}
```

Note that the domain-name-servers and option routers lines match the address you assigned to *sis1*.

The final step is to add *sis1* to the */etc/dhcpd.interfaces* file. For example:

```
# List of network interfaces served by dhcpd(8).
#
# ep0
# ed0 le0
# de1
sis1
```

Since the *dhcpd.conf* file can be a little tricky, you may want to run dhcpd manually to make sure there are no syntax errors:

```
# dhcpd sis1
```

If you see no output, the configuration file is fine. Otherwise, edit dhcpd. conf and fix the errors before proceeding.

A proxy for that old protocol

If you plan on using FTP clients on your internal systems, you'll want to run an FTP proxy on the gateway. FTP was developed in a time when all machines on the network had publicly routable addresses and security was not a major concern. In the default mode of operation, FTP servers establish TCP connections *back* to FTP clients when transferring data. Since you are using NAT and private address space, this technique won't work.

As a workaround, FTP "passive mode" was developed, whereby the client opens a connection to the server on a high-numbered port for data transfers. Unfortunately, many popular FTP clients either aren't capable of passive mode FTP or are set to active mode by default (notably Microsoft's Internet Explorer).

OpenBSD includes an FTP proxy that allows clients behind the proxy to use active mode FTP. The proxy handles these inbound connections and associates them with the proper machine on the internal network. To enable the proxy, edit */etc/inetd.conf* and uncomment the following line:

```
127.0.0.1:8021 stream tcp nowait root /usr/libexec/ftp-proxy ftp-
proxy
```

After making this change, send *inetd* a HUP signal to have it re-read the configuration file:

```
# kill -HUP `head -1 /var/run/inetd.pid`
```

Later, you'll use a packet-filter redirect rule to intercept outbound FTP connections and send them to the proxy.

Packet Filter (pf)

This home network gateway relies heavily on OpenBSD's packet filter, a.k.a. *pf*, for many of the features you want. In particular, it is responsible for Network Address Translation (NAT) and blocking unwanted packets. You'll also use it to improve the security of packets leaving the home network. We refer to these activities as *translating*, *filtering*, and *scrubbing*.

To enable the packet filter, make sure the pf line in */etc/rc.conf* looks like this:

```
pf=YES                    # Packet filter / NAT
```

With the packet filter enabled, your system automatically looks for pf instructions in */etc/pf.conf* when it boots. All of the example lines given in this section should be placed in that file. You'll probably find that *pf.conf* already contains a number of lines that are commented out. You can either just delete them, or copy the default *pf.conf* to a different filename if you'd like to refer to it later. For more additional information on OpenBSD's packet filter, have a look at **http://www.openbsd.org/faq/pf/**, the *pf(4)*, and the *pf.conf(5)* manual pages.

Options

The first statements in *pf.conf* deal with options that control the behavior of the firewall. There are many options and settings, but the defaults are usually acceptable. We'll cover just two important settings, `block-policy` and `optimization`.

block-policy

One important setting is the packet filter's default disposition when blocking a packet. There are two behaviors to choose from. The filter can return the appropriate message to the packet's sender when a packet is filtered, sending a packet with the RST (reset) flag set for blocked TCP packets or an "ICMP unreachable" for blocked UDP packets (`block-policy return`). Alternatively, the filter can silently drop the packet, giving no indication to the sender that a particular port is closed (`block-policy drop`). We suggest that you configure the filter to return resets and ICMP messages, rather than silently drop the packets. To do so, make this the first line in *pf.conf*:

```
set block-policy return
```

optimization

The packet filter can have *stateful* rules, meaning rules that create a *state* in the filter for traffic. Traffic passing through the filter is checked against all states before being matched to rules, allowing traffic associated with a stateful rule to pass through the filter even if there is only a rule for the initial connection.

For instance, the filter may have a stateful rule matching outbound SMTP (port 25) connections. The rule could match only the first packet in those connections (an outbound TCP packet with a destination of port 25 and the SYN flag set) and create a state. All traffic associated with that connection (inbound and outbound) would then match the state and pass through the filter.

For TCP, *pf* adds and removes table entries according to the rules of the protocol. For UDP and other stateless protocols, *pf* uses a set of timeouts to expire table entries created by inbound or outbound traffic. The *pf.conf* manpage describes these in great detail, but making individual adjustments to the timeouts is usually unnecessary. You can select the timeout policy with the `optimization` option, and you have four to choose from:

`normal`
> Suitable for almost all networks.

`aggressive`
> Aggressively expires connections, reducing firewall memory usage at the cost of sometimes dropping connection state prematurely.

`high-latency`
> Useful for extremely high-latency (long round-trip) networks such as satellite connections.

`conservative`
> Uses very long timeouts to avoid dropping any connection prematurely. The downside is increased memory usage.

We recommend that you stick with the `normal` optimization setting:

```
set optimization normal
```

Scrubbing

Scrubbing is a term that refers to *pf*'s features for cleaning up incoming and outgoing packets. OpenBSD also refers to this as normalization. One of the things that scrubbing does for you is buffer and reassemble IP fragments. The kernel buffers these fragments until the entire IP/TCP/UDP header is present. This allows it to avoid making bad decisions on incomplete packets.

Another cool scrubbing feature is *pf*'s ability to alter the IP ID field for outgoing packets. This is primarily used as a way to obfuscate some details about your internal network. A paper published in 2002 ("A Technique for Counting NATted Hosts," by Steve Bellovin, AT&T Labs Research) describes a technique for figuring out how many hosts are behind a NAT box by examining the IP ID field values. Some people worry that ISPs may use this technique to bill subscribers for using more than one computer on their home network. In response, OpenBSD added the `random-id` scrubbing feature to *pf*. Randomizing the IP ID fields makes it harder to differentiate multiple hosts sharing a single public IP address.

The following `scrub` statements implement normalization and randomizing. These should go at the beginning of your */etc/pf.conf* file:

```
scrub in  all
scrub out all random-id
```

Translation

pf can translate addresses for both incoming and outgoing packets. Outgoing address translation is also sometimes called *source NAT*, or SNAT. Inbound translation is sometimes called *destination NAT*, or DNAT. We'll show you how to implement both.

First, for outbound translation (SNAT), you need only a simple rule that maps addresses from the internal interface (*sis1*) to the external interface (*sis0*):

```
nat on sis0 from (sis1:network) -> (sis0)
```

The nice thing about this rule is that it works even if *sis0* has a dynamically assigned address. The token (`sis1:network`) matches any IP address corresponding to the network on the *sis1* interface. Similarly, (`sis0`) corresponds to the address, or addresses, assigned to *sis0*.

Any time that you can avoid hardcoding IP addresses in your configuration files is a big win.

The preceding rule applies only to connections initiated from the internal network. You need a DNAT rule if you have a server running on your internal network that you'd like to access from the outside. For example, let's say that you have a web server on an internal machine with a private address (as will be the case if you follow the instructions in this chapter). You can't directly reach the private address from the outside and you can't assign the gateway's public IP address to the web server, so what can you do? A `rdr` (redirect) packet filter rule bridges this gap:

```
rdr pass on sis0 inet proto tcp from any to (sis0) port 80 ->
10.0.23.2
```

The rule instructs the kernel to take any packets destined for port 80 on any (`sis0`) address and forward them to 10.0.23.2 instead. Note that this rule actually changes the destination IP address in the packet before forwarding. That behavior is different than the way FreeBSD's *ipfw* redirection works.

Some applications, such as BitTorrent, use more than one TCP port number. The *pf* syntax allows you to specify multiple ports if necessary. For example:

```
rdr pass on sis0 inet proto tcp from any to (sis0) port \
{ 6881, 6882, 6883, 6884, 6885, 6886, 6887, 6888, 6889 } \
-> 10.0.23.3
```

We've split the rule across multiple lines for readability. When breaking a rule or statement into multiple lines, be sure to escape the end of the line with a backslash, as in the preceding example.

Finally, here is an rdr rule for the FTP proxy. It intercepts outbound FTP connections coming from the internal network and sends them to the ftp-proxy application listening on port 8021 instead:

```
rdr pass on sis1 proto tcp to port ftp -> 127.0.0.1 port 8021
```

The pass keyword in the redirection rules tells *pf* to implicitly pass (allow) any traffic matching the redirection. If you omit pass here, you'll need additional rules later in the configuration file to explicitly pass the redirected packets.

Filtering

Filtering rules in *pf* start with either pass or block. This is where you decide which packets are allowed to reach their destination and which are simply dropped.

The OpenBSD kernel evaluates *pf.conf* rules in the same order that they appear. Additionally, the kernel evaluates every rule in the list until reaching the end or until finding a rule with the quick keyword. This is the opposite of the way that some other packet filters work, such as FreeBSD's *ipfw* and Linux's *iptables*. OpenBSD checks all the rules and applies the last one that is a match. This means that your filtering rules should proceed from the general to the very specific.

We'll start the filtering section with a block rule that matches all inbound traffic. Thus, any traffic that does not match a more specific rule later will be blocked and logged:

```
block in log
```

Next, you should allow all packets on the gateway's loopback interface. You may also want to implicitly trust hosts connected to the internal network interface (*sis1*) and allow all of their packets. We're using the quick keyword here to avoid processing any remaining rules:

```
pass quick on lo
pass quick on sis1
```

If you prefer not to implicitly trust all traffic outbound from the local network (perhaps you have some untrusted systems), the two rules above could be replaced by more restrictive ones. For instance, this ruleset limits traffic from the addresses in untrusted_hosts to TCP outgoing port 80 (HTTP) only:

```
untrusted_hosts="{ 192.168.23.66/32, 192.168.23.67/32 }"

pass quick on lo
pass on sis1
pass in on sis1 inet proto tcp from $untrusted_hosts to any port 80 \
  keep state
block in on sis1 from $untrusted_hosts to any
```

Without the `quick` keyword, the last matching rule for any given traffic applies.

If you're allowing all packets on *lo* and *sis1*, the rest of the rules deal with *sis0* only. First, here are a few rules for outgoing packets on the *sis0* interface:

```
pass out on sis0 inet keep state
pass out on sis0 inet proto udp keep state
pass out on sis0 inet proto tcp modulate state
```

The first of these three applies to all IPv4 packets. The `keep state` option instructs the kernel to dynamically create a temporary rule for these outgoing packets. Then, incoming packets that correspond to one of the dynamic state rules are automatically allowed in. This is a nice way to allow incoming packets only if they are in response to a conversation initiated by a host on your network.

The second rule is simply a more specific version of the first that applies only to UDP.

The third rule applies only to TCP connections. Here you must use the `modulate state` option. Its purpose is to generate new, random initial sequence numbers (ISNs) for outgoing TCP connections. Research has shown that many operating systems have poor ISN-selection algorithms, which in turn makes them susceptible to TCP hijacking and man-in-the-middle attacks. The `modulate state` feature improves security by making it harder for attackers to predict the TCP ISNs emanating from your home network. The `modulate state` statement implies `keep state`.

So far, the stateful filtering rules allow packets for connections initiated from inside the firewall. We call these *outgoing connections*. But what about *incoming connections*? We already showed you how to add a DNAT `rdr` rule that forwards incoming connections to an internal host. You may also want to allow incoming connections to the gateway itself, although we feel it weakens the security of your firewall. You'll need to add a rule for each service that should accept connections from the outside. For example, if you want to SSH in to your gateway from the outside, make sure that *sshd* is enabled in */etc/rc.conf* and add this rule:

```
pass in on sis0 proto tcp to (sis0) port ssh keep state
```

You may also want to accept *ident* connections. Some IRC and SMTP servers use this service to log the username associated with a client TCP connection. You shouldn't be too surprised to learn that OpenBSD's *ident* server doesn't send real usernames. Instead, it replies with a one-way hash value. The hash value and real username are logged locally, which allows you to figure out who did what after the fact if necessary.

OpenBSD's *inetd* runs *identd* by default, so you simply need to add this rule to accept incoming connections:

```
pass in on sis0 proto tcp to (sis0) port ident keep state
```

You already added an `rdr` rule for the FTP proxy. However, you need another rule to allow incoming FTP data connections (the connections that FTP servers make back to FTP clients). These connections use high-numbered TCP ports, above 49151 by default. Since other applications may use ports in the same range, it is a little unsafe to simply accept packets based on the port number. Fortunately, OpenBSD has a solution. You can allow packets for sockets that are opened by certain users or groups. Since the FTP proxy runs as the *proxy* user, this rule does the trick:

```
pass in on sis0 proto tcp to (sis0) port > 49151 user proxy keep state
```

We also suggest that you configure the gateway to respond to ICMP pings from the outside. Some people fear ICMP, but we feel it is safe and useful in a number of situations. Here's the rule for *pf.conf*:

```
pass in on sis0 inet proto icmp to (sis0) icmp-type echoreq keep
state
```

Note that you don't have to do anything special for ICMP_UNREACH_NEEDFRAG messages, which are used for path MTU discovery. The reason is that ICMP_UNREACH_NEEDFRAG messages are matched to firewall state for existing connections. In other words, if the ICMP_UNREACH_NEEDFRAG packet corresponds to a known connection (due to a `keep state` rule), it is allowed to pass through.

Trying it out

Here is a complete *pf.conf* based on the suggested configuration in the previous section:

```
set block-policy return
set optimization normal

scrub in all
scrub out all random-id

nat on sis0 from (sis1:network) -> (sis0)
rdr pass on sis0 inet proto tcp from any to (sis0) port 80 -> 10.0.23.2
rdr pass on sis0 inet proto tcp from any to (sis0) port \
        { 6881, 6882, 6883, 6884, 6885, 6886, 6887, 6888, 6889 } \
        -> 10.0.23.3
rdr pass on sis1 proto tcp to port ftp -> 127.0.0.1 port 8021


block in log
pass quick on lo
pass quick on sis1
```

```
# If you have untrusted hosts on your internal network, comment
# out the above "pass quick on sis1" line and then uncomment the
# following block

# untrusted_hosts="{ 192.168.23.66/32, 192.168.23.67/32 }"
# pass on sis1
# pass in on sis1 inet proto tcp from $untrusted_hosts to \
# any port 80 keep state
# block in on sis1 from $untrusted_hosts to any

pass out on sis0 inet keep state
pass out on sis0 inet proto udp keep state
pass out on sis0 inet proto tcp modulate state

pass in on sis0 proto tcp to (sis0) port ssh keep state
pass in on sis0 proto tcp to (sis0) port ident keep state
pass in on sis0 proto tcp to (sis0) port > 49151 user proxy keep state
pass in on sis0 inet proto icmp to (sis0) icmp-type echoreq keep state
```

You can check the file for syntax errors with this command:

```
# pfctl -nf /etc/pf.conf
```

Unfortunately, *pfctl* does not always give helpful messages about syntax errors. It will tell you the line number, but that's all. Once the rules are error-free, you can reboot or load them with this command:

```
# pfctl -f /etc/pf.conf
```

Extra Credit

At this point, you have a very nice, secure, and stable gateway that protects your home network from the evils of the Internet. In this section we have a few ideas and alternatives that you may wish to explore further.

Wi-Fi

A wireless network interface is an obvious improvement to this project. These days, even most of the off-the-shelf home gateway products support wireless Ethernet. Adding Wi-Fi to the net4501 isn't that difficult.

The net4501 has two connectors suitable for a wireless card: the 3.3V-only PCI slot and the Mini-PCI slot. Finding a 3.3V PCI wireless card can be tricky, although not impossible. You may have more luck with the Mini-PCI interface, since this is the standard used in most laptops. Given the popularity of wireless networking, many vendors stock Mini-PCI cards along with the necessary radio cable "pigtails" required to connect an antenna to the card.

OpenBSD currently supports a number of Wi-Fi card chipsets. We recommend that you use cards based on Intersil PRISM2.5 and Cisco Aironet if possible. You can also use an Atheros chipset with OpenBSD 3.7 and later. Also be aware that hardware vendors sometimes switch chipsets with only a minor change in the version number. For example, the older D-LINK DWL-520 used a PRISM2.5 chipset, but the newer DWL-520+ uses a Texas Instruments chipset. Before making a purchase, you should search the Web to find out if a particular product uses a supported chipset. The following URLs should get you started:

- http://www.openbsd.org/faq/faq6.html#Wireless

- http://wiki.personaltelco.net/index.cgi/Prism2Card

- http://www.seattlewireless.net/index.cgi/HardwareComparison

We also highly recommend the Netgate Mini-PCI wireless kit for Soekris boards. See **http://www.netgate.com/**.

After installing the wireless card, it appears as the *wi0* interface, or *an0* for Cisco Aironet chipsets. The kernel outputs the device when it boots:

```
wi0 at pci0 dev 16 function 0 "Intersil PRISM2.5 Mini-PCI WLAN" rev
0x01: irq 10
wi0: PRISM2.5 ISL3874A(Mini-PCI), Firmware 1.1.0 (primary), 1.4.9
(station), ad8
```

The least complicated way to extend the internal network out over the wireless interface is to configure a network bridge between the internal network Ethernet interface (*sis1*) and the wireless interface (*wi0*).

First, create the */etc/hostname.wi0* file with the configuration information for the wireless interface (network name, mode, channel). For example, these lines set the network name to "my network," the port type to hostap mode, and the frequency to channel 10:

```
up
!wicontrol \$if -n "my network" -p 6 -f 10
```

In OpenBSD, a network bridge has its own interface name, such as *br0*. You can configure a bridge by adding lines to a file named */etc/bridgename.br0*. First add the real interfaces that belong to the bridge, and then bring it up:

```
add sis1
add wi0
up
```

The packet filter configuration also needs a small change, since you want traffic to pass on both the wireless interface and the bridge. Add new rules for *wi0* and *br0* that unconditionally pass all traffic sent and received:

```
pass quick on lo
pass quick on sis1
pass quick on wi0
pass quick on br0
```

After a reboot, you will find that the internal network extends over both the *sis1* Ethernet interface and the *wi0* wireless interface. DHCP will work for clients connecting over either interface.

If you are a little more paranoid about your wireless network, you may want to use a routed, instead of bridged, configuration. In other words, use a different subnet for *sis1* and *wi0* and route packets between them. This also makes it easy to apply different firewall rules to each subnet.

Installing via a CF adapter

Instead of installing OpenBSD over the network, you can use a CF card adapter and copy files from an existing OpenBSD system. You'll need to use *fdisk*, *disklabel*, and *newfs* to prepare the filesystem on the CF card. Don't forget to make the CF card bootable and install the OpenBSD Master Boot Record with:

```
# fdisk -u -f /usr/mdec/mbr wd4
```

This approach can be a bit tedious, since you may have to omit certain files from the CF to make everything fit (another reason to the largest card that you can). You'll also need to edit a number of configuration files in the */etc* directory.

For an easy way to create a bootable OpenBSD CF card, check out "flash-dist" by visiting **http://www.nmedia.net/~chris/soekris/.**

Read-only CF card

With a little more work, you can make a read-only CF card. Any directories that must be writable, such as */dev* and */var*, are mounted as memory-based filesystems. This should extend the life of your CF card if that is a major concern for you. It's also nice from a security perspective because it becomes a little harder for attackers to overwrite and delete important files. Google for "openbsd read-only flash" to get started down this path.

Monitoring your ISP's nameserver

In "From Installation to Gateway," earlier in this chapter, we suggested that you should use your ISP's nameserver as a forwarder in *named.conf*. Since it will be hardcoded there, you'll want to know if your ISP moves the nameserver to a new IP address some day. You can use the following shell script in a *cron* job to make sure the upstream nameserver is still there. It extracts the value for forwarders and sends it a query using *dig*:

```
#!/bin/sh
nameserver=`awk '$1 == "forwarders" {print $3}' /var/named/etc/named.conf`
nameserver=`echo $nameserver | sed -e 's/;//'`
dig @$nameserver www.google.com >/dev/null
if test $? != 0 ; then
        echo ISP nameserver at $nameserver may be down or changed
fi
```

This simple script is likely to report false errors on occasion due to temporary network outages or other problems. You may want to make it more robust by pinging the nameserver first or by not reporting the outage until some number of consecutive errors occur.

Network Monitor

5

Time

a weekend

Difficulty

moderate

What You Need

- Soekris net4801-50 single-board PC and case

- 12 volt, 1.2 amp power transformer

- 2.5-inch hard drive mounting kit for the net4801

- 2.5-inch-wide, 9.5 mm high, laptop hard drive, preferably 4200RPM

- 2.5-inch laptop drive–to–40-pin/power adapter for connecting the laptop drive to a regular PATA (IDE) controller

- Desktop PC with a standard (non-serial) PATA controller and a CD-ROM

- FreeBSD installation CD

This network monitor can help you notice attacks or questionable traffic on your home or office network—without having to change the network's topology. As a bonus, you'll get graphs and statistics about network usage.

Depending on the features that you want in your monitoring system and the size of the network you are monitoring, you could spend anywhere from two to five days on this project. The core set of functionality (intrusion detection and simple network usage monitoring) should take less than two days to complete, depending on your experience and skill level.

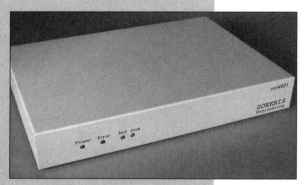

Figure 5-1. Soekris net4801, front view.

Figure 5-2. Soekris net4801, rear view.

Figure 5-3. Soekris net4801 with cover removed.

Introducing the Soekris net4801

The net4801 is ideal for this project because it has enough processing power to monitor a sizeable WAN connection (possibly up to several megabits) and the ability to use a disk drive for logs and graphs. Even with space for a laptop hard drive, the total form factor including the case is identical to the very small (8.5 × 6 × 1 in, 21.5 × 15 × 2.5 cm) net4501 discussed in Chapter 4.

The front of the net4801 is shown in Figure 5-1. It features four LEDs, indicating power, error conditions, network activity, and disk activity. The error LED is controllable from software and also remains lit until the board's power-on self-test (POST) has completed.

The rear of the net4801, shown in Figure 5-2, has three fast Ethernet ports, a DB-9 serial connector, a small power plug accepting 6–28 volts DC, and a USB connector.

Removing the cover, you can see the small mainboard pictured in Figure 5-3. A full-size PCI connector is prominent along one side of the board. Like the rest of Soekris's line of single-board computers, this PCI slot only supports 3.3V cards, so many PCI cards cannot work in the net4801. Carefully check specifications before purchasing a PCI card for use in your net4801.

On the opposite side of the board, you'll find a white Mini-PCI connector and a black Compact Flash (CF) slot. Next to the Mini-PCI connector are general purpose I/O (GPIO) pins and the header for a second serial port. Along the top of the board near the LEDs, you'll see a 44-pin connector for the laptop hard drive.

Designed for performance and low power, the net4801 is based on AMD's Geode SC2100 platform. The SC2100 is a 32-bit, x86-compatible chip running at 266 MHz. The net4801-50 has 128 MB of RAM soldered directly to the mainboard.

The net4801's 2.5-inch drive mounting kit, shown in Figure 5-4, is relatively straightforward. The U-shaped bracket sits directly on top of the mainboard. The kit comes with four hex standoff screws that replace the screws holding the mainboard in place. The short 40-pin parallel ATA (PATA) cable connects the drive to the mainboard. Note that you must use a 9.5 mm high hard drive. These have been standard for many years now. Older laptop hard drives are 12.5 mm high and do not fit inside the net4801's case.

Without a drive in place, the net4801 doesn't require any extra steps to keep cool, since it generates so little heat (barely warming up even under load). A laptop hard drive, however, may generate a little more heat than you'd like. Reports on the Soekris mailing list indicate that some drives in the net4801 case don't require any venting, while others do. If you want to be on the safe side, drill some small holes in the case so some of that heat can escape.

We purchased a 12 V, 1.2 A "mini switch mode" power supply for our net4801 directly from Soekris Engineering, along with the net4801 itself and the laptop drive mounting kit. This power supply is a regular wall wart transformer, but with a very slim form factor that means it won't eat up more than one outlet on a power strip. Since it is capable of 1.2 amps at 12 volts, it also has plenty of power to run the laptop drive. At any rate, even with the laptop drive, our measurements show the system pulling about 10–12 watts under load.

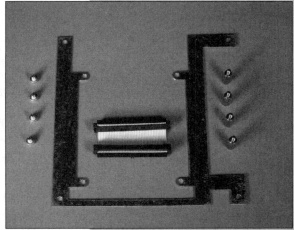

Figure 5-4. Soekris net4801 hard drive mounting kit.

Additional Hardware

The net4801 has two storage options: the CF slot on the board and the laptop hard drive connector. Since this monitor will be logging a fair amount of information to disk and generating graphs, we're using a laptop drive and leaving the CF clot empty. CF media have poor write performance and functional lifetime issues when subjected to frequent writes.

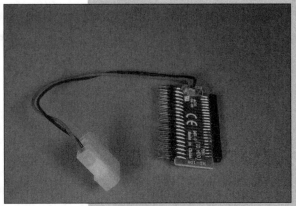

Figure 5-5. A 40-to-44 pin adapter for laptop hard drives.

This project doesn't require much drive capacity (1 GB would be fine), but storage has gotten so cheap that it is difficult to find new laptop drives smaller than even 20 GB. We choose a 30 GB Fujitsu drive for this project.

You should probably get a 2.5-inch hard drive adapter so you can connect the laptop drive to a standard desktop PC. This makes it much easier to install the operating system. The one that we used is shown in Figure 5-5. You'll notice that 2.5-inch hard drives have only one connector, providing both power and data transfer. The adapter has a standard 40-pin PATA connector on one side, plus a standard molex power connector. The other side is a 44-pin laptop drive connector.

Installing FreeBSD

The easiest way to install FreeBSD is from a CD-ROM. You can download and burn your own, or, if that is not an option, you can buy a CD-ROM online. In either case, visit **http://www.freebsd.org/where.html** to see your options.

At any given time, you'll probably find two major versions of FreeBSD available. For example, as we're writing this chapter, Version 4.11 is the latest (and perhaps last) release in the 4.X series, and 5.4 is the latest release in the 5.X series. If you are new to FreeBSD, it may not be immediately obvious which one you should choose. You may want to spend some time reading the release announcements and mailing list archives to get a feel for their stability. If you want to play it safe, install the latest version from the lower-numbered release.

At this time, we recommend using the latest 5.X release. We're using FreeBSD 5.4 throughout this chapter.

Download and burn the FreeBSD ISO image

If you have access to a CD writer, you can download and burn your own FreeBSD installation CD. Connect to one of the mirror sites and go to the *releases/i386/ISO-IMAGES* directory. Choose the appropriate version (e.g., 5.4) and go to that subdirectory. There you should see a number of *.iso* files. You'll only need *disc1* to install FreeBSD. Start downloading this large file to your computer and then go for a bike ride while waiting for it to complete.

After downloading, it's a good idea to check the size and MD5 checksum of the ISO file. Download the *CHECKSUM.MD5* file from the same directory. Then, use a MD5 checksum program to calculate the checksum of the ISO file. Windows users may need to install a program such as *winmd5sum* or *fastsum*. Unix users can use a program like *md5sum* or *md5*:

```
% md5 5.4-RELEASE-i386-disc1.iso
MD5 (5.4-RELEASE-i386-disc1.iso) = 3dbb37485535e129354bc099e24aed99
% cat CHECKSUM.MD5
MD5 (5.4-RELEASE-i386-bootonly.iso) = 2afe65af7e7b994c3ce87cefda27352e
MD5 (5.4-RELEASE-i386-disc1.iso) = 3dbb37485535e129354bc099e24aed99
MD5 (5.4-RELEASE-i386-disc2.iso) = e4b748415ca783fce64cfafd6bd56f57
```

If the checksums do not match, your ISO file is either the wrong size or corrupted. If it's too small, you can try to resume the transfer. Otherwise, delete the file and try the transfer again. Once the checksums match, go ahead and burn the image to a CD.

Connect the laptop drive

You need to get the laptop drive connected to the standard PATA cable inside the desktop computer that you'll be using to bootstrap the installation. First, connect the adapter to the laptop drive, taking care to honor pin order. Pin one should be labeled on the adapter. Pin one on the laptop drive will be on the right when viewing the laptop drive from the top down and the pins towards you. Ignore the smaller cluster of four pins on the extreme right, as these are used for jumpers to set the drive to master or slave—leave those pins empty so the laptop drive stays set to master (device 0).

Figure 5-6. Installing the laptop hard drive into a normal PC.

Now the adapter and drive need to be connected to the PATA controller in whatever machine you're using to do the installation. It is easiest to connect the drive to the primary PATA controller if your system has two PATA controllers, since this is the logical location of the drive once it is in the net4801. You want the laptop drive to be device 0 on controller 0 (master on the primary controller). When connecting the adapter to the standard PATA cable, be sure to pay attention to pin one. Pin one is typically colored red on PATA cables. You'll also need to connect the power cable on the adapter to a standard molex power connector inside the computer. Figure 5-6 shows the hard drive and adapter connected to a standard-sized PC.

Install FreeBSD from the CD

In this section we'll explain how to install FreeBSD onto the laptop hard drive. However, first timers may find our instructions somewhat terse. If you haven't installed FreeBSD before, you may want to have a look at the "Installing FreeBSD" chapter of the FreeBSD Handbook. You can find a link to the Handbook on the FreeBSD home page (**http://www.freebsd.org**).

Insert the FreeBSD install CD into the computer and turn it on. If the computer does not boot from the CD-ROM, you'll need to go to the BIOS setup and change the device boot order. When it works correctly, you should see a "Welcome to FreeBSD!" screen with some ASCII art of the FreeBSD daemon. You can hit Enter here or wait about ten seconds to automatically go to the install program, named *sysinstall*.

When you see the *sysinstall* menu, move the cursor to the "Standard" option and press Enter. The first step is to set up the DOS partition table with the FDISK Partition Editor. Note that FreeBSD also calls these partitions *slices*. Most likely your hard drive already has a slice. If so, delete it and then press "A" for Use Entire Disk. Then press "S" for Set Bootable. You should see something like this:

```
Disk name:    ad0                                    FDISK Partition
Editor
Disk Geometry 13424 cyls/15 heads/63 sectors = 12685680 sectors
(6194MB)
   Offset      Size       End    Name  PType    Desc  Subtype  Flags

        0        63        62      -      12   unused        0
       63  12685617  12685679   ad0s1      8  freebsd      165  A
```

Hit **Q** to quit and go on to the next screen, which has some information and options regarding the boot sector. We recommend using the FreeBSD Boot Manager (BootMgr), so simply press Enter here.

The next screen is the FreeBSD Disklabel Editor. Here, you'll create a number of partitions inside the slice. We recommend pressing **A** for the Auto Defaults option. This should give you a reasonable partitioning scheme. If you have your own preferences, feel free to use the other options to customize the partition sizes. When done, press **Q** to quit.

Next, you'll see a screen titled Choose Distributions. Here you can pick and choose which parts of FreeBSD to install. We recommend the Kern-Developer option. You'll need the kernel source to build a new FreeBSD kernel later on. Move the cursor to the Kern-Developer line and press the spacebar.

The next question is about the FreeBSD ports collection. This is a large directory hierarchy of *Makefiles* and other files used to download, compile, and install various free software packages. You'll use ports to build the application software for the project, so say "Yes" here.

Now you should be back at the Choose Distributions screen. Move the cursor up to the Exit line and press Enter.

Next, you'll see a screen that asks you to choose the installation media. Since you're installing from the CD-ROM, simply press Enter here.

Now you'll see a warning screen that gives you a last chance to abort the installation, in case you just realized that the disk drive contains the only copy of your very own Great American Novel. When you are ready to continue, press Enter. Then sit back and watch the fun.

You should see a few brief messages about creating filesystems, then some windows that display the progress of installing various software bundles. If you have better things to do than watch the progress, feel free to step away for a while and check back later. The ports collection in particular takes a long time to install. After some time you should see a "Congratulation!" screen. Press Enter here.

After installation you'll see a screen asking if you want to configure a network device. We recommend that you take up this offer (select **Yes**) and use the menus to configure your network. The installation procedure has about a dozen more questions for you. We've listed them, and the answers that we recommend, in Table 5-1.

Table 5-1. Questions and recommended answers for FreeBSD installation.

Question	Answer
Do you want this machine to function as a network gateway?	No
Do you want to configure inetd and the network services that it provides?	No
Would you like to enable SSH login?	Yes
Do you want to have anonymous FTP access to this machine?	No
Do you want to configure this machine as an NFS server?	No
Do you want to configure this machine as an NFS client?	No
Would you like to customize your system console settings?	No
Would you like to set this machine's time zone now?	Yes
Is this machine's CMOS clock set to UTC?	Yes
Would you like to enable Linux binary compatibility?	No
Does this system have a PS/2, serial, or bus mouse?	No
Would you like to browse the [package] collection now?	No
Would you like to add any initial user accounts to the system?	Yes
Now you must set the system manager's password.	Choose a good one

Figure 5-7. net4801 hard drive bracket position.

Figure 5-8. Attaching the hard drive to the bracket.

WARNING

If you pull too hard or twist the adapter, you might bend the pins on the drive.

Finally, you'll be asked if you want to set any last options. Answer **No** here, and you should find yourself back at the main *sysinstall* screen. Press Tab to move the cursor to the Exit Install option, then press Enter. Confirm your desire to exit the installation, eject the CD-ROM, and watch the computer reboot!

Configure the serial port for login

By default, FreeBSD does not spawn a *login* process on the serial port. This will be a problem when you move the hard drive to the net4801 unless you modify */etc/ttys* first. Bring up the file in an editor and find the line that starts with ttyd0. Change the off field to on, and change the default terminal type to vt100 or xterm, like this:

```
ttyd0    "/usr/libexec/getty std.9600"   vt100   on  secure
```

While you're at it, you should also disable the logins on *ttyv1* through *ttyv7*. These devices will not exist when FreeBSD runs on the net4801. Be sure to leave at least one login (on *ttyv0*) in case you need to put the hard drive back into a computer with a screen and keyboard.

Install the drive into the net4801

You are now ready to move the laptop hard drive from the installation computer to the net4801. First, make sure the computer is powered off. Carefully separate the laptop drive from the 40-to-44 pin adapter.

Open up the net4801 case by removing the four small screws on the bottom side. Then locate four screws that secure the mainboard to the bottom of the case. Remove these one by one and replace them with the hex-shaped standoff screws that came with the drive mounting kit. Tighten the hex screws with a socket or wrench. Set the U-shaped mounting bracket on top of the hex screws such that the open end is by the PATA connector, as shown in Figure 5-7. Do not attach the bracket yet.

WARNING

The bracket is not symmetric. One side is designed to avoid hitting the capacitors near the Mini-PCI connector.

Take the bracket off and attach the hard drive on top of it using the four screws from the mounting kit. Note that when the bracket is in place, the hard drive sits above the bracket, rather than below it. You'll find four holes underneath the hard drive that line up with the holes in the bracket (see Figure 5-8). Tighten the screws and place the assembly back on top of the net4801 mainboard. Take the four screws from the mainboard and insert them into the hex standoffs. Finally, connect the short PATA cable between the mainboard and hard drive. The cable should line up perfectly with the two connectors.

You may want to make sure everything works before you close up the net4801 case. Also, you may want to drill some ventilation holes in the case if you haven't done so already. Since the case is made of metal, be careful about the resulting metal shavings. You'll probably want to do this outside or in a garage, away from your computer equipment.

Connect a null modem serial cable between the net4801 and another computer. Start a terminal emulation program on the other computer and configure the serial port for 19,200 baud, 8 data bits, no parity, and one stop bit. When you power up the net4801, you should immediately see output similar to this in the terminal program:

```
comBIOS ver. 1.27  20041122  Copyright (C) 2000-2004 Soekris
Engineering.

net4801


0128 Mbyte Memory                   CPU Geode 266 Mhz

Pri Mas  TOSHIBA MK6412MAT          LBA Xlt 789-255-63  6342 Mbyte

Slot   Vend Dev  ClassRev Cmd  Stat CL LT HT  Base1     Base2    Int
-----------------------------------------------------------------
0:00:0 1078 0001 06000000 0107 0280 00 00 00  00000000  00000000
0:06:0 100B 0020 02000000 0107 0290 00 3F 00  0000E101  A0000000 10
0:07:0 100B 0020 02000000 0107 0290 00 3F 00  0000E201  A0001000 10
0:08:0 100B 0020 02000000 0107 0290 00 3F 00  0000E301  A0002000 10
0:18:2 100B 0502 01018001 0005 0280 00 00 00  00000000  00000000
0:19:0 0E11 A0F8 0C031008 0117 0280 08 38 00  A0003000  00000000 11

 5 Seconds to automatic boot.   Press Ctrl-P for entering Monitor.
```

If you don't get any output, double-check your serial connection and terminal emulation settings. If you don't see a drive listed below the memory and CPU information, power down the board and double-check the laptop drive installation. The pins on the hard drive connector are small, and it's easy to be off by one.

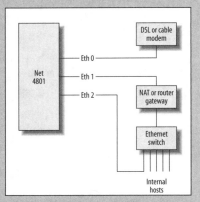

Figure 5-9. Connecting the network monitor in place.

You should make a few changes to some BIOS settings on the net4801. First, we recommend changing the console speed to 9,600 baud, since this is the default console speed under FreeBSD. Second, you want the system to treat the hard drive as primary. By default, the net4801 is set to treat the CF slot as primary. Hit Ctrl-P during the power-on self test to enter the comBIOS monitor:

```
comBIOS Monitor.   Press ? for help.
```

```
> set ConSpeed=9600
```

```
> set FLASH=secondary
```

Now, power down the net4801 and reconfigure your terminal emulator for 9,600 baud. Powering the system back up, you should see POST output much like before. If you see gibberish, start over (at 19,200 baud) and try to set the console speed again.

With everything in order, you'll see the FreeBSD boot loader run after the net4801 finishes its POST:

```
>> FreeBSD/i386 BOOT
Default: 0:ad(0,a)/boot/loader
boot:
```

The kernel will boot, displaying information about all the devices present in the system. Once you reach a login prompt, log in as root again and we'll show you how to configure the network.

Configuring the network interfaces

All three of the net4801's network interfaces are required to passively monitor a connection to the Internet while allowing you to view the logs and graphs the monitor will make. You'll configure two interfaces as a network bridge between the gateway (router or other gateway) and the Internet. A network bridge forwards Layer 2 (i.e., Ethernet) packets from one interface to the other. This allows the monitor to see all inbound and outbound traffic without requiring you to change (or obtain!) any IP addresses between your gateway and the Internet (most likely a DSL or cable modem). You'll place the third interface on your internal network ("inside" the gateway), as shown in Figure 5-9.

On the exterior of the net4801 case, the three Fast Ethernet interfaces are labeled Eth0, Eth1, and Eth2. In FreeBSD, these correspond to *sis0*, *sis1*, and *sis2*. Start by configuring *sis2*, since it's the easiest. If you want to assign this interface an address with your DHCP server, add this line to */etc/rc.conf*:

```
ifconfig_sis2="DHCP"
```

If you'd rather manually configure the IP address and netmask, use the appropriate *ifconfig* arguments instead of the keyword DHCP. For example:

```
ifconfig_sis2="inet 172.16.5.9 netmask 255.255.255.0"
```

You may see a similar line for another interface name (e.g., ifconfig_fxp0) from when you installed FreeBSD on the other computer. You can leave it there in case you need to move the hard drive back to the other computer sometime.

You may want to reboot at this point and make sure that your *ifconfig_sis2* configuration works as expected.

Now for the harder part: bridging the first two interfaces. The first step is to build a new kernel with the BRIDGE option enabled. We recommend creating a custom kernel configuration file based on the GENERIC configuration:

```
# cd /usr/src/sys/i386/conf
# cp GENERIC NET4801
# vi NET4801
```

Add the following line to the end of the *NET4801* file:

```
options   BRIDGE
```

This may also be a good time to remove some drivers and features from the kernel that you'll never use. For example, you probably don't need SCSI controllers, RAID, PCMCIA, FireWire, parallel port, or a floppy drive. But be careful when removing kernel drivers. If you are too ambitious, you may create a kernel that won't run on the hardware. Also, don't forget that you might need to take the hard drive out of the net4801 and put it into a normal PC to fix a problem sometime in the future.

We also recommend that you disable building of kernel modules, simply to speed up the process of building a kernel. To do so, add the following line to */etc/make.conf*:

```
NO_MODULES=true
```

Now you're ready to start building the kernel. Issue the following commands:

```
# config NET4801
# cd ../compile/NET4801
# make depend all install
```

As this runs, you'll begin to understand how slow the net4801's processor is. For us, it took 37 minutes to compile the kernel. If you lack the patience for this, you may want to move the laptop hard drive to a faster machine and do all the compiling there.

When the new kernel is installed, reboot the net4801. When it comes back up, you can configure Ethernet bridging with these commands:

```
# sysctl net.link.ether.bridge.config=sis0,sis1
# sysctl net.link.ether.bridge.enable=1
```

To see all the bridging configuration settings and statistics, run:

```
# sysctl net.link.ether.bridge
```

To have the system automatically configure bridging each time it boots, add these lines to *etc/sysctl.conf*:

```
net.link.ether.bridge.config=sis0,sis1
net.link.ether.bridge.enable=1
```

At this point, you can insert the net4801 into your network. Connect *Eth0* to your DSL/cable modem or other upstream device, and connect *Eth 1* to your router/gateway, as shown in Figure 5-9. After connecting the cables, make sure that packets are flowing through the net4801's bridged interfaces. Ping a few external hosts from an internal system. If something appears to be wrong, restore the original network connections until you debug the bridging configuration.

Arpwatch

Arpwatch is a nifty little program based around the simple idea that you would like to know about any Layer 2 (Ethernet) addressing changes to your network. As you may know, ARP is the Address Resolution Protocol. An *ARP table* provides a mapping between Ethernet and IP addresses. On Unix systems you can view the ARP table by running arp -a:

```
# arp -a
? (10.0.0.11) at 00:00:24:c4:3e:8a on sis1 [ethernet]
? (10.0.0.20) at 00:90:27:5c:87:56 on sis1 [ethernet]
? (10.0.0.21) at 00:90:27:16:aa:75 on sis1 [ethernet]
? (10.0.0.22) at 00:90:27:17:93:6e on sis1 [ethernet]
? (10.0.0.23) at 00:40:63:cb:38:52 on sis1 [ethernet]

? (10.0.0.27) at 00:02:b3:11:21:ec on sis1 [ethernet]
? (10.0.0.42) at 00:a0:c9:da:30:e9 on sis1 [ethernet]
? (10.0.0.98) at (incomplete) on sis1 [ethernet]
```

Arpwatch will notify you about changes to the ARP table. For example, you can find out if a new host joins the network. This might be especially useful if you have a wireless network. Arpwatch also lets you know if a device on your network changes its IP address.

To install Arpwatch, execute the following commands as *root*:

```
# cd /usr/ports/net-mgmt/arpwatch
# make all install
```

The install procedure creates a sample startup script named */usr/local/etc/rc.d/arpwatch.sh.sample*. We recommend that you rename or copy this file and use it to start Arpwatch automatically when your system boots:

```
# cd /usr/local/etc/rc.d
# cp arpwatch.sh.sample arpwatch.sh
```

You can tell the script which interfaces to monitor by setting the `arpwatch_interfaces` configuration variable in */etc/rc.conf*. You probably want Arpwatch to monitor your internal network, which is on *sis2*, so add this line:

```
arpwatch_interfaces="sis2"
```

You might be tempted to also monitor the other network interfaces. Unfortunately, it won't work because those interfaces are in bridged mode and do not have their own IP addresses.

Arpwatch uses both syslog and email to let you know about interesting events. Here's what the syslog message looks like:

```
Jun  3 01:01:47 arpwatch: new station 172.16.5.241 0:0:24:c4:3e:8a
```

And here's the corresponding email notification:

```
Date: Fri, 3 Jun 2005 01:01:48 -0600 (MDT)
From: arpwatch@net4801 (Arpwatch)
To: root@net4801
Subject: new station (dhcp241)

          hostname: dhcp241
        ip address: 172.16.5.241
  ethernet address: 0:0:24:c4:3e:8a
   ethernet vendor: CONNECT AS
         timestamp: Friday, June 3, 2005 1:01:47 -0600
```

Most likely you won't notice the syslog messages unless you specifically look for them. Email is a much better way to receive instant notifications. Messages are sent to *root* by default. You'll probably want to forward *root*'s mail to another address by defining an alias in */etc/mail/aliases*:

```
# cd /etc/mail
# vi aliases
# make
```

Alternatively, you can modify *arpwatch.sh* to include the `-m` option, followed by an email address, in the `arpwatch` command.

Nagios

Nagios is a popular open source program for monitoring hosts, services, and networks. Nagios uses active measurement and monitoring techniques. In other words, it sends periodic probes to hosts and services and uses the corresponding reply (or lack of a reply) to determine the state of the host or service. You can use Nagios to monitor your Internet connection, web server, mail server, and more.

Installing Nagios

As before, use FreeBSD's ports system to install Nagios. Begin by running make from the *net-mgmt/nagios* port directory:

```
# cd /usr/ports/net-mgmt/nagios
# make
```

You may notice that the ports system installs a number of dependencies before actually building Nagios. For example, Nagios requires *m4*, *autoconf*, and *libtool*, as well as the *png*, *jpeg*, and *freetype* libraries. If you compile Nagios on the net4801 itself, this step may take more than an hour.

After compiling Nagios, the next step is to actually install it with this command:

```
# make install
```

You should see a dialog box appear that asks you if you want to select certain optional plug-ins. These are not the only plug-ins that will be installed. This is only a list of plug-ins that require additional packages to be installed. We selected only the plug-ins that use SNMP:

```
              Options for nagios-plugins 1.4_1,1

 ---------------------------------------------------------------
|                                                               |
|     [ ] QSTAT    Game server query support                    |
|     [ ] FPING    Support for non-flooding fast ping           |
|     [X] NETSNMP  SNMP support                                 |
|     [ ] RADIUS   Radius support                               |
|     [ ] MYSQL    MySQL support                                |
|     [ ] PGSQL    PostgreSQL support                           |
|     [ ] LDAP     OpenLDAP support                             |
|                                                               |
 ---------------------------------------------------------------
```

Towards the end of the installation, you'll be asked about creating a *nagios* user and group. Answer yes to both of these questions.

To make FreeBSD automatically start Nagios when it boots, add this line to your */etc/rc.conf* file:

```
nagios_enable="YES"
```

Installing Apache

Nagios has a web-based user interface. You'll need an HTTP server with CGI support, such as Apache, to use Nagios. We suggest that you install the latest version of Apache 2.x from FreeBSD ports:

```
# cd /usr/ports/www/apache2
# make
# make install
```

To start Apache at boot time, add this line to */etc/rc.conf*:

```
apache2_enable="YES"
```

Note that Apache's default log files are */var/log/httpd-access.log* and */var/log/httpd-error.log*. You may want to add these to */etc/newsyslog.conf* so that they are periodically rotated and archived.

Another installation default is that the *data* directory is a symbolic link to *data-dist*. You'll probably be better off in the long term if you remove the symbolic link and create your own *data* directory:

```
# cd /usr/local/www
# ls -l data
lrwxr-xr-x  1 root  wheel  24 Jun 26 23:18 data -> /usr/local/www/data-dist
# rm data
# mkdir data
```

Configuring Apache

You need to tell Apache where to find the Nagios HTML files and CGI scripts. Also, we recommend that you use authentication-based access controls on the CGI scripts. You might feel that authentication is unnecessary since the server is inside your firewall. However, Nagios uses the authenticated username to determine the type and amount of information a user is allowed to see.

First, add `ScriptAlias` and `Directory` directives for the *cgi-bin* directory to the end of */usr/local/etc/apache2/httpd.conf*:

```
ScriptAlias /nagios/cgi-bin /usr/local/share/nagios/cgi-bin
<Directory "/usr/local/share/nagios/cgi-bin">
    AllowOverride AuthConfig
    Options ExecCGI
    Order allow,deny
    Allow from all

    AuthName "Nagios Access"
    AuthType Basic
    AuthUserFile /usr/local/etc/nagios/htpasswd.users
    require valid-user
</Directory>
```

Following that, add another pair of directives for the directory holding the HTML files:

```
Alias /nagios /usr/local/share/nagios
<Directory "/usr/local/share/nagios">
    Options None
    AllowOverride AuthConfig
    Order allow,deny
    Allow from all
</Directory>
```

Note that the order here is important. Be sure to put the *cgi-bin* directory first.

Start (or restart) Apache with this command:

```
# /usr/local/etc/rc.d/apache2.sh restart
```

If the configuration is correct, you can go to a web browser and enter the net4801's hostname or IP address. You should see a page that says "Index of /". Append */nagios/* to the URL, and you should see the Nagios welcome page. From there you can read the Nagios documentation, which will come in handy for the next section.

Configuring Nagios

Nagios uses a number of configuration files, located in */usr/local/etc/nagios*. The installation provides samples for each one. We'll go through them one at a time and let you know what to customize or leave alone.

The main configuration file is *nagios.cfg*. You can create it by copying the sample:

```
# cp nagios.cfg-sample nagios.cfg
```

You don't need to change many settings in this file. By default, Nagios encourages you to place different configuration "objects" into different configuration files. For example, *nagios.cfg* refers to *hosts.cfg*, *services.cfg*, and others. Multiple configuration files can be confusing for first-time users, so we recommend placing everything into one file, at least until you have a good understanding of the configuration syntax.

Find the following lines in *nagios.cfg* and either remove them or comment them out:

```
cfg_file=/usr/local/etc/nagios/contactgroups.cfg
cfg_file=/usr/local/etc/nagios/contacts.cfg
cfg_file=/usr/local/etc/nagios/dependencies.cfg
cfg_file=/usr/local/etc/nagios/escalations.cfg
cfg_file=/usr/local/etc/nagios/hostgroups.cfg
cfg_file=/usr/local/etc/nagios/hosts.cfg
cfg_file=/usr/local/etc/nagios/services.cfg
cfg_file=/usr/local/etc/nagios/timeperiods.cfg
```

Then add this line to take their place:

```
cfg_file=/usr/local/etc/nagios/mynet.cfg
```

You may have noticed other "include" files that are not commented out. You should create these by copying the sample versions:

```
# cp resource.cfg-sample resource.cfg
# cp checkcommands.cfg-sample checkcommands.cfg
# cp misccommands.cfg-sample misccommands.cfg
```

Now it's time to create *mynet.cfg*. The following sections describe each of the Nagios object types that you'll need in that file. You may want to refer to the Object Definitions page of the Nagios documentation as we go through them.

Hosts

Begin the configuration with objects that describe the hosts on your network. To keep things simple (for now), you should define only one host. However, you should also make use of Nagios's inheritance feature to simplify adding more hosts later. The first host object, named *generic-host*, is a template for the real hosts. This object contains the variables that are common to all hosts:

```
define host {
        name                   generic-host
        check_command          check-host-alive
        check_period           24x7
        check_interval         1
        max_check_attempts     5
        contact_groups         the-contact-group
        notification_interval  60
        notification_period    awake-times
        notification_options   d,r
        register               0
}
```

check-host-alive refers to a command object that exists in the *checkcommands.cfg* file. 24x7 and awake-times refer to time period definitions that you'll add to this configuration file later. Similarly, the-contact-group refers to a contact group object that you'll define later. The notification options d and r indicate that you want to be notified when the host goes down (d) and recovers (r). Finally, setting register to 0 indicates that this object is just a template and not a real host that should be monitored.

With the template object defined, you can easily add individual hosts, such as this one:

```
define host {
        host_name    gateway
        alias        Netgear Router
        address      172.16.5.1
        use          generic-host
}
```

The settings here should be intuitive. host_name is a short name for the host, and alias is a description of it. address can be either an IP address or a hostname. The use line refers to the generic-host template where all the other important values are defined. Note that you can override any of the other values in the real host definition if you need to.

Hostgroups

A *hostgroup* is simply a group of hosts that have something in common. It may be silly to have a hostgroup for very small networks, but Nagios complains unless your configuration has at least one hostgroup defined. The members field contains a comma-separated list of hostnames. In this simple configuration, the hostgroup has only one member:

```
define hostgroup {
        hostgroup_name          home-hosts
        alias                   Home Network Hosts
        members                 gateway
        }
```

Services

Nagios can monitor services in addition to hosts. A service usually corresponds to a daemon process running on a host, although it can be almost anything.

You should use the Nagios inheritance feature again here. The first service object is a template for checking a DNS server:

```
define service {
        name                    dns-service
        service_description     Check DNS Server
        max_check_attempts      5
        normal_check_interval   5
        retry_check_interval    3
        check_period            24x7
        notification_interval   30
        notification_period     24x7
        notification_options    w,c,r
        contact_groups          the-contact-group
        register                0
        }
```

Many of the parameters are similar to those in the host object. One difference is the notification_options field. Here, w refers to a warning state, c refers to a critical state, and r refers to a recovery. You can define a real service based on the dns-service template with just a few lines:

```
define service {
        host_name               gateway
        check_command           check_dns_name!localhost!127.0.0.1
        use                     dns-service
        }
```

The most interesting thing here is the check_command line. You can see it has three fields separated by exclamation points. The first field (check_dns_name) refers to a command that you'll define later. The remaining fields are command-line arguments that get passed to the command when it runs. In this case, you'll be calling a command that makes a DNS query to make sure that the name *localhost* resolves to the IP address 127.0.0.1. Note that the point of this service check is not necessarily to make sure that the value of `localhost` never changes, but rather just to make sure that your DNS server is up and responding to queries.

Contactgroups

You've probably noticed the `contact_groups` fields in the `host` and `service` objects. A contact group is, obviously, a group of contacts, which you'll define next. This simple configuration uses only one contact group, which in turn has only one member:

```
define contactgroup {
        contactgroup_name       the-contact-group
        alias                   The Only Contact Group
        members                 nagios
        }
```

Contacts

Here is a definition of a single contact, named `nagios`. Recall that contact names must correspond to the authentication usernames in the HTTP server password file. The definition has quite a few fields:

```
define contact {
        contact_name                    nagios
        alias                           Nagios User
        email                           root
        host_notification_period        awake-times
        service_notification_period     awake-times
        host_notification_options       d,r
        host_notification_commands      host-notify-by-email
        service_notification_options    w,c,r
        service_notification_commands   notify-by-email
        }
```

This example sets the contact's email address to `root`. You may want to choose a different address for your own installation. Note that the contact has different notification settings for hosts and services. The `host_notification_options` and `service_notification_options` settings match those found in the sample host and service definitions, although that is not a requirement. For example, you may have one contact that does not want to receive service warnings, while others do. The contact will be contacted only for states listed in both the host/service object and the contact object. The `host_notification_commands` and `service_notification_commands` settings refer to objects defined in the *misccommands.cfg* file.

Timeperiods

You've already seen a number of references to time periods in the previous objects. We recommend that you define two simple time periods: 24x7 (all day, every day) and `awake-times` for the times when you (or other people) are usually awake:

```
define timeperiod {
        timeperiod_name         24x7
        alias                   All Day Every Day
        sunday                  00:00-24:00
        monday                  00:00-24:00
        tuesday                 00:00-24:00
        wednesday               00:00-24:00
        thursday                00:00-24:00
        friday                  00:00-24:00
        saturday                00:00-24:00
        }

define timeperiod {
        timeperiod_name         awake-times
        alias                   Times people are usually awake
        sunday                  09:00-22:00
        monday                  07:00-21:00
        tuesday                 07:00-21:00
        wednesday               07:00-21:00
        thursday                07:00-21:00
        friday                  07:00-21:00
        saturday                09:00-22:00
        }
```

Commands

The final object definition is a special command to check your DNS server. The *checkcommands.cfg* already includes a command named `check_dns`. However, that command doesn't quite work the way we want it to. It always makes a query for **www.yahoo.com** and doesn't care what the answer is. With the following command, you can specify both the name to check (`$ARG1$`) and the expected answer (`$ARG2$`):

```
define command {
    command_name    check_dns_name
    command_line    $USER1$/check_dns -H $ARG1$ -a $ARG2$ -s $HOSTADDRESS$
    }
```

Recall that the `check_dns_name` command is referenced in the "Check DNS Server" service for the gateway host. The example we gave is:

```
        check_command           check_dns_name!localhost!127.0.0.1
```

In this case, `$ARG1$` (the name to query) becomes `localhost` and `$ARG22` (the expected answer) is `127.0.0.1`. The variable `$HOSTADDRESS$` is set to the address of the host for the corresponding service definition.

CGI Configuration

Nagios uses CGI programs to display information about the hosts and services it monitors. While the web interface is convenient to use, it is also a hassle to set up. CGI programs have certain security risks, and Nagios is no exception.

The Nagios CGI programs use a configuration file named *cgi.cfg*. It contains settings for a wide variety of things, including the directory for Nagios HTML files, other configuration files, authorization parameters, and presentation options. You can probably just copy and use the sample configuration file:

```
# cp cgi.cfg-sample cgi.cfg
```

If you read through *cgi.cfg*, you'll see a number of settings related to user authentication and privileges. Nagios internally enforces certain restrictions on what users can see and do. By default, a user can only see information on hosts and services for which it is listed as a contact. Most likely, your initial Nagios configuration will be simple, with just a single contact.

Note that Nagios does not have its own authentication database. Instead, it relies on the HTTP server to authenticate each user. Nagios assumes that the HTTP server is properly configured to execute CGI programs only when the user provides valid authentication credentials. Recall that we asked you to add a HTTP Basic authentication requirement to the Nagios *cgi-bin* directory back in "Configuring Apache."

Also note that the Nagios contact names must match the HTTP authentication usernames. Thus, you'll need to add a user to the *htpasswd.users* file for each contact listed in the Nagios configuration. To add a password for a contact named *nagios*, run this command:

```
# htpasswd -c /usr/local/etc/nagios/htpasswd.users nagios
New password:
Re-type new password:
Adding password for user nagios
```

Running Nagios

Nagios has a nice feature that you can use to check your configuration file for errors. Since the configuration is relatively complex, there is a good chance you'll make a few mistakes the first time. To validate the configuration, run:

```
# nagios -v /usr/local/etc/nagios/nagios.cfg
```

Any errors that you see must be fixed before Nagios runs. Warnings can be ignored, but may indicate a problem that you should fix anyway. When the configuration file is error-free, run Nagios in the foreground for the first time:

```
# nagios /usr/local/etc/nagios/nagios.cfg
```

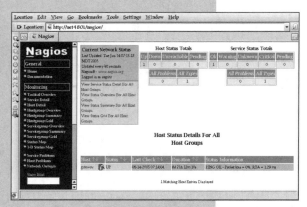

Figure 5-10. The Nagios Host Detail screen.

```
Nagios 2.0b2
Copyright (c) 1999-2005 Ethan Galstad (www.nagios.org)
Last Modified: 02-09-2005
License: GPL

Nagios 2.0b2 starting... (PID=18228)
```

Later, when you're sure it's all working correctly, start Nagios as a daemon process with the system startup script:

```
# /usr/local/etc/rc.d/nagios.sh start
Starting nagios.
```

Note that the startup script checks the value of nagios_enable from */etc/rc.conf*. Double-check that setting if Nagios does not start. If Nagios starts, but does not stay running, check */var/spool/nagios/nagios.log* for error messages.

Using Nagios

To use Nagios, go to your web browser and enter the URL containing the network monitor's hostname or IP address, followed by */nagios/* (e.g., *http://172.16.5.9/nagios/*). You should see the main Nagios page with a navigation menu on the left and some links to documentation in the main window.

Click on the Host Detail link under the Monitoring section. You should be prompted to enter a username and password. If you're following our example, enter *nagios* as the username and the password you created earlier in "CGI Configuration." Once you're authenticated, you should see a screen like the one shown in Figure 5-10.

Take some time to explore some of the other Nagios pages and features. Many of them won't be very interesting with just one host in the configuration. After some time, you'll probably be eager to add more hosts and services to your configuration. Adding new hosts should be simple, since we used the template feature. Simply copy the gateway entry and change the values as appropriate.

As you become more and more familiar with Nagios, you may want to use some of the advanced features, such as host/service dependencies, hierarchical relationships, passive monitoring, and more.

Snort

Snort is an open source intrusion detection system (IDS). It is designed to watch network traffic for certain patterns and signatures. When a packet (or sequence of packets) matches a Snort rule, the event is logged along with the source and destination addresses.

The number of alerts that you get from Snort is related to the number of services that you have running on your systems. For TCP-based services, such as SMTP and HTTP, your computers won't even receive the interesting traffic unless you have servers running to participate in the protocol conversation. For example, if you don't have an HTTP server running, then any attempt to establish a connection results in a TCP reset and there is no traffic for Snort to analyze. This may or may not be what you desire, depending on your level of paranoia. If you want to see IDS alerts for services that you don't normally run, you'll need to run those servers or set up some kind of a honey pot.

Installing Snort

As usual, installing a package such as Snort is simple with FreeBSD Ports:

```
# cd /usr/port/security/snort
# make all install
```

After typing make, you should see a dialog window that allows you to select a few optional features. Three of these are support for databases (MySQL, PostgreSQL, and ODBC). If you enable one or more of these, you can store alerts into a relational database instead of (or in addition to) a regular file. Another option is for a Snort feature called "flexible response," which gives Snort the ability to actively close dangerous connections. This feature is optional because it requires the *libnet* library. The final configuration option enables the code for Prelude integration. Prelude calls itself a "hybrid intrusion detection system," which means that it can collect intrusion alerts from a number of IDS systems.

We recommend that you enable MySQL support (or PostgreSQL if you prefer). Later in this chapter, we'll talk about installing an optional application called BASE, which requires an SQL database, to view Snort alerts. If you think you might want to use BASE, you might as well enable MySQL support now.

After installing Snort, add these two lines to */etc/rc.conf*:

```
snort_enable="YES"
snort_interface="sis0"
```

Note that *sis0* (a.k.a. Eth0) is the interface that should be connected to your Internet provider equipment (e.g., cable/DSL modem or router) as shown in Figure 5-9. If, after reading the Snort documentation, you want to use some different command-line options, you can add an *rc.conf* variable named snort_flags.

Configuring Snort

After Snort is installed, you'll need to customize its configuration file, */usr/ local/etc/snort.conf*. The file is installed read-only by default, so you may want to make it writable before editing it:

```
# chmod +w /usr/local/etc/snort.conf
# vi /usr/local/etc/snort.conf
```

Perhaps the most important *snort.conf* setting is the HOME_NET variable. This tells Snort the address (or addresses) corresponding to your local network. For example:

```
var HOME_NET 192.168.5.1
```

Note that if your network includes a Network Address Translator (NAT) connected to Eth1 as shown in Figure 5-9, HOME_NET should be set to your public IP address, rather than the private address space. Since Snort sits on the public side of your NAT box, the addresses won't have been translated yet when Snort processes packets.

If your public IP address is dynamically assigned, you may have to update the HOME_NET variable when the address changes. Snort has a feature to use whatever address is assigned to an interface, but that won't work for us since we are using a bridging configuration where Eth0 and Eth1 don't have assigned addresses.

If you are using Snort to monitor a number of non-NATed hosts (at the office perhaps), you can set HOME_NET to the whole subnet:

```
var HOME_NET 172.16.5.0/24
```

By default, Snort looks for all types of traffic on all hosts covered by HOME_ NET. However, if you have only certain services running on certain hosts, you can define those as well:

```
var DNS_SERVERS    [172.16.5.1,172.16.5.2]
var SMTP_SERVERS   [172.16.5.3,172.16.5.4]
var HTTP_SERVERS   172.16.5.5
var SQL_SERVERS    172.16.5.6
var TELNET_SERVERS 172.16.5.7
var SNMP_SERVERS   172.16.5.8
```

The *snort.conf* comments imply that setting these variables may make Snort more efficient. On the other hand, you'll probably want to know if an SMTP server suddenly appears on a host that does not normally serve SMTP. It is a trade-off, but we recommend leaving the *_SERVERS variables set to $HOME_NET.

The only other *snort.conf* change you should make at this point is to enable an output plug-in. We recommend using the *log_alert* plug-in, which sends alert messages to syslog:

```
output alert_syslog: LOG_AUTH LOG_ALERT
```

Towards the end of *snort.conf*, you'll see a number of `include` lines that refer to Snort rule files. We recommend leaving these as they are for now. After you have a little experience using Snort, you may want to revisit this section and add or delete certain rules. Also note that when you update the Snort software in the future, you may want to check the latest *snort.conf-sample* to see if any new rule sets have been added.

Running and using Snort

With some configurations, Snort writes log files to */var/log/snort*. Create this directory and leave it owned by *root*:

```
# mkdir /var/log/snort
```

Before actually running Snort, you should test your configuration file with the -T option:

```
# /usr/local/bin/snort -T |& less
```

Or, if you are using *bash* or *ksh*:

```
# /usr/local/bin/snort -T 2>&1 1>/dev/null | less
```

You'll see a fair amount of output describing how various Snort components are configured. Any errors should be at the end. If the configuration is error-free, go ahead and start it as a daemon:

```
# /usr/local/etc/rc.d/snort.sh start
Starting snort.
```

After starting Snort for the first time, run *top* and monitor its CPU usage for a while. Depending on the amount and type of traffic you have, Snort may have a hard time keeping up with the net4801. For example, here's what *top* reports after Snort has been running for a few minutes, monitoring our T1:

```
52 processes:  1 running, 51 sleeping
CPU states:  8.5% user,  0.0% nice,  3.1% system,  9.7% interrupt,
78.7% idle
Mem: 48M Active, 8072K Inact, 35M Wired, 1440K Cache, 22M Buf, 28M Free
Swap: 231M Total, 130M Used, 101M Free, 56% Inuse

  PID USERNAME PRI NICE   SIZE    RES STATE    TIME   WCPU    CPU COMMAND
21221 nagios    20    0  3376K  1148K kserel  55:29  0.00%  0.00% nagios
21924 root     -58    0 71556K 40344K bpf     37:21  6.98%  6.98% snort
69679 root      96    0  2392K   996K select   6:33  0.00%  0.00% top
```

With only the syslog output method, you should find that messages are written to */var/log/auth.log*. Unfortunately, these syslog messages are difficult to read. The lines are very long and don't always give you enough information to easily see if the threat is real. Here are some syslog entries from our monitor:

```
Jul  6 06:06:31 net4801 snort: [1:2570:7] WEB-MISC Invalid HTTP Version
```

```
String [Classification: Detection of a non-standard protocol or event]
[Priority: 2]: {TCP} 80.58.15.235:36217 -> 206.168.0.13:80
Jul  6 06:06:32 net4801 snort: [1:485:4] ICMP Destination Unreachable
Communication Administratively Prohibited [Classification: Misc
activity] [Priority: 3]: { ICMP} 213.204.200.2 -> 206.168.0.9
Jul  6 06:06:39 net4801 snort: [1:1560:6] WEB-MISC /doc/ access
[Classification: access to a potentially vulnerable web application]
[Priority: 2]: {TCP} 202.241.4.130:35303 -> 206.168.0.9:80
Jul  6 06:06:41 net4801 snort: [122:17:0] (portscan) UDP Portscan
{PROTO255} 195.251.229.5 -> 206.168.0.9
Jul  6 06:06:42 net4801 snort: [1:1560:6] WEB-MISC /doc/ access
[Classification: access to a potentially vulnerable web application]
[Priority: 2]: {TCP} 66.249.65.3:55601 -> 206.168.0.9:80
Jul  6 06:06:45 net4801 snort: [122:2:0] (portscan) TCP Decoy Portscan
{PROTO255} 59.120.106.128 -> 206.168.0.9
Jul  6 06:06:53 net4801 snort: [106:4:1] (spp_rpc_decode) Incomplete
RPC
 segment {TCP} 206.168.0.13:80 -> 24.118.57.248:32771
Jul  6 06:09:11 net4801 snort: [1:1852:3] WEB-MISC robots.txt access
[Classification: access to a potentially vulnerable web application]

[Priority: 2]: {TCP} 202.165.98.144:38898 -> 206.168.0.9:80
```

In addition to syslog, you should also have a number of subdirectories under */var/log/snort*. Here, there is a subdirectory for each source IP address, with one or more files in each subdirectory. These files have only a little more information about each alert (i.e., the IP header field values). But since they are organized by IP address, you might find them more useful. For example, you can use this simple command to see which address causes the most alerts:

```
# du | sort -n
```

If your network is moderately busy and Snort generates more than a few alerts, you'll probably find it difficult to sift through these files looking for important events. That's why we recommend you also install MySQL and BASE, as described in the following sections. Note that when you enable the MySQL output plug-in in *snort.conf*, Snort no longer writes to the IP address files in */var/log/snort*.

However, if you decide to not use MySQL and keep logging to */var/log/snort*, you'll need a *cron* job to make sure the directory doesn't fill up over time. For example, the following crontab entry deletes subdirectories that haven't been modified for 5 days:

```
0 4 * * * find /var/log/snort -type d -mtime +5 -print | xargs rm -rfv
```

Another long-term concern is how to keep up to date with new Snort rules. Perhaps the easiest way is to periodically check FreeBSD ports for updates to the Snort package. We have some tips for doing so in "Staying up-to-date with FreeBSD," at the end of this chapter. You can also download new rules from the Snort web site, **http://www.snort.org/**, but you must be either a paid subscriber or register for free to receive delayed updates.

MySQL

Instead of (or in addition to) logging alerts to a disk file, you can make Snort put them into a database. If you want to use BASE to view the alerts, then you'll need to install MySQL (or PostgreSQL).

You might be wondering if your little net4801 can really run MySQL in addition to Snort, Nagios, Apache, and any other monitoring tools you may install. This is a valid concern. The answer depends on the amount of traffic passing through the box. It may also depend on how cool you can keep the net4801. As the system works harder, both the CPU and hard drive generate more heat. If the box gets too hot, it may crash or fail in some other way. If you think this may be a problem, you can actually run MySQL and BASE on a different system. Snort can send updates to a remote database.

As usual, you should install MySQL from ports. Unfortunately, this is a little bit confusing because ports has a number of different MySQL directories for different MySQL versions. The ports *makefiles* define a default version, which is currently 4.1. If you enabled MySQL when building Snort, the default MySQL client port should have been installed. You can check by looking for a *mysql* directory in */var/db/pkg*:

```
# ls /var/db/pkg/mysql*
/var/db/pkg/mysql-client-4.1.12:
+COMMENT        +CONTENTS       +DESC           +MTREE_DIRS
+REQUIRED_BY
```

When you find the version of the installed MySQL client port, install the matching server port. In this case, we'll install MySQL version 4.1:

```
# cd /usr/ports/databases/mysql41-server
# make all install
```

Following installation, enable the MySQL server in */etc/rc.conf*:

```
mysql_enable="YES"
```

You may also want to tune MySQL for this relatively small system by placing these lines in */etc/my.cnf*:

```
[mysqld]
skip-locking
key_buffer = 64K
max_allowed_packet = 1M
table_cache = 4
sort_buffer_size = 64K
read_buffer_size = 256K
read_rnd_buffer_size = 256K
net_buffer_length = 2K
thread_stack = 64K
```

Snort Logging Locations

Snort may or may not create additional logfiles in */var/log/snort* depending on the types of output plug-ins that you use. When we use the *syslog* plug-in only, Snort creates IP address subdirectories there. When we use both syslog and MySQL, Snort does not create these additional files and directories. When we use MySQL alone, Snort writes data to */var/log/snort/alert*.

Be sure to check whether or not Snort is putting files in */var/log/snort*. If so, you'll need to do something to make sure the files do not grow endlessly, eventually consuming all the space on this partition. For simple files, such as */var/log/snort/alert*, you can add an entry to */etc/newsyslog.conf*:

For other situations, you'll probably have to write your own shell script and run it periodically from *cron*.

Then start the server with its startup script:

```
# /usr/local/etc/rc.d/mysql-server.sh start
Starting mysql.
```

You may want to take a minute to read */usr/local/share/doc/snort/README.database*. It describes how to set up the database and configure the Snort output processor. You'll probably want to create a special database user for Snort and BASE. We'll use the name *snortusr*. Since BASE actually requires more database privileges than Snort, we recommend the following grant command to set up the database privileges. We also need to create the Snort database itself:

```
# mysql mysql
mysql> create database snort;
Query OK, 1 row affected (0.01 sec)
mysql> grant INSERT,SELECT,UPDATE,CREATE,DELETE on snort.* to snortusr@
localhost identified by 'sekrit';
Query OK, 0 rows affected (0.01 sec)
```

The next step is to create the necessary tables in the Snort database. The Snort distribution includes a script to do just this. It is not installed anywhere when you run make install, so you'll need to get it from the ports *work* directory:

```
# cd /usr/ports/security/snort/work/snort-2.3.3
# mysql -D snort < schemas/create_mysql
```

Now you can add a new output method to *snort.conf* with the same username and password from the MySQL grant command:

```
output database: log, mysql, user=snortusr password=sekrit \
        dbname=snort host=localhost
```

Restart Snort after updating its configuration file. To make sure that everything is working, you can ask MySQL to count the number of entries in the *event* table:

```
# mysql -e 'select count(*) from event;' snort
+----------+
| count(*) |
+----------+
|       73 |
+----------+
```

BASE

The Basic Analysis and Security Engine (BASE) is a nifty web interface that displays and manages Snort alerts. Those of you who took a chemistry class will appreciate that BASE is a fork of the code from the Analysis Console for Intrusion Databases (ACID) project.

BASE relies on a number of additional software packages, such as Apache, PHP, and a number of PEAR (PEAR is the PHP Extension and Application Repository.) modules. Install it from FreeBSD ports:

```
# cd /usr/ports/security/base
# make all install
```

We found that, for some reason, the ports system did not install all of the necessary PHP dependencies for us. This may be due to the fact that the PHP source-code distribution was recently split into smaller modules. Or perhaps the BASE dependency list is a little out of date. Whatever the reason, we manually installed the following PHP ports:

```
/usr/ports/www/php4-session
/usr/ports/databases/php4-mysql
/usr/ports/devel/php4-pcre
```

The next steps are to configure PHP and then BASE. (You may want to read */usr/local/share/doc/base/README* for more verbose instructions.) Assuming that PHP was not already installed on your system, you'll need to create and edit */usr/local/etc/php.ini*. The easiest way is to copy the *php.ini-recommended* file that was installed with PHP:

```
# cd /usr/local/etc
# cp php.ini-recommended php.ini
```

You'll probably want to change one line in the *php.ini* file. By default, PHP has very verbose debugging output. Since the BASE code generates a lot of warnings, Apache's *httpd-error.log* quickly fills up with garbage. The following setting is more appropriate:

```
error_reporting = E_ALL & ~E_NOTICE
```

Next, make sure Apache knows what to do with a file that ends with *.php*. Add this line to */usr/local/etc/apache2/httpd.conf*:

```
AddHandler php-script .php
```

You may also need to uncomment the PHP LoadModule **directive in your** *httpd.conf*.

Next, you must add additional configuration lines to *httpd.conf*. The BASE files are installed in */usr/local/www/base*, which is one directory up from the Apache *data* directory. You can either make a symbolic link or, as we prefer, add this line to *httpd.conf*:

```
Alias /base/ "/usr/local/www/base/"
```

For convenience, we recommend that you add index.php to DirectoryIndex in *httpd.conf*:

```
DirectoryIndex index.html index.html.var index.php
```

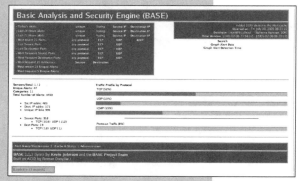

Figure 5-11. Screenshot of the main BASE page.

To configure BASE, copy the sample configuration file and bring it up in an editor:

```
# cd /usr/local/www/base
# cp base_conf.php.dist base_conf.php
# vi base_conf.php
```

Make sure the database name, database user, and password match those that you used in *snort.conf*. For example:

```
$alert_dbname   = "snort";
$alert_user     = "snortusr";
$alert_password = "sekrit";
```

As you can see from the `Alias` line that you added to *httpd. conf*, the URLs for BASE should begin with /base. You'll need to set `BASE_urlpath` to the same string in *base_conf.php*:

```
$BASE_urlpath = "/base";
```

At this point, you should be able to start using BASE. Fire up your browser and enter the net4801's hostname followed by /base/. For example:

```
http://172.16.5.9/base/
```

The first time, you'll probably see a message that says "use the setup page to configure and optimize the DB." Click on the setup page link, and then click on Create BASE AG. When you're done, go back to the main page. If it's working, you should see something like the screenshot in Figure 5-11.

Customizing Snort

It is likely that you'll need to customize Snort before it becomes useful to you. We found that Snort generates a lot of false positives, which tend to get in the way when trying to find real problems.

For example, our most common alert was "WEB-MISC Invalid HTTP Version String." This Snort rule was designed to catch a certain buffer overflow bug in an obscure email/web server. The rule says that there must be a newline character no less than five bytes after "HTTP/" in the request. However, Snort, or the rule, is not smart enough to limit its search to only the first line of the HTTP request. One of our busy servers receives many requests that look like:

```
GET /foo.html HTTP/1.1
...
Via: HTTP/1.1 silly inktomi proxy
```

The first line of the above request is valid, but the `Via` header (which is technically noncompliant, but of no real threat), sets off the alert. To avoid receiving these alerts, we edited */usr/local/share/snort/web-misc.rules* and commented out the line containing the description "Invalid HTTP Version String." We also commented out these other rules:

```
WEB-MISC /doc/ access
```

```
ICMP PING NMAP
WEB-MISC robots.txt access
```

Another annoyance we found with Snort is a large number of port-scan events. In particular, we found many "Open Port," "UDP Portscan," and "TCP portsweep" alerts in our database. It seems that they are often triggered by legitimate traffic, such as queries to our DNS server and outgoing SMTP connections. We chose to disable port-scan alerts by commenting out the `preprocessor sfportscan` line in *snort.conf*.

Obviously, the type and number of alerts that you get from Snort depends on how many hosts you have and the services that they run. You may find other types of false positives or alerts that you don't really care about. Use BASE's feature to show unique alerts sorted by total number of events to find out which ones are most common in your environment.

Snort maintenance

Neither Snort nor BASE automatically remove old alerts from MySQL. The database grows over time as more and more alerts are added. This might not be much of a problem if the database is running on a fast system. However, the net4801 becomes pretty slow as the database increases in size.

BASE has some features to help maintain the alert database. At the bottom of the pages that show alerts, you'll see a small HTML form labeled "ACTION." Here you can email, delete, archive, and move alerts into Alert Groups (AGs). You can use the delete and archive actions to keep the alert database small. However, these operations can be slow, especially if you forget to do them regularly.

To help keep our database size down, we came up with a shell script you can run from *cron*. Our script uses knowledge of the database structure, which is documented in the *schemas/create_mysql* file of the Snort distribution. If the schema changes in a future release, this script may need to be modified.

The script works by finding the first CID (the column name that represents an event id) older than 24 hours and then removing all entries with CIDs less than that. The one-day limit is pretty aggressive. If you want to keep alerts for a longer period of time, simply change the INTERVAL 1 DAY argument to whatever you like. Here is the script:

```
#!/bin/sh
set -e

DB=snort
TABLES="data iphdr tcphdr udphdr icmphdr opt event acid_event"

PATH=/sbin:/bin:/usr/sbin:/usr/bin:/usr/games:/usr/local/sbin:/usr/local/bin
export PATH
```

```
date

SENSORS=`mysql -N -e "select sid from sensor;" $DB`
for sid in $SENSORS ; do

  MAXCID=`mysql -N -e "select cid from event where sid = $sid \
    and timestamp < DATE_SUB(NOW(), INTERVAL 1 DAY) \
    order by cid desc limit 1;" $DB`

  test -z "$MAXCID" && continue
  echo "SENSOR=$sid, MAXCID=$MAXCID"

  for t in $TABLES ; do
    SQL="delete low_priority from $t where sid = $sid and cid <= $MAXCID;"
    echo $SQL
    mysql -e "$SQL" $DB
  done

done
echo -n 'Optimize:'
for t in $TABLES ; do
  echo -n " $t"
  SQL="optimize table $t;"
  mysql -e "$SQL" $DB >/dev/null
done
echo ''

# show how many rows in each table
for t in $TABLES ; do
  SQL="select count(*) from $t;"
  C=`mysql -N -e "$SQL" $DB`
  echo "$t          $C"
done

date
```

If you save the script as *trim_snort_db.sh* in *root*'s home directory, you can use this crontab entry:

```
0 0 * * * ./trim_snort_db.sh
```

RRDTool

The final network-monitoring technique we'll present uses RRDTool and some simple scripts to create graphs showing how much network traffic the hosts on your network send and receive over time. (Since the net4801 is configured as a bridge between two interfaces, it is relatively simple to count packets that pass through them.) This may help you understand why your network is occasionally slow or if certain hosts seem to be sourcing or sinking more traffic than they should be.

RRDTool (**http://people.ee.ethz.ch/~oetiker/webtools/rrdtool/**) is a system for storing and displaying data collected over time intervals, such as network interface counters, the number of spam emails in your inbox, and the price of gasoline. RRDTool is nice because it provides fixed-size, long-term storage and because it generates pretty good-looking graphs. The "RRD" in RRDTool stands for round-robin database. This apparently refers to the way that the database stores its data. An RRD file consists of one or more data sources (DSes) and one or more round-robin archives (RRAs). Data sources have attributes such as the data type and min/max values. An archive consists of some number of time slots and an aggregation function. For example, you can define an archive to store 24 hours worth of measurements at 5-minute intervals, plus a week's worth of data at 30-minute intervals.

We recommend installing RRDTool from FreeBSD ports:

```
# cd /usr/ports/net/rrdtool
# make all install
```

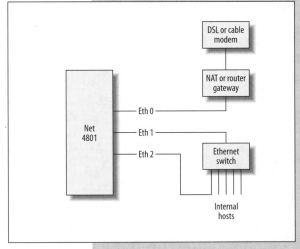

Figure 5-12. Alternative topology for the network monitor.

The trouble with NAT

Network Address Translation presents a problem with our goal of measuring per-host bandwidth. Recall from Figure 5-9 that the net4801 bridges the network between a cable/DSL modem and a router/gateway. If the router/gateway is configured for NAT, the net4801 only sees the public IP address. The addresses of the internal hosts are not in the packets flowing between Eth0 and Eth1.

If you are in this situation, you might prefer to change the topology so that the net4801 bridges the network between the router/gateway and the Ethernet switch. This topology is shown in Figure 5-12. The advantage is that you can monitor separate hosts with RRDTool, but Snort may see less traffic.

Setting up the counters

The goal is to see how many bytes and packets are sent to and from each host on our network. FreeBSD's *ipfw* utility has a good way to get this information. All you need to do is add a number of count rules to the *ipfw* configuration. First, make sure that the kernel has IPFIREWALL support. Go to the kernel configuration directory and edit the current configuration file:

```
# cd /sys/i386/conf
# vi NET4801
```

Add the following lines to the end of the file:

```
options        IPFIREWALL
options        IPFIREWALL_DEFAULT_TO_ACCEPT
```

Note that we are not suggesting that you configure this system to actually filter any packets. You only want to count the packets. Hence, the default-to-accept option ensures that you won't accidentally drop any packets. If you have IPv6 on your network (or plan to), you might want to add these lines as well:

```
options         IPV6FIREWALL
options         IPV6FIREWALL_DEFAULT_TO_ACCEPT
```

After editing, build and install the new kernel:

```
# config NET4801
# cd ../compile
# make depend all install
```

The FreeBSD firewall code does not, by default, receive bridged packets. To make this work, you also need to enable a sysctl variable. You can add this line to */etc/sysctl.conf*:

```
net.link.ether.bridge_ipfw=1
```

Another oddity is that the firewall only receives bridged packets on input. Bridged output packets do not go through the firewall code. But this is not a serious problem because packets entering your network are received on one interface, and packets leaving your network are received on the other.

This is probably a good time to reboot the system with the new kernel and *sysctl* setting. After the reboot, you can add the *ipfw* rules to start counting packets. You can customize the following shell script and save it as */etc/rc.firewall.count*:

```
#!/bin/sh

IPFW="/sbin/ipfw -q"
COUNT="$IPFW add count"
SUBNET="206.168.0"
FIRST=0
LAST=31
IF_IN=sis0
IF_OUT=sis1

$IPFW -f flush

i=$FIRST
while test $i -le $LAST ; do
        $COUNT ip from any to $SUBNET.$i in via $IF_IN
        $COUNT ip from $SUBNET.$i to any in via $IF_OUT
        i=`expr $i + 1`
done
```

Run the script manually a few times until you are satisfied that it works correctly. Note that with the -q option to *ipfw* you won't see any output unless there is an error. You can type ipfw show to see the rules and their counts, or to see only those rules with non-zero counts, use this command:

```
# ipfw show | awk '$2'
```

You should see something like this:

```
00700    1740     488595 count ip from any to 206.168.0.3 in via sis0
00800    1800     124940 count ip from 206.168.0.3 to any in via sis1
00900    2491     381248 count ip from any to 206.168.0.4 in via sis0
01000    2451     805783 count ip from 206.168.0.4 to any in via sis1
01100     692      88447 count ip from any to 206.168.0.5 in via sis0
01200     795     312687 count ip from 206.168.0.5 to any in via sis1
01300    7886    2114851 count ip from any to 206.168.0.6 in via sis0
01400    8699    1393426 count ip from 206.168.0.6 to any in via sis1
```

When you are satisfied with the *etc/rc.firewall.count* script, add the following lines to *etc/rc.conf* so that it is called when your system boots:

```
firewall_enable="YES"
firewall_script="/etc/rc.firewall.count"
```

Creating RRD files

Now you need to create the RRD files to store the counters. Recall that an RRD database is defined by a number of Data Sets (DSes) and Round Robin Archives (RRAs). You'll be updating the RRD databases with a *cron* job that runs every five minutes.

You should use one DS for each IP address on your network. Each DS definition has five parameters: name, type, heartbeat, min, and max. Here, for example, is the dataset definition that we recommend you use:

```
DS:a0:DERIVE:600:0:U
```

The dataset name is relatively straightforward. Our example uses a0 through a31 to represent the 32 IP addresses in a /27 subnet. The most appropriate dataset type is derive, which is like a derivative. It automatically calculates the rate of change for an ever-increasing counter. The heartbeat parameter specifies the maximum amount of time between data points. If, for some reason, the database is not updated within this period, RRDTool inserts unknown values. We suggest 600 seconds (10 minutes) for the heartbeat value, which is double the amount of time between normal updates. We also suggest 0 for the minimum and U (unknown) for the maximum to specify no limit. The zero minimum catches cases when the counters are reset to zero and which might otherwise result in a negative rate of change.

You'll also define five RRAs to store data at different granularity for different lengths of time between 1 day and 10 years. For example, the one-day RRA contains one value for each five-minute sample period. The 10-year RRA stores one value for each week. An RRA definition has four parameters and looks like this:

```
RRA:AVERAGE:0.99:1:288
```

The first parameter defines the aggregation, or consolidation, function. In this case, values are averaged as they are aggregated into each RRA. The second value is a number between 0 and 1 that specifies the fraction of input data values that may be unknown before the aggregate value is also declared unknown. We recommend a relatively high value (99%) so that you almost never have unknown values in the low-granularity RRAs. The third parameter specifies how many primary data points constitute an aggregated data point. The suggested step size is 300 seconds (five minutes). The final parameter is the number of aggregated data points to store for this RRA. These are called *rows* in the RRDTool documentation. When you multiply the step size, the number of steps, and the number of rows, you'll have the total time period covered by the RRA. For example, $300 \times 1 \times 288$ results in 86400 seconds, or one day.

If you want to count packets in, packets out, bits in, and bits out, you should use four separate RRD files. Each RRD file has the same internal structure and differs only in the name of the file. We recommend that you create a simple shell script to create the databases. For example:

```
#!/bin/sh
set -e
for f in pktsin pktsout bitsin bitsout ; do
    test -f $f.rrd || rrdtool create $f.rrd \
        --step 300 \
        DS:a0:DERIVE:600:0:U \
        DS:a1:DERIVE:600:0:U \
        DS:a2:DERIVE:600:0:U \
        DS:a3:DERIVE:600:0:U \
        DS:a4:DERIVE:600:0:U \
        DS:a5:DERIVE:600:0:U \
    ...
        DS:a31:DERIVE:600:0:U \
        RRA:AVERAGE:0.99:1:288 \
        RRA:AVERAGE:0.99:6:336 \
        RRA:AVERAGE:0.99:12:744 \
        RRA:AVERAGE:0.99:288:365 \
        RRA:AVERAGE:0.99:2016:520
done
```

Obviously you'll need to customize the DS lines for your particular network. You may have more or fewer addresses to monitor. You might be tempted to omit DS lines for addresses that you are not currently using. Be warned, however, that once an RRD database is created, you cannot go back and modify it. If you need to add more DS lines later, you must create a new RRD, then export and import the old data to the new database. Speaking from experience, you will not enjoy that procedure.

Select somewhere on your system for the RRD files to reside. If you don't have any other preferences, we suggest */usr/local/var/rrd*. We also suggest placing the creation script here so that you can use it again in the future if necessary. Once you have the location chosen, execute the script there to create the RRD files:

```
# mkdir -p /usr/local/var/rrd
# cd /usr/local/var/rrd
# mv ~/create-rrds.sh .
# sh create-rrds.sh
# ls -l
total 2434
-rw-r--r--  1 root  wheel     1312 Jul 11 16:32 create-rrds.sh
-rw-r--r--  1 root  wheel   597672 Jul 11 16:32 bitsin.rrd
-rw-r--r--  1 root  wheel   597672 Jul 11 16:32 bitsout.rrd
-rw-r--r--  1 root  wheel   597672 Jul 11 16:32 pktsin.rrd
-rw-r--r--  1 root  wheel   597672 Jul 11 16:32 pktsout.rrd
```

Updating the RRDs

Now you need a way to periodically parse *ipfw* output and insert the values into the RRDs. Like many of life's little problems, this one can be solved with Perl. You can run the following script from *cron* every five minutes. Note that it has some hardcoded IP addresses. You'll need to modify it before trying to use it on your own network:

```perl
#!/usr/bin/perl

use strict;
use warnings;
use FindBin;
use RRDs;

my @rrds = qw (pktsin pktsout bitsin bitsout);
my $maxidx = 0;
my $data;
my $IPFW_CMD="/sbin/ipfw show|";
my $now = time;

# ipfw output looks like this:
# 00900    25715     5083121 count ip from any to 206.168.0.4 in via sis0
# 01000    25734    10182547 count ip from 206.168.0.4 to any in via sis1

my $INPUT_PAT = '\d+\s+(\d+)\s+(\d+)\s+count ip from any ' .
  'to 206.168.0.(\d+) in via sis0';
my $OUTPUT_PAT = '\d+\s+(\d+)\s+(\d+)\s+count ip from 206.168.0.(\d+) ' .
  'to any in via sis1';

chdir $FindBin::Bin || die "$0: $!";

open (IPFW_CMD, $IPFW_CMD) || die "$IPFW_CMD: $!";
while (<IPFW_CMD>) {
        my $idx;
        chomp;
        if (/$INPUT_PAT/) {
                $idx = $3;
                $data->{pktsin}[$idx] += $1;
                $data->{bitsin}[$idx] += ($2 * 8); # convert to bits
        } elsif (/$OUTPUT_PAT/) {
```

```
                     $idx = $3;
                     $data->{pktsout}[$idx] += $1;
                     $data->{bitsout}[$idx] += ($2 * 8); # convert to bits
            } else {
                     next;
            }
            $maxidx = $idx if ($idx > $maxidx);
    }
    close IPFW_CMD;

    exit 1 if (0 == $maxidx);

    foreach my $rrd (@rrds) {
            my @idxes = grep {$data->{$rrd}[$_] > 0} 0..$maxidx;
            my $Tmpl = join(':', map {"a$_"} @idxes);

            my $Vals = join(':', $now, @{$data->{$rrd}}[@idxes]);
            RRDs::update("$rrd.rrd", '--template', $Tmpl, $Vals);
            my $ERR = RRDs::error;
            die "ERROR while updating $rrd.rrd: $ERR\n" if $ERR;
            if (open(LOG, ">>$rrd.log")) {
                print LOG "rrdtool update $rrd.rrd --template $Tmpl $Vals\n";
                close(LOG);
            }
    }
```

This script uses two Perl modules: *FindBin* and *RRDs*. The first is a part of the standard Perl installation. The second is installed along with RRDTool.

The INPUT_PAT and OUTPUT_PAT variables contain regular expressions to match the input and output rules in the *ipfw* output. Again, this sample script is hardcoded to match specific IP addresses. Make sure to modify these for your own network.

This script assumes that it lives in the same directory as the RRD files (i.e., */usr/local/var/rrd*). Rather than hardcoding this directory name in the script, it calls chdir $FindBin::Bin to change the current directory to wherever the script is stored. You'll need to modify this line if you want to place the script and RRD files in different directories.

The script also assumes that host numbering starts with .0. You may need to modify the assignment of $idx if your hosts are on a subnet that does not start with .0.

Note that the script creates a log of the RRD updates. You can use these logfiles to repopulate the RRD database if you accidentally lose them or need to re-create them for some reason. If you don't want the logfiles, you can remove or comment out those lines.

To run this script from *cron* every five minutes, add a line like this to *root*'s crontab:

```
*/5 * * * * /usr/local/var/rrd/update-rrds.pl
```

Viewing RRD graphs

The best way to view your RRD graphs is in your web browser. RRDTool includes a program named *rrdcgi* that enables you to write CGI scripts to generate RRD graphs. First, create a directory to hold the CGI scripts and image files:

```
# mkdir /usr/local/www/hoststats
# chgrp www /usr/local/www/hoststats
# chmod 775 /usr/local/www/hoststats
```

Note that the directory must be writable by the Apache user ID so that *rrdcgi* can create images there. Next, you need to tell Apache how to access the directory and to execute CGI programs found there. Add these lines to *httpd.conf*:

```
Alias /hoststats/ "/usr/local/www/hoststats/"
<Directory "/usr/local/www/hoststats">
    Options ExecCGI
</Directory>

AddHandler cgi-script .cgi
```

Then restart Apache:

```
# /usr/local/etc/rc.d/apache2.sh restart
```

That was the easy part. The hard part is writing the *rrdcgi* script, or scripts. This is hard for a number of reasons:

- You'll probably find a lot of repeated "code" in the *rrdcgi* file. For example, if you want to display four graphs on a page (one each for packets in, packets out, bits in, and bits out), you'll have four very similar RRD::GRAPH definitions. Multiply this by the number of time scales (day, week, month, year, decade), and now you have 20 graphs.

- Each host that you want to display requires at least 2 lines in the RRD::GRAPH definition. If you want to show 10 hosts, the code to generate the graph may be more than 20 lines long. It becomes a real hassle when you need to change a few of these lines in each of 20 graphs.

- There are a limited number of distinct colors that you can use on a graph. If you have more than 10 or so hosts, you'll either need to aggregate them or separate them.

Some of these difficulties can be solved by writing scripts to generate your *rrdcgi* files. You can also embed HTML forms into the script, allowing the user to select different graphs and time scales. We won't get that fancy here. Instead we'll show you the basic design of an *rrdcgi* script and leave the fancy stuff for you to explore on your own.

An *rrdcgi* script looks a lot like an HTML file. In fact, the *rrdcgi* interpreter acts only on special tags that begin with <RRD::. Any text outside of these tags is passed through unchanged. Here is a simple example:

```
#!/usr/local/bin/rrdcgi
<HTML>
<BODY>
<H1>Simple Graph</H1>

<RRD::GRAPH simple.png
        --start -1day
        --imgformat PNG
        --width 300 --height 200
        DEF:var1=/usr/local/var/rrd/bitsin.rrd:a3:AVERAGE
        LINE1:var1#FF0000:host2
        >

</BODY>
</HTML>
```

As you can see, the script starts off with some HTML markup, but the interesting parts are the instructions for drawing the graph. Everything inside the <RRD::Graph ... > tags is simply *rrdgraph* command-line arguments. You'll want to read the *rrdgraph* documentation (e.g., manpage) to really understand how to make graphs.

This simple example has a few options, such as --start and --imgformat. The DEF line defines a variable. In this case it says to take the average value of a3 from the */usr/local/var/rrd/bitsin.rrd* file. The LINE1 line instructs RRDTool to draw a 1-pixel-wide line representing the var1 data in red and label it "host2."

Save the script under */usr/local/www/hoststats/* with a name like *simple.cgi*. Go to your browser and enter the URL corresponding to this file. When *rrdcgi* executes the code, it does two things. First it generates a PNG file named *simple.png* in the same directory as the script. Then it replaces the RRD::Graph section with the following HTML:

```
<IMG SRC="./simple.png" WIDTH="380" HEIGHT="255">
```

If everything is working correctly, you should see an image in your web browser when you access the CGI file. If not, you may see an error message where the graph belongs. Also, check the Apache error log for messages. Once you have it working, it's time to move on to a more complex graph.

This one displays the bandwidth used by six different hosts over the last 24-hour period:

```
#!/usr/local/bin/rrdcgi
<HTML>
<HEAD><TITLE>Host Network Statistics</TITLE></HEAD>
<BODY>
<H1>Host Statistics</H1>

<RRD::GRAPH hoststats.bitsin.day.png
        --title="Bits In -- 1day"
        --start -1day
        --imgformat PNG
        --vertical-label "bits/sec"
        --width 500 --height 200
        --lower-limit 0
        --no-minor

    DEF:i4=/usr/local/var/rrd/bitsin.rrd:a4:AVERAGE
    DEF:i5=/usr/local/var/rrd/bitsin.rrd:a5:AVERAGE
    DEF:i6=/usr/local/var/rrd/bitsin.rrd:a6:AVERAGE
    DEF:i9=/usr/local/var/rrd/bitsin.rrd:a9:AVERAGE
    DEF:i13=/usr/local/var/rrd/bitsin.rrd:a13:AVERAGE
    DEF:i18=/usr/local/var/rrd/bitsin.rrd:a18:AVERAGE

    AREA:i4#FF0000:host1
    STACK:i5#FFFF00:host2
    STACK:i6#00FF00:host3
    STACK:i9#00FFFF:host4
    STACK:i13#0000FF:host6
    STACK:i18#FF00FF:host7

    >

</BODY>
</HTML>
```

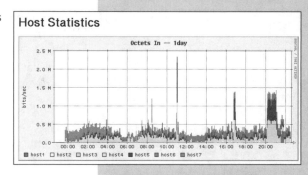

Figure 5-13. A sample RRDTool graph.

The first section of the graph sets a number of options. Many of them are self-explanatory. The `--start -1day` option specifies that the graph starts at the current time minus one day. The `--lower-limit` option ensures that the Y-axis starts at zero. The `--no-minor` option disables minor grid lines and makes the graph look a little less cluttered.

The next section defines six variables based on the data in */usr/local/var/rrd/bitsin.rrd*. Note that RRDTool automatically takes data from the appropriate RRA, depending on the `--start` value. We've specified AVERAGE as the consolidation function in case the chosen RRA has too many data values to fit in the width of the graph.

The final section instructs RRDTool how to display the data. We'll display the first variable as an AREA and then STACK subsequent variables on top of that. This allows you to quickly see the total bandwidth used by all hosts. You can see how it looks in Figure 5-13. Alternatively, you might prefer to plot each variable as a LINE2.

Don't forget the final angle bracket (>) to close the RRD::Graph tag.

Once you get a good-looking graph, you can use it as a template to create more graphs. For example, to change the "bits in" graph to "bits out," you need to change the DEF lines, the title, and the PNG image filename. To change the one-day graph to a one-week graph, change the start value and the image filename. You may find it easier in the long run to write a Perl script that generates *rrdcgi* scripts.

Extra Credit

Now that you have a decent network-monitoring platform, we have a few ideas for making it even better.

Staying up to date with FreeBSD

We recommend that you periodically update your FreeBSD system to stay on top of security issues, bug fixes, and to take advantage of new features. Updating the software is a multi-step process. First you'll download the updates from a server over the Internet. Then you'll build and install the new software. We'll show you how to do so for both the operating system itself and the applications you've installed from ports.

One of the best ways to receive software updates is with a program called *cvsup*. It is similar to, and more efficient than, anonymous CVS. It is also a little more complicated to set up, but we'll tackle it anyway. You'll need to install the *cvsup* client from ports. We recommend the non-GUI version:

```
# cd /usr/ports/net/cvsup-without-gui
# make all install
```

Next, you'll create a "supfile" for each collection that you want to update. We'll discuss this separately for *usr/src* and *usr/ports*.

Updating /usr/src

usr/src contains all the source code for the FreeBSD operating system, including the kernel and userland application such as *ls*, *vi*, and *grep*. Here is a sample supfile for *usr/src*, which you might save as *etc/usrsrc.supfile*:

```
*default host=cvsup12.us.FreeBSD.org
*default base=/var/db
*default prefix=/usr
*default release=cvs tag=RELENG_5
*default delete use-rel-suffix
*default compress
src-all
```

Briefly, that configuration instructs *cvsup* to update all the files in *usr/src* tagged with RELENG_5 from the server named **cvsup12.us.FreeBSD.org**. Refer to the "Using CVSup" section of the FreeBSD Handbook for a deeper explanation of each line in the file. The handbook also has a current list of *cvsup* servers around the world.

To update the files, simply run *cvsup* with this filename as a command-line argument:

```
# cvsup /etc/usrsrc.supfile
```

After you've updated *usr/src* for the first time, you may want to add these lines to *etc/make.conf*:

```
SUP_UPDATE=true
SUPFILE=/etc/usrsrc.supfile
```

Then, in the future, you can just run:

```
# cd /usr/src
# make update
```

After the files have been updated, you can compile and install the operating system. The standard method is:

```
# cd /usr/src
# make buildworld
# make buildkernel KERNCONF=NET4801
# make installkernel KERNCONF=NET4801
# make installworld
# mergemaster
# reboot
```

Note that the buildworld and buildkernel steps will take a very long time on the net4801. If you don't have the patience, you may want to pull the hard drive from the system and temporarily mount it in a box with a faster processor. You may also want to do so if your net4801 seems to overheat under the stress of compiling so much software.

The *mergemaster* program is designed to keep your system configuration files up to date. Since some of them may have been modified by you, they are not overwritten by the `installworld` command. Instead, *mergemaster* identifies files that have changed and asks you whether to use the new file, the old file, or to merge them.

Updating /usr/ports

The supfile for */usr/ports* is similar, with only a couple of changes. Here is a sample */etc/usrports.supfile*:

```
*default host=cvsup12.us.FreeBSD.org
*default base=/var/db
*default prefix=/usr
*default release=cvs tag=.
*default delete use-rel-suffix
*default compress
ports-all
```

Note that the `cvs tag` is set to `.` for the ports collection. To fetch the files, run:

```
# cvsup /etc/usrports.supfile
```

Alternatively, add this line to */etc/make.conf*:

```
PORTSSUPFILE=/etc/usrports.supfile
```

Then run:

```
# cd /usr/ports
# make update
```

Updating the applications you've installed from ports is a little more complicated than for rebuilding the operating system. A program called *portupgrade* makes this a little easier. Without it, you'd have to recompile and reinstall each application manually. You can install *portupgrade* from ports:

```
# cd /usr/ports/sysutils/portupgrade
# make all install
```

Then, we recommend running the following set of commands to update all your ports applications:

```
# portsdb -Uu
# pkgdb -F
# portversion -vL =
# portupgrade -avr
# /usr/local/sbin/portsclean --workclean
# /usr/local/sbin/portsclean --distclean
# /usr/local/sbin/portsclean -DD
```

Again, this will take a long time on the net4801, so you may want to perform these steps on a faster machine.

Additional Nagios features

Nagios has a number of additional features and plug-ins that we haven't mentioned yet. For example, you can use SNMP to monitor various host resources such as disk space, memory usage, and CPU load. Nagios can warn you before a filesystem totally runs out of disk space and when the system load average exceeds a threshold. Install the *net-mgmt/nagios-snmp-plug-ins* port to use these features.

Another interesting Nagios-related port is the Nagios Remote Plug-in Executor (NRPE). It allows you to execute a Nagios plug-in on a remote host. That means you must have Nagios installed on the remote host as well. The NPRE port is *net-mgmt/nrpe*.

You can find more Nagios-related software by searching for "nagios" in the FreeBSD ports collection.

Additional software for Snort

The FreeBSD ports collection includes a number of useful Snort-related packages as well. Oinkmaster (found in *security/oinkmaster*) is a tool that helps keep your rules up to date. It also helps you retrieve rule sets from different sources. Oinkmaster even shows you the rules that are changed in each update.

snort-rep (found in *security/snort-rep*) is a little utility that generates either HTML or text reports from a syslog file. A similar program is SnortSnarf (found in *security/snortsnarf*). If you are using the BASE application, these tools may not be especially useful to you.

User authentication in BASE

By default, anyone that has access to Apache can use BASE to query the Snort alert database. If you would like a somewhat more secure installation, you can use BASE's internal user-authentication system. First, click on the Administration link from the main BASE page. Here you'll see links for creating users and roles. Add a role first, and then a user. Then edit */usr/local/www/base/base_conf.php* and set:

```
$Use_Auth_System = 1;
```

Wi-Fi Extender 6

Time

a day

Difficulty

easy

What You Need

- 4G Systems Access Cube
- 9–20 volt, 1 amp power supply
- 2 Mini-PCI Wi-Fi cards
- 2 Wi-Fi antennas
- Parts for custom console cable (optional)

Have you ever been in a situation where you wanted to use a nearby wireless network but the signal was too weak where you were sitting? How many times have you held your laptop up to your hotel room window desperately searching for an open network? With this project, you can build a portable device that acts as a gateway between two wireless networks. You can use it to extend wireless connectivity to your office, living room, or hotel room. Figure 6-1 shows a situation where the extender comes in handy. The Wi-Fi extender is actually quite simple: it routes traffic between two wireless networks, using standard protocols such as DHCP and NAT.

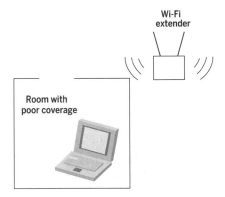

Wi-Fi
extender

Room with
poor coverage

Existing
Wi-Fi network

Figure 6-1. This diagram shows a situation where the Wi-Fi extender comes in handy.

Figure 6-2. Front view of the Access Cube.

Figure 6-3. Rear view of the Access Cube.

Introducing the Access Cube

The Access Cube is a small black box measuring $7 \times 5 \times 7$ cm, or $3 \times 3 \times 2$ inches. Figure 6-2 shows the front of it, where you'll find an RJ45 Ethernet jack (10/100 Mbps), a USB type A and another USB type mini-B port, and a power connector. This side also has two small screws that secure the two halves of the case.

On the rear you'll see two RP-SMA antenna connectors, shown in Figure 6-3. A pair of wires inside the case connects each antenna to one or more 802.11 cards. The wires have U.FL connectors, which are standard for Mini-PCI wireless cards. We'll show you how to connect them later in the chapter.

The Access Cube is designed for wireless networking applications. You can add two Wi-Fi cards to the cube with the two-sided Mini-PCI adapter. Since the Access Cube runs Linux, it supports a wide variety of 802.11 cards. 4G Systems sent us an 802.11b card based on the Prism chipset. You should be able to use any other Prism-based card, as well as those based on Atheros, Aironet, and Hermes chipsets.

A 400 MHz MIPS CPU powers the Access Cube. The CPU runs cool enough to not require any active cooling (i.e., fans). However, some Access Cube users have reported overheating issues when using the cube outdoors. Certainly the black color of the case does not help in that situation. We used the cube indoors only and did not experience any heat-related problems.

In terms of memory, the Access Cube has 64 MB of RAM and 32 MB of flash. The flash memory holds the Linux filesystem. While it may not seem like much space, 32 MB turns out to be plenty. In the default configuration, some of the RAM is used as a temporary filesystem mounted on */var*.

The Access Cube accepts a wide range of input voltages: between 7 and 24 volts DC. Our power meter says that it consumes only 2–3 watts. The Access Cube also supports Power-over-Ethernet (PoE), although we won't be using it in this project.

Our Access Cube kit, delivered from the manufacturer in Germany, came with a 9-volt, 1.2-amp power transformer. Unfortunately it has a European power plug and does not fit in North American sockets. The transformer can handle 110v AC, so you can use it if you have the necessary socket adapter. Since we didn't have such an adapter, we looked for a different transformer. We quickly found a 9 volt North American transformer in the closet, but it was rated for only 0.4 amps and did not provide enough power to the Access Cube. We found that a 12-volt, 1 amp transformer works great.

You may have noticed that the Access Cube doesn't have a serial port interface for console access. Actually, it does, but it's not accessible with the case in place, and it's not a standard RS-232 interface. This isn't a huge problem because the cube comes preloaded with Linux and you can log in over either the wired or wireless network interface. If you do a lot of tinkering with the system, you may find a serial console cable useful. You can either build one as described later in this chapter, or buy one directly from 4G Systems when ordering your cube.

Figure 6-4. Access Cube mainboards sandwiched together.

Assembling the System

When you receive your Access Cube, you'll probably have to assemble everything. This is actually very easy, since it has only a few different parts. Start by identifying the components. You should have:

- The two mainboards, sandwiched together
- The Mini-PCI adapter
- Two 802.11 Mini-PCI cards
- Two "rubber duck" antennas
- A 7–24 volt power supply

Find the mainboards, which are shown in Figure 6-4. If you are curious, you can carefully pry the two boards apart, as shown in Figure 6-5. It looks like CPU and memory live on the upper board, while the relatively bulky connectors are on the lower board. Carefully reconnect the boards if you've taken them apart.

Figure 6-5. Access Cube mainboards pulled apart.

> Before you insert the Mini-PCI cards, you may want to jot down their MAC addresses somewhere (they should appear on the cards), so this information is not sealed away inside the unit. This is especially important if your Wi-Fi network uses MAC address filtering to decide which hosts are allowed to connect to it, but could come in handy in other situations.

Figure 6-6. Access Cube Mini-PCI adapter.

The Mini-PCI adapter shown in Figure 6-6 fits on top of the two mainboards. But before attaching them, you'll need to insert the two 802.11 cards. Insert the Mini-PCI card shown in Figure 6-7 into the slot at an angle, as shown in Figure 6-8. Make sure the card is inserted as far as it will go (still at an angle), then press down on the other end of the card so that it is parallel to the adapter. You should see two small clips that line up with notches in the Mini-PCI card and keep it in place. Insert the second 802.11 card on the other side in the same way.

Figure 6-7. A Mini-PCI 802.11b Wi-Fi card .

The next step is to attach the small, circular U.FL connectors to the 802.11 card as shown in Figure 6-9. Your Wi-Fi card probably has two connectors: one labeled MAIN and another labeled AUX. Attach the two antenna cables to the MAIN connectors on each card. This is tricky because the connectors are very small. Use your thumb and finger to line up the connectors and slowly apply pressure until you hear them click. If the connectors are not aligned and you press too hard, you may bend the metal on the cable connector.

Now attach the Mini-PCI adapter (with 802.11 cards) to the top of the mainboard, as shown in Figure 6-10. The only awkward part here is that the antenna cables are already attached and might get in your way. Make sure they don't accidentally become detached. Then, slide the whole assembly into the bottom half of the case, as shown in Figure 6-11. As you slide it in, make sure the wires don't get in the way or become pinched between the case and boards.

Finally, slide the top half of the case in place and secure it with the two small screws. Again, watch the cables closely so they don't become pinched somewhere. When you're ready to try it out, connect the power supply. If you look closely, you'll see both a red and green LED somewhat hidden behind the case, between the USB and power connectors. The red LED should turn off after a few seconds, while the green one remains lit. Now it's time to go exploring!

Figure 6-8. Inserting the Wi-Fi card into the Mini-PCI adapter.

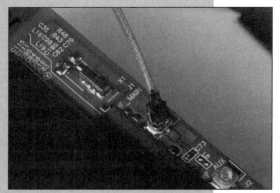

Figure 6-9. Attaching the internal antenna cable to the Wi-Fi card.

Exploring the Access Cube

Assuming that you don't have a serial console cable for your Access Cube, you'll need to log in with SSH. By default the Access Cube enables both a wired and wireless interface when it boots. The wired interface has an alias or "backdoor" address which, in theory, you can always use to reach the cube. The default backdoor address is 192.168.0.250 and the default wireless interface address is 10.0.0.1.

Logging In Through the Wired Interface

To log in through the wired interface, connect the Access Cube to your local area network. Or, if you don't have a LAN, connect it to another computer with an Ethernet crossover cable. The green light next to the Ethernet RJ45 jack lights up when the link has been established on the interface.

The Access Cube makes DHCP queries on *eth0*, so if you have a DHCP server on your network, it may get an address that way. Unfortunately, you may have to guess or look at the DHCP server logs to figure out exactly which address it receives.

If DHCP doesn't seem to work, you can always use the cube's backdoor address. You'll need to configure your PC with an IP address (or an alias) on the same subnet that the Access Cube is using (192.168.0.0/24). You can use any address other than 192.168.0.250, so let's choose 192.168.0.1. Here's how to add an alias to the first Ethernet interface on a Linux system:

```
# ifconfig eth0:0 192.168.0.1 netmask 255.255.255.0 broadcast\
192.168.0.255
```

Or, if you're using BSD (and assuming the Ethernet interface is named *fxp0*):

```
# ifconfig fxp0 alias 192.168.0.1 netmask 255.255.255.0
```

Figure 6-10. Attaching the Mini-PCI adapter to the top mainboard.

Microsoft Windows users can add an IP alias in the Advanced TCP/IP Properties dialog for the appropriate network connection.

After adding the address or alias to the interface, test it with a simple ping. You should immediately see some ping replies:

```
# ping 192.168.0.250
PING 192.168.0.250 (192.168.0.250): 56 data bytes
64 bytes from 192.168.0.250: icmp_seq=0 ttl=64 time=0.850 ms
64 bytes from 192.168.0.250: icmp_seq=1 ttl=64 time=0.387 ms
64 bytes from 192.168.0.250: icmp_seq=2 ttl=64 time=0.400 ms
^C
--- 192.168.0.250 ping statistics ---
3 packets transmitted, 3 packets received, 0% packet loss
round-trip min/avg/max/stddev = 0.387/0.546/0.850/0.215 ms
```

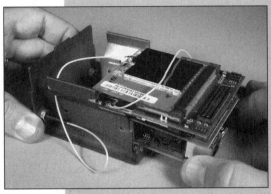

Figure 6-11. Sliding all the boards into the case.

Then, log in with SSH as *root*:

```
# ssh -l root 192.168.0.250
The authenticity of host '192.168.0.250 (192.168.0.250)' can't be
established.
DSA key fingerprint is ee:8f:e2:14:64:50:a8:28:73:7b:fc:0a:00:be:5e:4e.
Are you sure you want to continue connecting (yes/no)? yes
Warning: Permanently added '192.168.0.250' (DSA) to the list of known
hosts.
root@192.168.0.250's password: sekrit
root@mtx-1:~#
```

Note that your Access Cube comes with a preset, unique root password. You can find it on the "Configuration Sheet" that came with the Access Cube kit. If you happen to install a filesystem image update from 4G Systems, the root password will be changed or cleared. See the meshcube.org Wiki page titled Frequently Asked Questions (**http://www.meshcube.org/meshwiki/FrequentlyAskedQuestions**) for the current default root password.

Logging In Through the Wireless Interface

You can also log into the Access Cube through one of its wireless interfaces. By default, the first wireless interface (*wlan0*) is given the SSID *cube-ap* and the IP address 10.0.0.1. A DHCP server runs on this interface by default as well. If you plan to log in this way, be sure to attach an antenna to *wlan0*.

Your wireless-enabled laptop (or other computer) may automatically associate with the Access Cube's network and get an IP address. You may need to pick the *cube-ap* network from a list or set it explicitly if other Wi-Fi networks are nearby.

If for some reason DHCP is not working, you can try manually assigning an address such as 10.0.0.2. However, it is more likely that you have a problem with the wireless network configuration. Once your laptop has an IP address, test the network by pinging the Access Cube:

```
# ping 10.0.0.1
PING 10.0.0.1 (10.0.0.1): 56 data bytes
64 bytes from 10.0.0.1: icmp_seq=0 ttl=64 time=4.337 ms
64 bytes from 10.0.0.1: icmp_seq=1 ttl=64 time=4.399 ms
64 bytes from 10.0.0.1: icmp_seq=2 ttl=64 time=4.664 ms
^C
--- 10.0.0.1 ping statistics ---
3 packets transmitted, 3 packets received, 0% packet loss
round-trip min/avg/max/stddev = 4.337/4.467/4.664/0.174 ms
```

Once you've verified IP connectivity, log in with SSH as described previously for the wired network interface. Instead of using 192.168.250, use 10.0.0.1.

Poking Around

Before getting serious, you'll probably want to spend a little time checking out the Access Cube's operating system and marvel that it's really running Linux. For example, check out the processes that are running:

```
root@mtx-1:~# ps ax
  PID  Uid      VmSize Stat Command
    1 root         592 S    init [2]
    2 root              SW   [keventd]
    3 root              SWN  [ksoftirqd_CPU0]
    4 root              SW   [kswapd]
    5 root              SW   [bdflush]
    6 root              SW   [kupdated]
    8 root              SW   [mtdblockd]
    9 root              SW   [khubd]
   43 root              SWN  [jffs2_gcd_mtd0]
  279 root         708 S    udhcpc -b -p /var/run/udhcpc.eth0.pid -i eth0
 1102 root         828 S    /usr/sbin/crond -c /etc/cron/crontabs
 1107 nobody       812 S    /usr/bin/dnsmasq
 3368 root         592 S    /usr/sbin/ifplugd -i eth0 -fwI -u0 -d10
 3379 root        1060 S    /usr/sbin/olsrd -d 0
 3414 root        1692 S    /usr/sbin/sshd
 3418 root         660 S    /sbin/syslogd -n -C 500 -m 20
 3420 root         620 S    /sbin/klogd -n
```

```
3432 root        584 S   /sbin/getty 115200 tts/0 vt100
3473 root       2064 S   sshd: root@pts/0
3475 root       1768 S   -sh
4046 root        792 R   ps ax
```

Not surprisingly, it looks like a minimal Linux system. You have *cron*, *sshd*, and a DNS/DHCP server (*dnsmasq*). The *ifplugd* process executes commands to configure (and unconfigure) network interfaces when it notices that cables are plugged in (and unplugged). The *olsrd* process sends Optimized Link State Routing packets out the wireless interfaces, hoping to find nearby nodes and join or create a mobile adhoc network.

Now let's look at the filesystems:

```
root@mtx-1:~# df -h
Filesystem              Size      Used Available Use% Mounted on
/dev/root               28.0M    12.1M     15.9M  43% /
tmpfs                   10.0M    32.0k     10.0M   0% /var

root@mtx-1:~# mount
/dev/root on / type jffs2 (rw)
none on /dev type devfs (rw)
/proc on /proc type proc (rw)
tmpfs on /var type tmpfs (rw)
devpts on /dev/pts type devpts (rw)
usbdevfs on /proc/bus/usb type usbdevfs (rw)
```

The Access Cube's primary filesystem is 28 MB and only 43% full. Not bad! The 10 MB */var* memory filesystem seems a bit excessive, however. We'll show you how to change it in the next section. In the mount output we see that the primary filesystem is using the Journaling Flash File System (JFFS). As the name states, this is a filesystem designed specifically for use with flash memory storage. For example, JFFS distributes writes evenly to maximize the lifetime of the flash memory.

You might also note that syslog messages are written to */var/log*. This means that the syslog messages won't waste precious flash write cycles. It also means that syslog messages are not preserved between reboots.

How about network interfaces?

```
root@mtx-1:~# ifconfig -a
eth0      Link encap:Ethernet  HWaddr 00:0E:56:00:01:9E
          inet addr:10.0.0.87  Bcast:10.0.0.255  Mask:255.255.255.0
          UP BROADCAST RUNNING MULTICAST  MTU:1500  Metric:1
          RX packets:3070 errors:0 dropped:0 overruns:0 frame:0
          TX packets:4076 errors:2 dropped:0 overruns:0 carrier:4
          collisions:0 txqueuelen:1000
          RX bytes:1264335 (1.2 MiB)  TX bytes:408405 (398.8 KiB)
          Interrupt:28

eth0:0    Link encap:Ethernet  HWaddr 00:0E:56:00:01:9E
          inet addr:192.168.0.250  Bcast:192.168.0.255
```

```
                    Mask:255.255.255.0
                    UP BROADCAST RUNNING MULTICAST  MTU:1500  Metric:1
                    Interrupt:28

          lo        Link encap:Local Loopback
                    inet addr:127.0.0.1  Mask:255.0.0.0
                    UP LOOPBACK RUNNING  MTU:16436  Metric:1
                    RX packets:0 errors:0 dropped:0 overruns:0 frame:0
                    TX packets:0 errors:0 dropped:0 overruns:0 carrier:0
                    collisions:0 txqueuelen:0
                    RX bytes:0 (0.0 B)  TX bytes:0 (0.0 B)

          wifi0     Link encap:UNSPEC
                    HWaddr 00-90-4B-0A-DF-9E-00-00-00-00-00-00-00-00-00-00
                    UP BROADCAST RUNNING MULTICAST  MTU:1500  Metric:1
                    RX packets:2 errors:0 dropped:0 overruns:0 frame:0
                    TX packets:1695 errors:0 dropped:0 overruns:0 carrier:0
                    collisions:0 txqueuelen:1000
                    RX bytes:132 (132.0 B)  TX bytes:138584 (135.3 KiB)
                    Interrupt:4 Memory:c01af000-c01b0000

          wifi1     Link encap:UNSPEC
                    HWaddr 00-02-6F-03-56-58-00-00-00-00-00-00-00-00-00-00
                    UP BROADCAST RUNNING MULTICAST  MTU:1500  Metric:1
                    RX packets:0 errors:0 dropped:0 overruns:0 frame:0
                    TX packets:1675 errors:0 dropped:0 overruns:0 carrier:0
                    collisions:0 txqueuelen:1000
                    RX bytes:0 (0.0 B)  TX bytes:137268 (134.0 KiB)
                    Interrupt:5 Memory:c01b1000-c01b2000

          wlan0     Link encap:Ethernet  HWaddr 00:90:4B:0A:DF:9E
                    inet addr:10.0.0.1  Bcast:10.255.255.255  Mask:255.0.0.0
                    UP BROADCAST RUNNING MULTICAST  MTU:1500  Metric:1
                    RX packets:0 errors:0 dropped:0 overruns:0 frame:0
                    TX packets:1695 errors:0 dropped:0 overruns:0 carrier:0
                    collisions:0 txqueuelen:0
                    RX bytes:0 (0.0 B)  TX bytes:138584 (135.3 KiB)
                    Interrupt:4 Memory:c01af000-c01b0000

          wlan1     Link encap:Ethernet  HWaddr 00:02:6F:03:56:58
                    inet addr:172.16.0.1  Bcast:172.31.255.255  Mask:255.240.0.0
                    UP BROADCAST RUNNING MULTICAST  MTU:1500  Metric:1
                    RX packets:0 errors:0 dropped:0 overruns:0 frame:0
                    TX packets:1675 errors:0 dropped:0 overruns:0 carrier:0
                    collisions:0 txqueuelen:0
                    RX bytes:0 (0.0 B)  TX bytes:137268 (134.0 KiB)
                    Interrupt:5 Memory:c01b1000-c01b2000
```

And the Wi-Fi interfaces:

```
root@mtx-1:~# iwconfig
lo        no wireless extensions.

eth0      no wireless extensions.

wifi0     IEEE 802.11b  ESSID:"cube-ap"
          Mode:Master  Frequency:2.412GHz  Access Point: 00:90:4B:0A: DF:9E
          Bit Rate:11Mb/s    Sensitivity=1/3
          Retry min limit:8    RTS thr:off    Fragment thr:off
```

```
            Encryption key:off
            Power Management:off
            Link Quality:0  Signal level:0  Noise level:0
            Rx invalid nwid:0  Rx invalid crypt:0  Rx invalid frag:0
            Tx excessive retries:1  Invalid misc:1840   Missed beacon:0

   wlan0    IEEE 802.11b  ESSID:"cube-ap"
            Mode:Master  Frequency:2.412GHz  Access Point: 00:90:4B:0A DF:9E
            Bit Rate:11Mb/s    Sensitivity=1/3
            Retry min limit:8    RTS thr:off    Fragment thr:off
            Encryption key:off
            Power Management:off
            Link Quality:0  Signal level:0  Noise level:0
            Rx invalid nwid:0  Rx invalid crypt:0  Rx invalid frag:0
            Tx excessive retries:1  Invalid misc:1840   Missed beacon:0

   wifi1    IEEE 802.11b  ESSID:"cube-mesh"
            Mode:Ad-Hoc  Frequency:2.462GHz  Cell: 02:02:64:2D:56:58
            Bit Rate:2Mb/s    Sensitivity=1/3
            Retry min limit:8    RTS thr=250 B    Fragment thr:off
            Encryption key:off
            Power Management:off
            Link Quality:0/70  Signal level:-100 dBm  Noise level:-100 dBm
            Rx invalid nwid:0  Rx invalid crypt:3506  Rx invalid frag:0
            Tx excessive retries:252  Invalid misc:13586   Missed beacon:0

   wlan1    IEEE 802.11b  ESSID:"cube-mesh"
            Mode:Ad-Hoc  Frequency:2.462GHz  Cell: 02:02:64:2D:56:58
            Bit Rate:2Mb/s    Sensitivity=1/3
            Retry min limit:8    RTS thr=250 B    Fragment thr:off
            Encryption key:off
            Power Management:off
            Link Quality:0/70  Signal level:-100 dBm  Noise level:-100 dBm
            Rx invalid nwid:0  Rx invalid crypt:3506  Rx invalid frag:0
            Tx excessive retries:252  Invalid misc:13586   Missed beacon:0
```

Notice that the *wlan0* and *wifi0* interfaces are very similar, as are *wlan1* and *wifi1*. The *wifi* interfaces exist to provide access to low-level aspects of the 802.11 protocols. They may be used by the wireless tools (`iwconfig`, `iwlist`, etc) and programs such as `kismet`. We ignore these low-level interfaces in this book. You should always use the *wlan* versions in your commands and configuration files.

If you run `ls -l` on a directory like */bin* you'll notice something interesting:

```
root@mtx-1:~# ls -l /bin | head
lrwxrwxrwx   1 root     root                 7 May 26 18:33 addgroup ->
busybox
lrwxrwxrwx   1 root     root                 7 May 26 18:33 adduser ->
busybox
-rwxr-xr-x   1 root     root           1396204 May 26 18:33 bash
-rwxr-xr-x   1 root     root            916316 May 26 18:33 busybox
lrwxrwxrwx   1 root     root                 7 May 26 18:33 cat -> busybox
lrwxrwxrwx   1 root     root                 7 May 26 18:33 chgrp ->
busybox
lrwxrwxrwx   1 root     root                 7 May 26 18:33 chmod ->
busybox
lrwxrwxrwx   1 root     root                 7 May 26 18:33 chown ->
busybox
```

```
lrwxrwxrwx   1 root      root            7 May 26 18:33 cp -> busybox
lrwxrwxrwx   1 root      root            7 May 26 18:33 cpio -> busybox
```

Most of the system executables are symbolic links to something called busybox. BusyBox (**http://www.busybox.net/**) is a very cool project that combines stripped-down versions of Unix utilities into a single executable. This technique is very space-efficient because it eliminates the overhead of having a separate binary file for each command and maximizes code reuse. The downside is that some BusyBox commands lack features found in their GNU equivalents. For example, the BusyBox *ps* command produces only one kind of output. Any special options that you pass are silently ignored.

You may notice that the name "mtx" appears in some places, including your shell prompt. This is 4G System's project name for the Access Cube, and is actually a shortened version of "matrix."

Customizing the System

The Access Cube is designed to work out-of-the-box in a *meshrouting* environment. In this mode, the Cube tries to locate nearby nodes and use a meshrouting protocol to establish connectivity. As cool as this sounds, it is something that we won't be using. So the first thing you should do is disable the meshrouting startup scripts. In particular:

```
root@mtx-1:~# cd /etc/rc2.d
root@mtx-1:~# mkdir disabled
root@mtx-1:~# mv S20olsrd disabled
root@mtx-1:~# mv S14hostap disabled
```

If you want to change the backdoor address (on *eth0*), edit */etc/nylon/configip. conf*. Edit */etc/network/interfaces* to change the default address for *wlan0*.

You may want to define one or two nameservers in the */etc/resolv.conf* file. The nameservers allow you to use DNS names instead of IP addresses. Note that these are usually overwritten when the DHCP client program (*udhcpc*) gets a lease from a DHCP server.

At some point you should make sure the Access Cube's system clock is set accurately with the Network Time Protocol (NTP). Although the Cube doesn't come with *ntpd*, it does have *ntpdate* (one of the few non-BusyBox binaries). The boot scripts use *ntpdate* to synchronize the clock with an NTP server. If you have an NTP server on your network, place a line like this in */etc/default/ntpdate*:

```
NTPSERVERS="192.168.0.1"
```

If you don't have an NTP server on your network, don't worry. The script uses a public NTP server by default. We wish that the Access Cube also had the *ntpd* program so that it could automatically keep the clock synchronized as it runs. Since it has only *ntpdate*, you may want to add a cron job like this:

```
37 1 * * * /etc/init.d/ntpdate restart | /usr/bin/logger
```

You'll probably want to set the system's time zone as well. The time zone files are organized by continent and city. Find your continent in */usr/share/zoneinfo*. Then, in that directory, look for the name of a major nearby city. The Unix convention is to make a symbolic link from */etc/localtime* to the file you just found. For example:

```
root@mtx-1:~# ls /usr/share/zoneinfo
Africa      Arctic     Australia   Indian      zone.tab
America     Asia       CVS         Pacific
Antarctica  Atlantic   Europe      iso3166.tab
root@mtx-1:~# ls /usr/share/zoneinfo/America
Adak        Denver     Louisville  Rainy_River
Anchorage   Detroit    Maceio      Rankin_Inlet
...
root@mtx-1:~# rm -f /etc/localtime
root@mtx-1:~# ln -s /usr/share/zoneinfo/America/Denver /etc/localtime
root@mtx-1:~# date
Sun Nov  7 11:42:55 MST 2004
```

This is also a good time to add user accounts and change the root password. You can use the adduser command to add a new user:

```
root@mtx-1:~# adduser -g 'Stewie Griffin' stew
Changing password for stew
Enter the new password (minimum of 5, maximum of 8 characters)
Please use a combination of upper and lower case letters and numbers.
Enter new password: die-Lois
Re-enter new password: die-Lois
Password changed.
```

Don't forget to set or change the root password:

```
root@mtx-1:~# passwd
Changing password for root
Enter the new password (minimum of 5, maximum of 8 characters)
Please use a combination of upper and lower case letters and numbers.
Enter new password: sekrit
Re-enter new password: sekrit
Password changed.
```

If you feel that a 10 MB */var* partition is excessive (as we do), you can decrease the value in */etc/fstab*:

```
tmpfs           /var        tmpfs    size=2m       0     0
```

Wi-Fi Configuration

Up to this point you've seen how the Access Cube works and made a few minor tweaks to the operating system. Now it's time to get your hands dirty with some wireless network configuration.

We'll use the *wlan0* interface for the internal network. This is where you'll connect your laptop and/or other systems. You can give it a fixed IP address from RFC 1918 private address space. A DHCP server listens on the interface and hands out IP addresses to hosts joining the internal network. You'll also configure Network Address Translation (NAT) so that the internal hosts can communicate with the rest of the Internet.

We'll use *wlan1* as the upstream connection to the other wireless network. In most cases, you should get an IP address and DNS configuration from the upstream DHCP server. The only tricky part here is choosing the right wireless network when there is more than one.

wlan0

Let's start with the internal wireless interface. This one uses a static network name and a static IP address. You can configure everything in */etc/network/interfaces*:

```
iface wlan0 inet static
        address 172.17.0.1
        netmask 255.255.255.0
        wireless_mode ad-hoc
        wireless_essid foo
        wireless_channel 1
        #wireless_txpower 30
```

Those lines put the wireless interface into ad-hoc, or IBSS mode.

The example uses channel 1 and foo for the SSID. You should adjust these parameters as necessary for your own situation. Note that the wireless_ txpower line is commented out. The prism driver does not allow us to set the transmit power. If you try to do so, you'll get this error message:

```
Error for wireless request "Set Tx Power" (8B26) :
    SET failed on device wlan0 ; Operation not supported.
```

If you're using another wireless chipset, you should be able to set the transmit power. We suggest setting it to a relatively low value, such as 30 dBm, if you can. The transmit power should be set according to the distance between your laptop and the Access Cube. If the power is high and the distance is short, the wireless network may actually perform poorly. Plus, a lower transmit power reduces interference for other networks and makes it harder for others to eavesdrop on you.

Test your new settings by bringing the interface up and down a few times:

```
root@mtx-1:~# ifdown wlan0
root@mtx-1:~# ifup wlan0
root@mtx-1:~# ifdown wlan0
root@mtx-1:~# ifup wlan0
```

With the interface in the "up" state, run *ifconfig* and *iwconfig* to verify the settings:

```
root@mtx-1:~# ifconfig wlan0
```

Prefer Master/BSS Mode?

You may want to use master/ BSS mode instead. But if you do that, you should always set the wlan1 SSID explicitly. Otherwise, the cube will associate with itself. That is, *wlan1* in managed mode is likely to associate with *wlan0* in master mode

```
wlan0      Link encap:Ethernet  HWaddr 00:90:4B:0A:DF:9E
           inet addr:172.17.0.1  Bcast:172.17.255.255
           Mask:255.255.255.0
           UP BROADCAST RUNNING MULTICAST  MTU:1500  Metric:1
           RX packets:0 errors:0 dropped:0 overruns:0 frame:0
           TX packets:0 errors:0 dropped:0 overruns:0 carrier:0
           collisions:0 txqueuelen:0
           RX bytes:0 (0.0 B)  TX bytes:0 (0.0 B)
           Interrupt:4 Memory:c01af000-c01b0000

root@mtx-1:~# iwconfig wlan0
wlan0      IEEE 802.11b  ESSID:"foo"
           Mode:Ad-Hoc  Frequency:2.412GHz  Cell: 02:90:45:92:DF:9E
           Bit Rate:2Mb/s   Sensitivity=1/3
           Retry min limit:8   RTS thr:off   Fragment thr:off
           Encryption key:off
           Power Management:off
           Link Quality:0/70  Signal level:-73 dBm  Noise level:-73 dBm
           Rx invalid nwid:0  Rx invalid crypt:0  Rx invalid frag:0
           Tx excessive retries:0  Invalid misc:25   Missed beacon:0
```

You probably also want to have the Access Cube answer DHCP requests on *wlan0*. The *dnsmasq* program provides both DNS and DHCP. You'll need to edit */etc/dnsmasq.conf* and find the first uncommented dhcp line:

```
dhcp-range=10.0.0.10,10.0.0.200,2h
```

Make sure the address range there matches the subnet that you're using for *wlan0*. If you're sticking with our example configuration, change that line to:

```
dhcp-range=172.17.10,172.17.200,2h
```

You may want to look at other parts of the *dnsmasq.conf* while you have it in your editor, although most of the defaults are perfectly acceptable.

Finally, with *wlan0* in the "up" state, go to your laptop and make sure that you can associate with the wireless network (e.g., SSID foo in our example), get an IP address from the DHCP server, and log into the Access Cube.

wlan1

Configuring the other wireless interface, *wlan1*, is a little simpler. You can use these lines in */etc/network/interfaces*:

```
iface wlan1 inet dhcp
        wireless_mode managed
        wireless_essid linksys
```

These lines set the mode to managed, which makes this interface a client of an access point. The example also sets the network name (SSID) to a specific value: linksys in this case. You'll probably need to change this setting as you move the Access Cube from location to location. linksys is a common network name because it is the default value for Linksys equipment, but it won't always be available. If you set the network name to any, the card tries to associate with the network having the strongest signal. That may work in some situations, but not all. You'll probably find that it is less trouble to occasionally edit */etc/network/interfaces*, rather than leave the network selection up to chance. Note that whenever you edit the *interfaces* file, you should reconfigure the interface with a pair of ifdown and ifup commands.

Note the dhcp setting on the iface line. This tells the system to make a DHCP request for an address. When *udhcpc* is successful, the output looks like this:

```
root@mtx-1:~# ifup wlan1
udhcpc (v0.9.9-pre) started
Sending discover...
Sending select for 192.168.1.104...
Lease of 192.168.1.104 obtained, lease time 86400
adding dns 216.148.227.68
adding dns 204.127.202.4
```

Once *wlan1* has an IP address, try running a few pings and traceroutes to see if you can reach the public Internet:

```
root@mtx-1:~# ping www.oreilly.com
PING www.oreilly.com (208.201.239.36): 56 data bytes
64 bytes from 208.201.239.36: icmp_seq=0 ttl=44 time=51.9 ms
64 bytes from 208.201.239.36: icmp_seq=1 ttl=44 time=47.1 ms
64 bytes from 208.201.239.36: icmp_seq=2 ttl=44 time=48.7 ms
64 bytes from 208.201.239.36: icmp_seq=3 ttl=44 time=48.9 ms
```

NAT

The Access Cube comes preconfigured for NAT on *eth0* and possibly on *wlan1* as well. You can see the current NAT rules with this command:

```
root@mtx-1:~# iptables -t nat --list --verbose
Chain POSTROUTING (policy ACCEPT 0 packets, 0 bytes)
 pkts bytes target     prot opt in     out     source        destination
Chain POSTROUTING (policy ACCEPT 0 packets, 0 bytes)
 pkts bytes target     prot opt in     out     source        destination
    0     0 eth0_masq  all  -- any    eth0    anywhere      anywhere
    0     0 wlan1_masq all  -- any    wlan1   anywhere      anywhere

Chain eth0_masq (1 references)
 pkts bytes target     prot opt in     out     source        destination
    0     0 MASQUERADE all  -- any    any     anywhere      anywhere

Chain wlan1_masq (1 references)
 pkts bytes target     prot opt in     out     source        destination
    0     0 MASQUERADE all  -- any    any     anywhere      anywhere
```

If you don't see *wlan1* in the output, edit */etc/shorewall/masq* and add *wlan1* to the bottom of that file:

```
#INTERFACE          SUBNET          ADDRESS        PROTO   PORT(S)
eth0                0.0.0.0/0
wlan1               0.0.0.0/0
```

Then reboot, or run:

```
root@mtx-1:~# /etc/init.d/shorewall restart
```

Install Kismet

Since you'll probably be using the Wi-Fi extender in unknown environments, you'll need a good utility for finding nearby wireless networks. One of the best tools out there for Linux is called Kismet. Kismet puts interfaces into monitoring mode and then eavesdrops on all wireless traffic. It provides a wealth of information about nearby networks, including their operating mode (e.g., BSS, IBSS), signal strength, whether WEP is in use, how many clients are using the network, and much more. Kismet also breaks WEP encoding if it can capture enough packets. Unfortunately, the Access Cube does not come with Kismet pre-installed, but that's pretty easy to fix.

You can install Kismet from a precompiled binary package hosted on the 4G Systems web server. First, it's a good idea to update the local package database:

```
root@mtx-1:~# ipkg update
Downloading http://meshcube.org/nylon/stable/binary-feed/Packages.gz
Inflating http://meshcube.org/nylon/stable/binary-feed/Packages.gz
Updated list of available packages in /usr/lib/ipkg/lists/nylon-bin
Downloading http://meshcube.org/nylon/stable/feed/Packages.gz
Inflating http://meshcube.org/nylon/stable/feed/Packages.gz
Updated list of available packages in /usr/lib/ipkg/lists/nylon
```

Then, install the Kismet package:

```
root@mtx-1:~# ipkg install kismet
Installing kismet (2004-04-R1-r0) to root...
Downloading http://meshcube.org/nylon/unstable/feed/kismet_2004-04-R1-
r0_mtx-1.ipk
Configuring kismet
```

Kismet should run just fine without any special configuration. You may want to check that sound is disabled in */etc/kismet.conf*, anyway:

```
sound=false
```

The first time we ran Kismet, it refused to start and we got this error message:

```
Error opening terminal: xterm.
```

That happened because our TERM environment variable was set to *xterm* and there is no definition for *xterm* under */etc/terminfo*. Since there is a definition for *xterm-color*, we use that instead:

```
root@mtx-1:~# export TERM=xterm-color
```

Now we can finally start Kismet. We like to use the -n option to disable logging:

```
root@mtx-1:~# root@mtx-1:~# kismet -n
```

We'll talk more about using Kismet later in this chapter.

Antenna Options

You have a number of choices for Wi-Fi antennas. The antenna that you use may affect the quality of the wireless network connection, as well as the maximum distance between the Cube and another network.

Rubber Duck Antennas

"Rubber duck" refers to the short, black, semi-flexible antennas that you often find on access points and PCI Wi-Fi cards. 4G Systems will happily include one or two of these in your order. They usually have a rotating joint on the connector end so that you can easily orient the antenna as you please.

Rubber ducks are so-called omnidirectional antennas. They have the strongest signal in all directions perpendicular to the antenna and weaker signal in the parallel direction. The shape is very similar to a doughnut. This type of antenna is perfectly fine for most situations. You may want to consider one of the more "directional" antennas if you plan to use the Wi-Fi extender in locations where the upstream network might be farther away.

4G Systems describes their rubber duck antenna as a "+5 dBi probe." All this means is that it provides 5 dB gain (about a factor of 3) compared to an imaginary isotropic (perfectly spherical) antenna. While this is low compared to a more directional antenna, it's probably good enough for use within your house or office.

Parabolic Reflector

You can boost the signal strength of a rubber duck antenna by adding an inexpensive parabolic reflector. Hack #83 in *Wireless Hacks,* Second Edition (O'Reilly) explains how to do this. In theory, a parabolic reflector should provide about 10 dBi gain, or a factor of 10 increase in power levels.

Waveguide Antennas

Chances are you've heard of the famous "Pringles can" antenna. The Pringles can makes a very inexpensive, but effective, waveguide. The Pringles can is not a requirement, however. Other types of cans make even better waveguide antennas.

You can build your own can antenna for about $10 or less. Hacks #85 and #86 in *Wireless Hacks,* Second Edition (O'Reilly) provide good instructions. You should have no problems finding a number of web sites that also show you how. If you're lazy, you can buy a pre-made can antenna from a site such as **www.cantenna.com**. Figure 6-12 shows how the Access Cube looks next to a Cantenna.

You should be able to achieve about 12–15 dBi, or a factor of 15–30, with a can antenna.

Using the Wi-Fi Extender

We've described how to configure Linux on the Access Cube, but we haven't really explained how to use your little Wi-Fi extender. Here's how.

Find a Good Location

Figure 6-12. A Cantenna connected to the Access Cube.

Location is one of the most important factors in how well the Wi-Fi extender works. In particular, the upstream antenna (*wlan1*) should be in a location with a good signal to an existing 802.11 network. This might mean placing the cube right next to, or on the other side of, a window. Or perhaps it needs to be up high or at a corner where two walls meet. A can antenna gives you a little more flexibility because it can be placed a short distance away from the Cube itself, and can be aimed in a particular direction.

Boot Up the Access Cube and Log In

Power up the Access Cube and make sure that your laptop is configured to use the internal wireless network. The examples earlier in this chapter used the network name (SSID) *foo*. Set the network name on your laptop, if necessary, and check that it associates properly with the Access Cube.

Once the wireless network is associated, try to get an address from the Access Cube DHCP server. This usually happens automatically on Windows. On Unix systems you may need to run *dhclient*, *dhcpcd*, or *udhcpc*.

When your laptop has an IP address, you should be able to log in to the Access Cube through its *wlan0* interface. Log in as *root*, or a nonprivileged user if you created one.

Finding Wireless Networks with iwlist

In some cases you may get lucky enough that the Access Cube automatically latches on to a nearby wireless network. For that to work, the *wlan1* SSID must be set to any. Remember *wlan0* should be in ad hoc/IBSS mode if you want to use this wildcard SSID.

Most likely, however, you'll need to log in to the Access Cube and manually set the upstream network parameters.

You'll have to hunt for a suitable nearby Wi-Fi network if you don't already know of one. The yucky way to find nearby networks is with the iwlist command:

```
root@mtx-1:~# iwlist wlan1 scan
wlan1     Scan completed :
          Cell 01 - Address: 00:0F:B3:35:83:6F
                    ESSID:"moelter"
                    Mode:Master
                    Frequency:2.437GHz
                    Quality:0/92  Signal level:-76 dBm  Noise level:-97
dBm
                    Encryption key:off
                    Bit Rate:1Mb/s
                    Bit Rate:2Mb/s
                    Bit Rate:5.5Mb/s
                    Bit Rate:11Mb/s
                    Bit Rate:22Mb/s
                    Extra:bcn_int=200
                    Extra:resp_rate=110
          Cell 02 - Address: 00:30:AB:0A:E3:2B
                    ESSID:"plugh"
                    Mode:Master
                    Frequency:2.437GHz
                    Quality:0/92  Signal level:-67 dBm  Noise level:-97
dBm
                    Encryption key:off
                    Bit Rate:1Mb/s
                    Bit Rate:2Mb/s

                    Bit Rate:5.5Mb/s
                    Bit Rate:11Mb/s
                    Extra:bcn_int=100
                    Extra:resp_rate=10
          Cell 03 - Address: 00:90:4B:0A:DF:9E
                    ESSID:"xyzzy"
                    Mode:Master
                    Frequency:2.462GHz
                    Quality:0/92  Signal level:-61 dBm  Noise level:-95
dBm
                    Encryption key:off
                    Bit Rate:1Mb/s
                    Bit Rate:2Mb/s
                    Bit Rate:5.5Mb/s
                    Bit Rate:11Mb/s
                    Extra:bcn_int=100
                    Extra:resp_rate=10
```

We're mostly interested in the SSID values in this output. The other parameters don't matter as much. Notice that *iwlist* always reports the link quality as 0/92 for some reason. To really find the link quality you need to configure one of the network names and then run *iwconfig*:

```
root@mtx-1:~# iwconfig wlan1 essid plugh
root@mtx-1:~# iwconfig wlan1
wlan1     IEEE 802.11b  ESSID:"plugh"
          Mode:Managed  Frequency:2.437GHz  Access Point: 00:30:AB:0A E3:2B
```

```
Bit Rate:11Mb/s   Tx-Power:200 dBm   Sensitivity=1/3
Retry limit:8   RTS thr=250 B   Fragment thr=65534 B
Encryption key:off
Power Management:off
Link Quality:52/92   Signal level:-66 dBm   Noise level:-99 dBm
Rx invalid nwid:0   Rx invalid crypt:11   Rx invalid frag:0
Tx excessive retries:450   Invalid misc:555410   Missed beacon:0
```

When you get associated with a network, you can see if it is open by making a DHCP query:

```
root@mtx-1:~# udhcpc -i wlan1
```

Then try some pings and see if you can reach the Internet. If that works, then you should be all set. The Access Cube should happily NAT and forward packets from your internal network to this other.

Finding Wireless Networks with Kismet

One of the great things about Kismet is that it is so easy to use. The text-based screen is easy to understand and help is readily available. We like to start Kismet with logging disabled:

```
root@mtx-1:~# kismet -n
```

Most likely you'll see a welcome message that explains how to get help. When you close that message, you'll see the main Kismet screen, as shown in Figure 6-13. The large section lists known wireless networks, their operating mode, channel, packet counts, and IP address ranges. A smaller area below describes recent interesting events.

Press h or ? to see the Kismet help screen. It shows you the available commands and describes some of the cryptic codes used in the main display. For example, access points (in BSS mode) are marked with the letter A under the T (type) column. Ad hoc networks (IBSS mode) are listed with H.

Figure 6-13. Kismet main screen.

When looking for a network that you can connect to, you'll probably want to avoid those that use WEP (or WPA), indicated by a Y in the W column, unless you are authorized and have the necessary keys. Although Kismet can (in theory) crack WEP keys, we do not recommend that you attempt it.

You'll probably want to choose a network with good signal strength. Kismet can sort the list of networks by signal strength (press s then Q). Choose a network at the top of the list.

Once you have a few candidate network names to try, use the procedure from the previous section. Assign the network name to *wlan1*, then try to get an IP address with *udhcpc*. Alternatively, edit */etc/network/interfaces* and run ifup wlan1.

RFC1918 addresses are: 10.0.0.0 through 10.255.255.255, 172.16.0.0 through 172.31.255.254, and 192.168.0.0 through 192.168.255.255.

Gotchas

Watch out for situations where both network interfaces use the same subnet. It is common to find RFC1918 private addresses in use all over the place. The default configuration is to use 10.0.0.0/24 on *wlan0* and 192.168.0.0/24 on *eth0*. It's quite possible that the Access Cube will get a DHCP-assigned IP address on *wlan1* that falls within one of these existing networks. If that happens, you won't be able to send packets out the *wlan1* interface. Since you can't change the remote DHCP server, you'll need to change the conflicting subnet on the Access Cube interface.

Building a Console Cable

The Access Cube has a "Debug Connector" that you can use to access the system console. The connector itself is a very small miniature IDC header with 2 rows of 6 pins, shown in Figure 6-14. Three of these 12 pins are used for the serial console. Pin 1 is Transmit Data, pin 2 is Receive Data, and pin 11 is Signal Ground.

Unfortunately you can't just connect these pins to a standard serial cable. The Access Cube uses 3.3 volt signal levels, whereas standard RS-232C uses 12 volts. A page in the MeshCube Wiki provides instructions for building a level shifter using a MAX3232 chip, a Mini-IDC connector, four small capacitors, and a small circuit board. However, a MeshCube user discovered a simpler way.

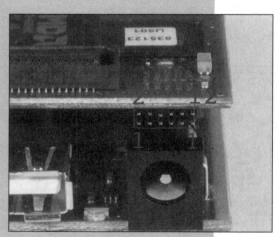

Figure 6-14. Closeup of the Debug Connector.

Some mobile phones have serial interfaces that also use 3.3 volt signal levels. You can buy a data cable for these phones that does exactly what we need. Most likely, the data cable includes a level shifter, similar to the one on the MeshCube Wiki, embedded in the DB9 plug. Since the mobile phone uses a proprietary connector, the only other thing we need is the Mini-IDC connector.

From the MeshCube Wiki, we found that Samtec (**www.samtec. com**) manufactures Mini-IDC cables and connectors in various styles. We contacted a local distributor and ordered a few 2x6-pin connectors with cables, as shown in Figure 6-15.

This fits perfectly onto the Access Cube's Debug Connector. We also ordered a data cable for Siemens mobile phones, as shown in Figure 6-16, which is an aftermarket accessory sold for Siemens model S46, M46, C35, S35, C3508, C25, S25, 6688, and SL45 phones. The only tricky part is connecting the tiny wires of the phone cable to the tiny wires of the Samtec ribbon cable.

You'll need to cut off the end of the phone cable that plugs into the phone. Do not cut off the RS232 connector! Cut away the outer insulation and expose the inner wires. If your cable is like ours, it has only three wires: blue, black, and white. Then crack open the phone-side connector and make note of which wires connect to which pins. The phone connector has 12 pins. Pin 1 (black wire) connects to Signal Ground, pin 5 (white wire) to Transmit Data, and pin 6 (blue wire) to Receive data.

Figure 6-17 is a schematic diagram of the cable you must build. DB9 pin 2 should connect to pin 1 on the Mini-IDC. Similarly, DB9 pin 3 should connect to IDC pin 2, and pin 5 to pin 11.

If you're not really sure how the datacable is wired, you can figure it out with a continuity tester. The circuitry inside the phone cable seems to isolate the transmit and receive wires on the two ends of the cable, such that you cannot test their continuity. However, you'll be able to identify the ground wire. Then you'll know that the other two are the transmit/receive pair. You have a 50% chance of correctly guessing which one is transmit and which is receive. If it looks like you've guessed wrong, swap them and try again.

But how should you physically connect them? After considering the best way to connect these two cables, we settled on using RJ45 connectors, just like you find on the end of an Ethernet cable. This was an easy route because we already had the RJ45 plugs and a crimper tool. The Samtec and phone cable wires are smaller than those in typical Cat5 cable, but it still works. Figure 6-18 shows how our cables look after adding the RJ45 connectors. Then we use an RJ45 coupler to join the two cables together, as shown in Figure 6-19.

For the phone cable, we connected the blue wire to pin 1 of the RJ45 plug, white to pin 2, and black to pin 8. Then, on the Samtec ribbon cable we connected pins 1 and 2 of the cable to pins 1 and 2 of the plug. (Note that pin 1 is marked with a red stripe on the ribbon cable.) Finally, we connected pin 11 of the ribbon cable to pin 8 of the RJ45 plug.

Testing the new console cable is relatively straightforward. You'll need to remove the Access Cube's cover to access the debug connector. Carefully slide the small IDC header onto the 12 pins. If you've done it right, the red stripe on the ribbon cable should be on the side closer to the USB connector. When the cable is connected, open a serial port communication program on the other computer. Set it for 115,200 bps, 8 data bits, no parity, and 1 stop bit. When you type Enter, you should see a login prompt from the Access Cube. If you shut down the cube and watch it boot, you should see something like this on the console:

```
YAMON ROM Monitor, Revision 02.17mtx1.
```

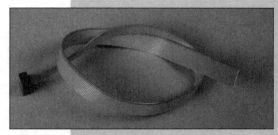

Figure 6-15. Mini-IDC connector and cable, Samtec P/N FFSD-06-S-10.00-01-N.

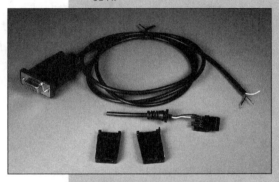

Figure 6-16. Cell phone data cable, with phone connector cut off.

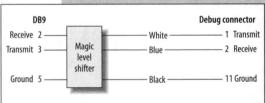

Figure 6-17. Cross-connecting the two ends of the serial cable.

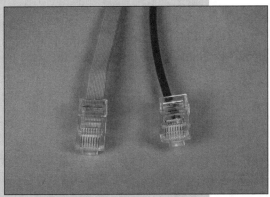

Figure 6-18. RJ45 jacks crimped on to the end of each cable.

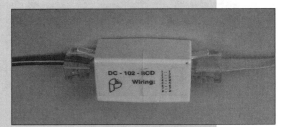

Figure 6-19. An RJ45 straight-through coupler joins the two cables.

```
Copyright (c) 1999-2000 MIPS Technologies, Inc. - All Rights
Reserved.

For a list of available commands, type 'help'.

Compilation time =            Aug 19 2003  13:49:58
MAC address =                 00.0e.56.00.01.9e
Processor Company ID =        0x03
Processor ID/revision =       0x02 / 0x02
Endianness =                  Little
CPU =                         324 MHz
Flash memory size =           32 MByte
SDRAM size =                  64 MByte
First free SDRAM address =    0x8008ac24

Environment variable 'start' exists. After 2 seconds
it will be interpreted as a YAMON command and executed.
Press Ctrl-C to bypass this.
```

Extra Credit

Can't get enough of the Access Cube? Here are a couple more tips and ideas that should keep you busy for a while.

Updating the Access Cube Software

The Access Cube uses a package management system called *ipkg*, which you've probably already used to install extra software. You can use the same program to update any or all of the software on the system. To upgrade everything, simply type:

```
root@mtx-1:~# ipkg upgrade
```

If the **meshcube.org** server has updated packages, they'll be downloaded and installed. You can also upgrade or remove particular packages by specifying the package name on the command line. To see the list of packages currently installed, type:

```
root@mtx-1:~# ipkg status | grep ^Package | less
```

To see the list of all available packages, type:

```
root@mtx-1:~# ipkg list | less
```

When upgrading, you may be prompted about whether or not certain files should be overwritten. A package may have files that are specifically marked as configuration files. If *ipkg* detects that you've edited a configuration file, you'll be asked whether you want to keep the current version, use the file from the package update, or see how they differ. In most cases you'll probably want to keep the current version. If you're not sure, see how they differ and then make your decision.

Loading a New Software Image

4G Systems provides an easy, albeit somewhat dangerous, way to "start over" with a fresh install of the latest Access Cube software. Read **http://www.meshcube.org/meshwiki/InstallingImages** before considering this approach. Note that this procedure entirely replaces the filesystem. Any files that you have created or modified will be lost.

The Access Cube software includes a script called *install-image*. Your cube must be connected to the Internet so that it can download the new image from the **meshcube.org** server. First, it's always a good idea to get an up-to-date copy of the *install-image* script:

```
root@mtx-1:~# cd /tmp
root@mtx-1:/tmp# wget http://meshcube.org/nylon/utils/install-image
```

Then execute it:

```
root@mtx-1:/tmp# bash install-image

*** INSTALL NEW NYLON IMAGE ***

**************************************************************
*** !!! WARNING !!!                                       ***
*** you will loose all your data!!!                       ***
*** if you continue you will loose all your configuration, ***
*** all files and other changes you made to your cube!    ***
***                                                       ***
*** do not power off the cube while flashing!!!           ***
**************************************************************

this script will download the nylon distribution image from a
server, write it to the flash and then reboot the cube.
this process will take about 10 minutes after the download has
completed, and is not without risk. if the cube does not reboot
after 10 minutes, something went wrong and you may have to use
the serial cable to recover it.

use install-image -h to see command line options

GETTING IMAGE FROM:    http://meshcube.org/nylon/stable/images
IMAGE NAME:            nylon.imgz

*** do you really want to continue? (yes/no) yes

* remounting /tmp to fit new images
* downloading image from http://meshcube.org/nylon/stable/images
Connecting to meshcube.org[217.160.210.161]:80
nylon.imgz          100% |*************************| 10600 KB
* preparing flash environment (chroot)
* switching to single user mode

**************************************************************
*** FLASHING IN PROGRESS                                  ***
***                                                       ***
*** !!!do not power off the cube in the next 10 minutes!!! ***
**************************************************************

if you are connected via ssh you will not see any output up from
this point. the flash process will continue nevertheless...

*** please wait approximately 10 minutes until the cube reboots ***

afterwards you will be able to login with empty password to the
new system on

ethernet:    192.168.0.250
accesspoint: 10.0.0.1          essid cube-ap
mesh:        172.16.0.1        essid cube-mesh
```

At this point, the instructions say to wait 10 minutes. During this time the Access Cube is unpacking the files from the image and placing them onto the flash. It's hard to predict exactly how long this takes, and if you interrupt the process before it's complete, you may be left with a broken Access Cube. After ten minutes, you should be able to log in again as root, with no password.

WARNING

To be on the safe side, make sure your Access Cube's power supply is connected to an uninterruptible power supply (UPS).

Don't forget that this procedure has wiped out all of your configuration files and customizations. IP addresses and other configuration settings have been reset back to their initial default values.

You'll probably want to install extra packages that you don't get with the update. For example, after you update the *ipkg* database you must manually install Kismet:

```
root@mtx-1:/tmp# ipkg update
root@mtx-1:/tmp# ipkg install kismet
```

PoE Wi-Fi Access Point

The Access Cube also makes a great wireless access point, especially since it supports Power over Ethernet (PoE). This means that you need to run only one cable up to the Access Cube.

PoE works by placing DC power on the unused wires of an Ethernet cable. Even though Ethernet cables have 8 wires (four pairs), only two pairs are used for data transmission for speeds up to 100 Mb/sec. The PoE standard (802.3af) supports two modes: A and B. In mode A, power is sent over the same pairs used for data transmission. In mode B, the power is sent over the two unused pairs. The Access Cube supports only mode B, which technically means it is not 802.3af compliant.

A PoE injector is the best way to put power onto the Ethernet cable. These cost anywhere from $10 to $75. The PoE injector has two RJ45 ports and a power source. One RJ45 jack is for the unpowered Ethernet cable and the other is for the powered cable, which connects to the Access Cube. Note that the cheaper injectors often require a third-party power supply.

Using the Access Cube as a Wi-Fi access point is relatively straightforward, especially if you use only one wireless card. Place the *wlan0* in master mode and assign it a network name. Configure the DHCP server (*dnsmasq*) as described under "wlan0" in "Wi-Fi Configuration," earlier in this chapter. You can choose to either route and NAT two subnets (one wireless, one wired), or bridge the two networks together as a single subnet. If you have only one Wi-Fi card, you can connect it to both antennas for improved coverage.

Small Form Factor PCs

A Portable, USB-Powered, Bridging Firewall

Time

a weekend

Difficulty

moderate

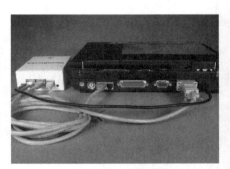

What You Need

- OpenBlockS/266 micro-server
- Ethernet crossover cable
- PC running Linux/BSD
- USB cable with type A male connector
- DC power plug with 4.0mm outer diameter and 1.7mm inner diameter
- Compact Flash card, 128–256 MB
- Soldering iron

Have you ever wanted a simple little firewall box that you could easily take with you? Perhaps you could bring it along when you visit your friends and family to upgrade and fix their computers. Or perhaps it could protect your Windows-based laptops while connected to strange networks. In this chapter we'll show you how to build a small, Linux-based bridging firewall that can be powered from a standard USB port.

A bridge is a *layer two networking device* that joins two network segments together. It is essentially just an Ethernet switch with two ports. It simply forwards Ethernet (layer two) frames from one side to the other. Bridges aren't nearly as popular today as they once were, because most people use switches and routers for their Ethernet networks. However, a bridge is a neat hack for this project because it means you don't have to change the IP addresses of any devices connected to it as you roam from one network to another. See the sidebar on page 191 for an explanation of the difference between a bridge and a switch.

This project is based around the OpenBlockS micro-server from Plat'Home in Japan. The OpenBlockS is small and consumes very little power, about six watts (even less with a Compact Flash card instead of a hard drive). To get everything working you'll also need a standard USB cable, a DC power plug, a soldering iron, a crossover cable or Ethernet switch, and a machine that can be configured as an NFS server.

Figure 7-1. The OpenBlockS266, front view.

Figure 7-2. The OpenBlockS266, rear view.

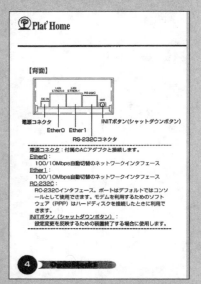

Figure 7-3. A page from the Japanese OpenBlockS manual.

The OpenBlockS comes with a 128 MB Compact Flash (CF) card, which barely holds the Unix binaries. You should purchase a larger CF card to make your life a little easier, or if you just want more storage. This firewall project doesn't need any additional storage, however. Be somewhat careful when purchasing third-party CF cards since not all of them work well as mini IDE drives. We've never had any problems with SanDisk CF cards.

Introducing the OpenBlockS

OpenBlockS is a series of products made by a company in Japan called Plat'Home (**http://www.plathome.co.jp**). We asked a friend of ours, Kenjiro Cho, if he could get one for us from Japan. If you'd like to order one from outside of Japan, visit the FATGadget site at **http://www.fatgadget.jp/e_products/openblocks.html**.

We received an OpenBlockS266. It is an ivory-colored box, measuring 3.25 x 4.5 x 1.5 inches, and is shown in Figure 7-1. On the front are four lights, one for disk activity and the other three for user applications. The front also has a 10-pin header labeled AUX that seems to be for communication with a UPS (it is probably just a second serial port with a special connector).

On the other side, shown in Figure 7-2, you'll find two 100 Mbps Ethernet ports, a serial port, a push-button labeled INIT, and a small 5V power connector. We haven't yet figured out what the INIT button does, but we know it does not reset the box.

Since the product line is targeted towards Japanese users, all of the documentation is in Japanese. This makes it a little difficult, but actually quite fun, to figure out how the OpenBlockS really works. For example, Figure 7-3 shows a page in the manual that describes the power, Ethernet, and serial ports.

Figure 7-4 shows the OpenBlockS internals, which consist of a small mainboard and, on top of that, an IDE-to-Compact Flash adapter. You can remove this adapter, as shown in Figure 7-4, and insert a laptop hard drive in its place! The mainboard, which sits under the heat-conducting aluminum frame, is shown by itself in Figure 7-5.

This particular OpenBlockS model has a 266 MHz PowerPC CPU, 8 MB of Flash memory, and 64 MB of 133 Mhz RAM.

It is, apparently, not possible to boot directly from the ATA/compact flash device. The OpenBlockS really wants to boot from its internal flash memory. You can, with some effort, boot "diskless" over the network too.

The OpenBlockS266 comes with an external universal power supply that outputs 5V. The system has no fans, so it relies on passive cooling. Inside there are a number of small pads that touch both the aluminum frame and various chips on both sides of the mainboard. These seem to be heat-conducting pads designed to transfer heat to the case. The case becomes warm, but not hot, after the box has been running for some time. Our measurements show that the system draws 4 watts with the CF card, which is less than a standard ATX power supply consumes when the computer is off! With a laptop hard drive the OpenBlockS consumes 6–8 watts.

Plat'Home includes a CD-ROM in the OpenBlockS package as well. It contains documentation, binary packages, source code, and some utilities that run under Microsoft Windows. You can use these utilities to install software on the OpenBlockS. However, chances are that you'll find more up-to-date versions on the Plat'Home FTP server at **ftp://ftp.plathome.co.jp/pub/OpenBlockS266/**.

Figure 7-4. OpenBlockS internals.

SSD Linux

The OpenBlockS comes with Linux pre-installed on the internal flash memory. However, it is a stripped-down version with only a subset of the GNU/Linux utilities. You'll probably want to install a larger set of the GNU/Linux utilities from the CDROM onto the CF card. But before you do that, you should play with the box a little.

The OpenBlockS comes with a short cat5 (Ethernet) cable and RJ45-to-DB9 adapter. Plug the cable into the console port as shown in Figure 7-6. Then connect the RJ45-to-DB9 adapter to the other end of the cable, and plug that into a serial port of another PC as shown in Figure 7-7.

Open a terminal emulation program on the PC (e.g., *hyperterm*, *minicom*, *cu*, *screen*, or *tip*) set for 9,600 bps, 8 data bits, no parity, and one stop bit (8N1). The OpenBlockS does not have an on/off switch, so when you plug the power cable into the little "DC IN" socket, you should immediately see some output like this on the screen:

Figure 7-5. The OpenBlockS/266 mainboard.

Figure 7-6. The OpenBlockS serial console cable.

```
405GPr 1.2 ROM Monitor (5/25/02) OBS266 1.3

--------------------- System Info ----------------------
Processor            = 405GPr (New mode),   PVR: 50910951
CPU speed            = 266 MHz
PLB speed            = 133 MHz
OPB speed            = 66 MHz
EBC speed            = 66 MHz
PCI Bus speed        = 33 MHz (Async)
VCO speed            = 800 MHz
Feedback Clock       = CPU
Amount of SDRAM      = 64 MBytes
Internal PCI arbiter enabled
---------------------------------------------------------
```

If you don't see any output, check your serial cable connections and software settings. Terminal emulation programs can be finicky and difficult to configure, so try a different program if the current one isn't working out for you.

Figure 7-7. Connecting OpenBlockS to another PC.

Hubs, Bridges, Routers, and Switches

So, what's the difference between a hub, switch, bridge, and router? Hubs, switches, and bridges all operate at layer two of the network stack. That means these devices do not have IP addresses. They forward packets based on Ethernet addresses.

Hubs are "dumb" network devices that copy each packet received on a port to every other port. The simplicity of a hub used to mean that it was the cheapest option for joining network segments.

These days, however, switches are so inexpensive that hubs are becoming extinct. Back in the good old days when hubs were more common, bridges took on the role of today's switches. A bridge usually has two ports, whereas switches have anywhere from four to 48.

A router is a layer three device, which means that it uses IP addresses to make forwarding decisions. Routers are used to connect different IP subnets. Many of the small home/office routers available today also provide network address translation (NAT) and firewall features.

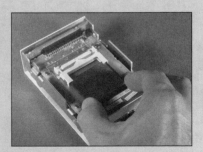

Figure 7-8. Inserting a Compact Flash card into the adapter slot.

When the OpenBlockS boots Linux from the flash memory, it loads the kernel and then creates a RAM disk within its 64 MB of system memory. The RAM disk is mounted as */dev/ram1* and populated with a few low-level system utilities.

After a short amount of time, you'll see a Linux login prompt. The *root* password is *root*. Perhaps the first thing you'll want to do is explore the filesystem—find out what's there and what's missing. Try to execute some of the common Unix commands (ls, ps, top, df). At some point you'll probably find that certain useful programs are missing.

Note that the system is running from a RAM disk. Any changes that you make will be lost when the system reboots. You'll probably want to use the CF card to build a more usable system.

One of the first things you should do is set the system time. Strictly speaking, it is not necessary. However, if the clock is significantly off, you'll see a lot of warnings later when using *tar* to copy files to the new filesystem. Unfortunately, you'll have to use the date command, which has an awkward syntax:

```
# date mmddHHMMYYYY.SS
```

Note the odd ordering. It goes: month, day, hours, minutes, then *year*, followed by seconds. If it's 12:15 on October 26th, 2005 you would run:

```
# date 102612152005.00
```

You should also set the TERM environment variable so that you can use *vi* and other full-screen applications:

```
# export TERM=xterm
# eval `resize`
```

Putting Linux on the Compact Flash Card

The OpenBlockS comes with a 128 MB CF card, which is initially blank. Given that 512 MB CF cards were selling for $30 at the time of this writing, you should consider replacing the 128 MB card with something bigger. With the system powered off, insert the CF card as shown in Figure 7-8. Now we'll show you one way to load it up with SSD/Linux.

The CF card looks just like a normal ATA device (i.e., hard drive) to the operating system. The first thing to do is run *fdisk* and create a Linux partition. If the CF card already was already partitioned, you must delete the existing partitions first:

```
obs# fdisk /dev/hda
 hda: hda1

Command (m for help): d
Selected partition 1
```

With an unpartitioned CF card, use these *fdisk* commands to create the Linux partition:

```
Command (m for help): n
Command action
   e   extended
   p   primary partition (1-4) p
Partition number (1-4): 1
First cylinder (1-978, default 1):
Using default value 1
Last cylinder or +size or +sizeM or +sizeK (1-978, default 978):
Using default value 978

Command (m for help): p

Disk /dev/hda: 128 MB, 128188416 bytes
8 heads, 32 sectors/track, 978 cylinders
Units = cylinders of 256 * 512 = 131072 bytes

   Device Boot    Start      End    Blocks   Id  System
/dev/hda1               1      978    125168   83  Linux

Command (m for help): w
The partition table has been altered!

Calling ioctl() to re-read partition table.
 hda: hda1
 hda: hda1
Syncing disks.
```

After *fdisk*, create a filesystem with *mke2fs*:

```
obs# mke2fs /dev/hda1
mke2fs 1.32 (09- hda:Nov-2002)
 hda1
 hda: hda1
Filesystem label=
OS type: Linux
Block size=1024 (log=0)
Fragment size=1024 (log=0)
31360 inodes, 125168 blocks
6258 blocks (5.00%) reserved for the super user
First data block=1
16 block groups
8192 blocks per group, 8192 fragments per group
1960 inodes per group
Superblock backups stored on blocks:
        8193, 24577, 40961, 57345, 73729

Writing inode tables: done
Writing superblocks and filesystem accounting information: done

This filesystem will be automatically checked every 24 mounts or
180 days, whichever comes first.  Use tune2fs -c or -i to override.
```

Then, mount the new filesystem:

```
obs# mount /dev/hda1 /mnt
```

Using a CF Card Reader

If the NFS server is not an option, you should also be able to use a Compact Flash card reader with an existing Linux box. You should have no trouble finding an inexpensive "All-in-1" reader/writer with a USB interface. Search your favorite shopping site for "flash card reader." Another option is to use a PC Card/PCMCIA adapter, if your laptop has suitable slot.

Once you have the CF card inserted into the reader/adapter, the commands are essentially the same. You'll need to `fdisk` and `mke2fs` the CF card, and then use `rsync` to copy the filesystem over.

Where Am I?

Since you'll be issuing a lot of commands from the shell on both the NFS server and OpenBlockS, things could get confusing. So, we'll use the `nfs#` prompt to show when you should be on the server and `obs#` to show when you should be issuing the commands from a terminal session with the OpenBlockS.

That was pretty easy, but the next step can be hard. Now that you have a blank filesystem, how can you get the GNU/Linux binaries onto it? If you are a Windows user, you can try one of the setup tools on the CD-ROM. Since we are not Windows users and we don't read Japanese, we chose to NFS-export the files from an existing Unix system, mount that directory on the OpenBlockS, and then copy over the necessary files. See the Appendix, "Running an NFS Server" for some hints on setting up an NFS server.

We recommend that you download the most recent SSD/Linux ISO image from the Plat'Home FTP server at **ftp://ftp.plathome.co.jp/pub/ssdlinux/iso/**. If you don't want to download that much, you can instead download specific files from **ftp://ftp.plathome.co.jp/pub/OpenBlockS266/LATEST/**. You'll need at least *installation/zImage.initrd.treeboot*, *installation/ramdisk.image.gz*, and all of the files in the *binary* directory. Alternatively, you can also use the CD-ROM that came with your OpenBlockS kit, but it may be out of date.

For the examples in this chapter, we assume that you have a recent ISO image burned to CD-ROM and mounted on your NFS server. If not, some of the pathnames may be different for you.

First, create a scratch directory on the NFS server that you can export to the OpenBlockS and use as a staging area for extracting and manipulating files. Then, create a directory under which you can mount the OpenBlockS CD-ROM:

```
nfs# mkdir /disk/openblocks
nfs# mkdir /cdrom
nfs# mount -t cd9660 /dev/cd0c /cdrom
nfs# vi /etc/exports
```

The directories that you just made should be exported by the NFS server. Add these lines to your */etc/exports* file on the server:

```
/disk/openblocks        -maproot=root
/cdrom  -alldirs
```

Restart or reconfigure *mountd* after updating */etc/exports*. Test the new configuration by running `showmount -e`.

Connect the OpenBlockS to the NFS server with a crossover cable or through an Ethernet switch. On the OpenBlockS, assign it an IP address (replace 10.0.0.19 with an available address on your network) before you try to mount the NFS filesystem:

```
obs# ifconfig eth0 10.0.0.19 netmask 255.255.255.0
```

If you have a DHCP server on your network, you can use this command to automatically configure the first network interface:

```
obs# dhclient eth0
```

When the OpenBlockS has an IP address, you can mount the two NFS-exported directories. Here we assume the NFS server's IP address is 10.0.0.1, but yours will almost certainly be different:

```
obs# mkdir /nfs
obs# mkdir /cdrom
obs# mount 10.0.0.1:/disk/openblocks /nfs
obs# mount 10.0.0.1:/cdrom /cdrom
```

The CD-ROM files should be accessible as /cdrom:

```
obs# ls -lR /cdrom
total 60
lr-xr-xr-x  1 root wheel      1 May 20 16:27 0.2-STABLE -> .
-r--r--r--  1 root wheel    175 May 20 16:43 AUTHORS
-r--r--r--  1 root wheel  29476 May 20 16:43 ChangeLog
-r--r--r--  1 root wheel   1823 May 20 16:43 LICENCE
-r--r--r--  1 root wheel   2048 May 20 19:56 boot.catalog
dr-xr-xr-x  2 root wheel  18432 May 20 06:41 distfiles
dr-xr-xr-x  4 root wheel   2048 May 20 06:36 i386
dr-xr-xr-x  4 root wheel   2048 May 20 11:37 powerpc-obs200
dr-xr-xr-x  4 root wheel   2048 May 20 16:27 powerpc-obs266
dr-xr-xr-x  2 root wheel   2048 May 20 06:40 source
```

The first step is to install the *zImage.initrd.treeboot* onto the internal flash. The easiest way to do this is with the `flashcfg` command from within SSD/Linux itself. For example:

```
obs# flashcfg -f /cdrom/powerpc-obs266/installation/zImage.initrd.
treeboot
Load boot image to FlashROM
##################################################
##################################################
done
```

There is a similar file named *zImage.initrd.treeboot-product*. It includes utilities that allow you to setup and manage the OpenBlockS from a web browser.

The next step is to extract the contents of the *base*, *etc*, and *kern* packages onto the CF card. The version that came on our CD-ROM, dated 20030708, did fit with only a few MB to spare. The more recent releases, however, are too big. The contents of *base.tgz* won't fit onto the 128 MB CF card.

We noticed that Perl 5.8, with all of its header files and modules, takes about 30 MB. If you need Perl on the system, you should get a larger CF card (256 MB cards are about $20 these days). Otherwise, you'll have to omit the Perl files from the filesystem. Normally we could exclude the *usr/lib/perl5* directory when extracting the files with *tar*. However, it seems that the `--exclude` option is broken on the version of *tar* found on the OpenBlockS boot image. Sigh...

To get around these problems, we extract the files into the scratch directory on the NFS server and then manually remove *usr/lib/perl5* before copying everything over to the CF card. For example, we ran these commands on the NFS server:

```
nfs# mkdir CF-root
nfs# cd CF-root
nfs# tar xzfp /cdrom/powerpc-obs266/binary/base.tgz
nfs# tar xzfp /cdrom/powerpc-obs266/binary/etc.tgz
nfs# tar xzfp /cdrom/powerpc-obs266/binary/kern.tgz
nfs# rm -rf usr/lib/perl5
nfs# du -hs
116M
```

Now that we are below the CF size limit, we're ready to copy these files to the mounted CF partition on the OpenBlocks. Note we use *tar* instead of *cp* because *tar* preserves hard and symbolic links in the filesystem:

```
obs# cd /nfs/CF-root
obs# tar cf - . | (cd /mnt; tar xvfp -)
```

The CF partition doesn't have any */dev* entries yet. Use these commands to create them:

```
obs# cd /mnt/dev
obs# ./MAKEDEV generic
```

You also need to create an */etc/fstab* file so Linux knows to mount the root filesystem from the CF card (*/dev/hda1*). You can just copy the existing */etc/fstab* file and change */dev/ram1* to */dev/hda1*:

```
obs# cp /etc/fstab /mnt/etc/fstab
obs# vi /mnt/etc/fstab
```

It should look like this:

```
/dev/hda1        /                ext2    defaults     1 1
none             /proc            proc    defaults     0 0
```

Next, you need to tell the OpenBlockS to mount the CF card instead of creating a RAM disk. Use `flashcfg` with the `-c` option to set the root device for subsequent reboots. For example:

```
obs# flashcfg -c harddisk
```

At this point you can reboot the system. If you want to double check your work before rebooting, make sure that you've performed all of these steps correctly:

1. Copy *zImage.initrd.treeboot* to the flash memory with *flashcfg*.

2. Copy *CF-root* to */mnt* with *tar*.

3. Create device entries in */mnt/dev* with MAKEDEV.

4. Copy */etc/fstab* to */mnt/etc/fstab*, then change the first line to */dev/hda1*.

5. Tell the system to mount the *harddisk* filesystem with `flashcfg -c`.

When you're ready, reboot!

```
obs# reboot
```

Watch the console as the OpenBlockS reboots. If you screwed up something, you might not get a login prompt after rebooting. For example, the first time we tried this, we forgot about the */dev* entries and the system could not open */dev/console* for the *getty* process. If it happens to you, power-cycle the box. When it boots again, type a key (e.g., the spacebar) when it pauses on the following line:

```
Linux/PPC load: root=/dev/hda1
```

Edit the command line and change hda1 to ram so that it uses the RAM disk instead of the CF card. Then you can mount the CF card on */mnt* and fix whatever needs fixing.

Customizing the Installation

SSD/Linux is a little different than most Linux installations because it uses BSD-style configuration files and startup scripts. One of the first things you should do is edit */etc/rc.conf* and set a few parameters. For example, these three lines set the hostname, specify the IP address for the first Ethernet interface, and start the *ssh* daemon:

```
hostname="obs.example.com"
ifconfig_eth0="10.0.0.19 netmask 255.255.255.0"
sshd=YES
```

Or, if you have a DHCP server on your network, you may want to use this configuration instead:

```
dhclient=YES
dhclient_flags=eth0
```

If you run *df* at this point, you'll see that the CF card is pretty much full. After installing the *base*, *etc*, and *kernel* packages, you'll have only about 5 MB left. That doesn't leave much for adding your own applications and data. Fortunately, you can probably free up enough space by removing unnecessary files and directories. For example, go to the */usr/bin* directory and list the files sorted by their size. For example:

```
obs# cd /usr/bin
obs# ls -l | sort -n +4 | tail
-rwxr-xr-x  1 root kmem     633400 Jan 19  2005 troff
-rwxr-xr-x  1 root kmem     900009 Jan 19  2005 localedef
-rwxr-xr-x  2 root kmem    1021680 Jan 19  2005 perl
-rwxr-xr-x  2 root kmem    1021680 Jan 19  2005 perl5.8.6
-r-xr-xr-x  1 root wheel   1088272 Jan 19  2005 nsupdate
-r-xr-xr-x  1 root wheel   1102948 Jan 19  2005 host
-r-xr-xr-x  1 root wheel   1103800 Jan 19  2005 nslookup
-r-xr-xr-x  1 root wheel   1109972 Jan 19  2005 dig
-rwxr-xr-x  1 root wheel   2291888 Jan 19  2005 run
-rwxr-xr-x  1 root wheel   5037680 Jan 19  2005 gdbtui
# rm perl* nsupdate host nslookup dig gdbtui
```

Turning the OpenBlockS into an Ethernet Bridge

Our goal is to turn the OpenBlockS into a bridging firewall. Unfortunately it takes a little tweaking to make that work. We'll need to recompile the Linux kernel and build some additional tools. We are unlikely to find RPMs for this particular platform, so we'll go to the trouble of compiling them from source.

Compiling a Linux Kernel

Since the CF card doesn't have enough space to hold the compiler and associated files, we created an entire OpenBlockS filesystem on our NFS server. We'll chroot to the NFS-mounted filesystem on the OpenBlockS, do our compiling, and then copy the binaries over to the CF card. First let's build the compiling filesystem and verify that the compiler works. On the NFS server:

```
nfs# mkdir comp-chroot
nfs# cd comp-chroot
nfs# tar xzfp /cdrom/powerpc-obs266/binary/base.tgz
nfs# tar xzfp /cdrom/powerpc-obs266/binary/etc.tgz
nfs# tar xzfp /cdrom/powerpc-obs266/binary/kern.tgz
nfs# tar xzfp /cdrom/powerpc-obs266/binary/comp.tgz
nfs# tar xzfp /cdrom/powerpc-obs266/binary/man.tgz
```

On the OpenBlockS, you should set up a chroot environment on the NFS server, including the /dev directory:

The obs-chroot# prompt indicates the command should be executed on the OpenBlockS under a chroot environment. Whenever we use this convention, it will be right after using a chroot command to get there in the first place.

```
obs# mkdir /nfs
obs# mount 10.0.0.1:/disk/openblocks /nfs
obs# cp /etc/resolv.conf /nfs/comp-chroot/etc/resolv.conf
obs# chroot /nfs/comp-chroot /bin/sh
obs-chroot# mount -t proc none /proc
obs-chroot# cd /dev
obs-chroot# ./MAKEDEV std
```

Now, let's see if we can compile something:

```
obs-chroot# cd /tmp
obs-chroot# gcc /usr/share/automake-1.9/ansi2knr.c
obs-chroot# ls -l a.out
-rwxr-xr-x  1 root wheel 25514 May 19 12:31 a.out
```

Looks like it worked! Now onto something more difficult: the kernel. The following instructions are based on Plat'Home's document for building SSD/Linux from source (**http://openlab.plathome.co.jp/ssdlinux/develop.html.en**). We are going to cheat a little bit and deviate from that document because we want to compile only the kernel, rather than the entire system. The first step is to extract the SSD/Linux source archive in our *comp-chroot* directory. This can be done on the NFS server:

```
nfs# cd /disk/openblocks/comp-chroot
nfs# rm -rf usr/src
nfs# tar xzf /cdrom/source/src.tgz
```

We'll be using some scripts from the SSD/Linux distribution. They look for certain files in a *distfiles* directory. If you have the OpenBlockS CD-ROM, it's probably easiest to just copy these files from the CD-ROM to the correct directory:

```
nfs# mkdir -p usr/src/dist/distfiles
nfs# cp -Rp /cdrom/distfiles usr/src/dist
```

Otherwise, the install process will try to download the distfiles that it needs from **ftp.plathome.co.jp**. So if you don't have the CD-ROM, make sure that your OpenBlockS can reach that server before proceeding.

On the OpenBlockS you need to set some environment variables and then run bmake from the appropriate directory:

```
obs-chroot# export HOSTTYPE
obs-chroot# export MACHTYPE
obs-chroot# export SHELL
obs-chroot# export WITH_X11=no
obs-chroot# cd /usr/src/mkdist/kernel
obs-chroot# bmake
```

The bmake command extracts the kernel source code and applies a number of patches. At this point we have a kernel source tree that we can compile on the OpenBlockS266. But before we do that, we need to apply another kernel patch that allows the netfilter code to work with bridging. The patch file is available from **http://ebtables.sourceforge.net** on the downloads page.

The ebtables project also has a userland program called *ebtables*. It provides functionality similar to *iptables*, but for layer two (Ethernet) packets. We don't need this utility for normal IP packet filtering because the ebtables kernel patch makes bridged packets pass through the kernel's normal iptables tables. If you want to filter packets based on MAC addresses or other layer two characteristics, the *ebtables* utility is easy to compile and install. We won't cover it in this book, however.

At the time of writing, the ebtables project has patches for kernel Version 2.4.21 through 2.4.31. The latest SSD/Linux kernel is Version 2.4.20, so we might have some problems applying this patch. We're going to give it a try anyway. We downloaded *ebtables-brnf-10_vs_2.4.21.diff* from **http://ebtables. sourceforge.net/download.html** and applied the patch on the NFS server:

```
nfs# cd comp-chroot/usr/src/linux
nfs# patch -s -p1 < /tmp/ebtables-brnf-10_vs_2.4.21.diff
```

Whew, the patch applies cleanly! Whatever the differences are between the 2.4.20 and 2.4.21 kernels, they don't affect the same code that this patch does. Looks like there should be no problems compiling the patched kernel. You are now ready to configure the new kernel on the OpenBlockS:

```
obs-chroot# cd /usr/src/linux
obs-chroot# make menuconfig
```

When the configuration menu appears, move the cursor down to "Networking options" and press Enter. Then scroll down to enable both 802.1d Ethernet Bridging and ebtables:

```
<*> 802.1d Ethernet Bridging
<*>    Bridge: ebtables (NEW)
< >      ebt: filter table support
< >      ebt: nat table support
< >      ebt: broute table support
< >      ebt: log support
< >      ebt: IP filter support
< >      ebt: ARP filter support
< >      ebt: among filter support
< >      ebt: limit filter support
< >      ebt: 802.1Q VLAN filter support
< >      ebt: 802.3 filter support
< >      ebt: packet type filter support
< >      ebt: STP filter support
< >      ebt: mark filter support
< >      ebt: arp reply target support
< >      ebt: snat target support
< >      ebt: dnat target support
< >      ebt: redirect target support
< >      ebt: mark target support
```

Since you'll be using *iptables* and not *ebtables*, you don't need any of the sub-options marked with "ebt:". However, if you plan to experiment with *ebtables*, feel free to enable the options that seem interesting.

Finally, exit and save the new configuration and compile the kernel:

```
obs-chroot# make dep clean
obs-chroot# time make
...
real    85m59.389s
user    61m38.320s
sys     15m23.730s
```

After the kernel has been built, the next step is to create the *initrd* image that you'll load onto the OpenBlockS internal flash. The *initrd* file consists of a kernel, plus a compressed filesystem that gets loaded into RAM. Normally the filesystem is built by compiling all the userland programs and copying them to a "loop" filesystem. However, you don't really want to spend the time compiling all the userland programs, so you can cheat by using a pre-built ramdisk image from the OpenBlockS CD-ROM:

```
nfs# cp -p /cdrom/powerpc-obs266/installation/ramdisk.image.gz \
/disk/openblocks/comp-chroot/usr/src/linux/arch/ppc/boot/images
```

Now, on the OpenBlockS, execute a command to build the *zImage.initrd. treeboot* file:

```
obs-chroot# cd /usr/src/linux
obs-chroot# make zImage.initrd
```

When *make* is done, you should find the *initrd* file in the *arch/ppc/boot/ images* directory. You can use *flashcfg* from outside the chroot environment to load the image to the OpenBlockS internal flash memory:

```
obs-chroot# exit
obs# flashcfg -f /nfs/comp-chroot/usr/src/linux/arch/ppc/boot/images/
zImage.initrd.treeboot
```

One final step is to copy the new *System.map* file to the root directory:

```
obs# cp -p /nfs/comp-chroot/usr/src/linux/System.map \
/System.map.20050119
obs# rm /System.map
obs# ln /System.map.20050119 /System.map
obs# reboot
```

The *System.map* file is used by a handful of Linux system utilities, such as *klogd*, *depmod*, and *top*. The file contains a list of program addresses (such as *0x451223a*) and symbol names (such as *use_extra_magic*). In other words, the *System.map* file helps translate numeric program addresses into meaningful source code names, and vice-versa.

After the system boots, you can log in and use the uname command to verify that the new kernel is running:

```
obs# uname -a
Linux obs 2.4.20 #2 Fri Sep 23 13:02:40 JST 2005 ppc ppc405 OpenBlockS
SSD/Linux 0.2-20050119
```

The date should correspond to the time when you compiled the new kernel, and the version number (e.g., 0.2-20050119) should correspond to the files from your CD-ROM or from the **ftp.plathome.co.jp** FTP server.

Installing the Bridge Utilities

Now that your kernel has support for Ethernet bridging, you also need a utility to configure the interfaces for bridging. This software comes from **http:// bridge.sourceforge.net**. You can use the NFS-mounted chroot environment to compile this program as well. Download the latest *bridge-utils* tar file from SourceForge and place it in the chroot filesystem. On the OpenBlockS, mount the NFS filesystem as before, and issue the chroot command:

```
obs# mount 10.0.0.1:/disk/openblocks /nfs
obs# chroot /nfs/comp-chroot /bin/sh
```

Then, extract the software, and run *./configure* and make:

```
obs-chroot# cd /tmp
obs-chroot# tar xzf bridge-utils-1.0.6.tgz
obs-chroot# cd bridge-utils-1.0.6
obs-chroot# ./configure
obs-chroot# make
```

After the bridge utilities have been compiled, install them into */usr/local*:

```
obs-chroot# make install
```

Remember that you are in the chroot environment, and the filesystem is really on the NFS server. Now you need to copy the files that you just installed from the NFS server directory to the OpenBlockS CF card. You can use *rsync* for this simple task:

```
obs-chroot# exit
obs# rsync -av /nfs/comp-chroot/usr/local /usr
```

We'll show you how to use the new *brctl* in just a bit. While you're still in compiling mode, however, we recommend that you also install *tcpdump*.

Installing tcpdump

Installing *tcpdump* is optional, but chances are that you will want to have it while debugging your *iptables* rules.

You'll need both *tcpdump* and *libpcap* packages from **http://www.tcpdump. org**. Save the tar files and extract them on the NFS server—under *comp-chroot/tmp*, for example. Then on the OpenBlockS, compile them like this:

```
obs# chroot /nfs/comp-chroot /bin/sh
obs-chroot# cd /tmp/libpcap-2005.08.25
obs-chroot# ./configure && make && make install

obs-chroot# cd /tmp/tcpdump-3.8.3
obs-chroot# ./configure && make && make install
```

To copy the recently installed files from the chroot directory to the CF card, use the same rsync command as before:

```
obs# rsync -av /nfs/comp-chroot/usr/local /usr
```

Then, try it out and see if it actually works:

```
obs# tcpdump -n -i eth0 -c 10
tcpdump: verbose output suppressed, use -v or -vv for full protocol
decode
listening on eth0, link-type EN10MB (Ethernet), capture size 96 bytes
14:26:13.292815 IP 10.0.0.90.22 > 10.0.0.21.2627: P 3557754178:35577542
90(112) ack 679062017 win 11088 <nop,nop,timestamp 206621 31069398>
14:26:13.292963 IP 10.0.0.21.2627 > 10.0.0.90.22: . ack 112 win 57808
<nop,nop,timestamp 31069404 206616>
14:26:13.293997 IP 10.0.0.90.22 > 10.0.0.21.2627: P 112:224(112) ack 1
win 11088 <nop,nop,timestamp 206621 31069404>
14:26:13.295932 IP 10.0.0.90.22 > 10.0.0.21.2627: P 224:400(176) ack 1
win 11088 <nop,nop,timestamp 206622 31069404>
```

rsync or tar?

rsync is usually better at copying directory structures. However, we had to use two tar commands earlier because rsync is not included on the smaller *initrd* filesystem.

```
14:26:13.296078 IP 10.0.0.21.2627 > 10.0.0.90.22: . ack 400 win 57744
<nop,nop,timestamp 31069405 206621>
14:26:13.297259 IP 10.0.0.90.22 > 10.0.0.21.2627: P 400:544(144) ack 1
win 11088 <nop,nop,timestamp 206622 31069405>
14:26:13.298338 IP 10.0.0.90.22 > 10.0.0.21.2627: P 544:704(160) ack 1
win 11088 <nop,nop,timestamp 206622 31069405>
14:26:13.298478 IP 10.0.0.21.2627 > 10.0.0.90.22: . ack 704 win 57760
<nop,nop,timestamp 31069405 206622>
14:26:13.299675 IP 10.0.0.90.22 > 10.0.0.21.2627: P 704:864(160) ack 1
win 11088 <nop,nop,timestamp 206622 31069405>
14:26:13.300747 IP 10.0.0.90.22 > 10.0.0.21.2627: P 864:1008(144) ack 1
win 11088 <nop,nop,timestamp 206622 31069405>
10 packets captured
28 packets received by filter
0 packets dropped by kernel
```

Configuring the Bridge

In Linux, a bridge is sort of a virtual network interface. You create it with
the brctl command. Then you add real interfaces to the bridge, also with
the brctl command.

Bridging does not work if one of the real Ethernet interfaces already has an
IP address. Thus, you should remove any ifconfig_eth0, ifconfig_eth1, and
dhclient lines from /etc/rc.conf. If your interfaces already have IP addresses
you can zero them out with these commands:

```
obs# ifconfig eth0 inet 0.0.0.0
obs# ifconfig eth1 inet 0.0.0.0
```

To configure a bridge, execute the following commands:

```
obs# brctl addbr br0
obs# brctl addif br0 eth0
obs# brctl addif br0 eth1
obs# ifconfig eth0 up
obs# ifconfig eth1 up
```

Shortly after, you should see some messages like this from *syslog*:

```
device eth0 entered promiscuous mode
device eth1 entered promiscuous mode
br0: port 2(eth1) entering listening state
br0: port 1(eth0) entering listening state
br0: port 2(eth1) entering learning state
br0: port 1(eth0) entering learning state
br0: port 2(eth1) entering forwarding state
br0: topology change detected, propagating
br0: port 1(eth0) entering forwarding state
br0: topology change detected, propagating
```

Only after the bridge interface is up and working can you assign an IP
address to it as well:

```
obs# ifconfig br0 inet 10.0.0.19 netmask 255.255.255.0
```

Or, if you prefer, with DHCP:

```
obs# dhclient br0
```

Once you have it all working, put the same commands into */etc/rc.local* so they get executed each time the OpenBlockS boots:

```
brctl addbr br0
brctl addif br0 eth0
brctl addif br0 eth1
ifconfig eth0 up
ifconfig eth1 up
dhclient br0
```

Assigning an IP address to the OpenBlockS is entirely optional. It will function perfectly well as a bridge without any IP address. The best reason to give it an IP address is so that you can log in to debug problems. You'll need an IP address to use programs such as *ping* and *traceroute* on the OpenBlockS. If you are comfortable using the serial port console, then you don't need to automatically assign the IP address when the system boots—just assign it whenever you need it.

Configuring the Firewall

Linux's netfilter (*iptables*) has too many features to fully cover here. You can find numerous references on using *iptables*, starting with **http://www.netfilter. org/**, or by entering "iptables" into any search engine. For now we'll provide a couple of simple examples to help get you started.

Web and DNS only

One of our favorite ideas for this project is to implement the OpenBlockS as a firewall that you can use to protect an unpatched Microsoft Windows box while downloading patches from the Internet. With so many Windows viruses scanning the Internet these days, many people have a hard time downloading and applying patches before their system becomes infected. We'll configure the bridging firewall to pass only packets necessary for a Windows Update session.

One way to accomplish the task is to allow only packets to and from Microsoft servers. This is, unfortunately, a little difficult because you can't simply configure your system to talk only to **.microsoft.com*. The Windows Update procedure uses numerous servers on different IP addresses and networks. If you take this route, you'll probably need a tool like *tcpdump* to find out where Windows Update is trying to get to. In my tests, Windows Update communicated with three separate servers on three different subnets.

The optimal approach is to restrict communication based on TCP and UDP ports. For Windows Update to work, the system needs to send and receive DNS queries on UDP port 53, HTTP on port 80, and HTTPS on port 443. If you are using DHCP, the firewall should pass UDP ports 67 and 68 as well. Here is a shell script that sets up netfilter for these ports:

```
#!/bin/sh
I="iptables -A FORWARD"

iptables --flush

# allow HTTP and HTTPS
for p in 80 443 ; do
    $I --proto tcp --dport $p -j ACCEPT
    $I --proto tcp --sport $p -j ACCEPT
done

# allow DNS and DHCP
for p in 53 67 68; do
    $I --proto udp --dport $p -j ACCEPT
    $I --proto udp --sport $p -j ACCEPT
done

# allow ICMP for Path MTU Discovery
$I --proto icmp --j ACCEPT

# uncomment the LOG line for debugging
#$I -j LOG

$I -j DROP
```

Note that these rules use the FORWARD table because that is where *iptables* looks for packets that get forwarded through the OpenBlockS. If you are worried about attacks against the OpenBlockS itself, you'll want to block packets to or from the OpenBlockS IP address using the INPUT and/or OUTPUT tables.

You may be able to get by without the rule to accept ICMP packets. In our case, we were connecting through a VPN tunnel that had a lower-than-normal MTU. We had to accept ICMP responses so that path MTU discovery worked correctly.

To utilize these rules each time the OpenBlockS boots, save the script as */etc/rc.iptables* and add this line to */etc/rc.conf*:

```
iptables=YES
```

Connection tracking

Linux *iptables* has a nifty feature called *connection tracking*. This is a kernel option that should be enabled by default. When enabled, the kernel keeps track of established connections for both TCP and UDP. You can then use this information to allow or deny packets based on the state of their associated connection. It is primarily useful for allowing packets associated with connections initiated inside the firewall and denying incoming connections from the outside.

Using connection tracking with bridging is a little bit confusing. Our first attempts didn't quite work the way we expected them to. We eventually worked it out by trial and error. The following script allows outgoing TCP and UDP connections, while blocking unsolicited traffic coming in from the outside:

```
#!/bin/sh
I="iptables -A FORWARD"

iptables --flush

# Note this rule set assumes that the device-to-be-protected
# is connected to ETH1 and the upstream network is
# connected to ETH0.

# Allow TCP connections we initiate
$I -p tcp -m state --state ESTABLISHED -i eth0 -j ACCEPT
$I -p tcp -m state --state NEW,ESTABLISHED -i eth1 -j ACCEPT

# Allow UDP connections we initiate
$I -p udp -m state --state ESTABLISHED -i eth0 -j ACCEPT
$I -p udp -m state --state NEW,ESTABLISHED -i eth1 -j ACCEPT

# allow ICMP for Path MTU Discovery
$I --proto icmp --j ACCEPT

# uncomment the LOG line for debugging
#$I -j LOG

$I -j DROP
```

As noted in the script comments, these rules assume that "inside the firewall" is connected to *eth1*, while *eth0* connects to the Big Bad Internet.

If you like to use FTP, the connection-tracking rules may cause a problem for FTP data connections. Unless you enable "passive" mode, an FTP server may try to establish a connection back to your FTP client. To allow that, add this rule to the script before the final DROP rule:

```
# for incoming FTP data connections
$I -p tcp -m state --state NEW,ESTABLISHED --sport 20 -i eth0 -j ACCEPT
```

If you want to make these rules permanent, save the *iptables* commands to */etc/rc.iptables* and add this line to */etc/rc.conf*:

```
iptables=YES
```

Using the Firewall

Now that the firewall is complete, we will tell you how to actually use it. This firewall is designed so that you can easily protect a host (or network of hosts) by placing the OpenBlockS between the host and its network device (i.e., switch or router). Figure 7-9 shows how this works for a single PC connected to a DSL router.

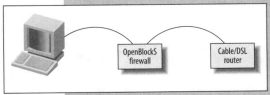

Figure 7-9. Using the OpenBlockS to protect a PC.

When connecting the OpenBlockS to a desktop or laptop computer, you must use an Ethernet crossover cable. They are easy to make if you have the necessary tools. Otherwise, you can purchase one for $10 or less. The easiest way to connect the OpenBlockS is to remove the Ethernet cable from the PC and insert it into one of the OpenBlockS ports. Then use the crossover cable to connect the PC to the other OpenBlockS port.

If you're using the simple firewall configuration ("Web and DNS only") it does not matter which OpenBlockS port goes to the PC. The simple firewall rules do not refer to IP addresses or interface names, so they are symmetrical.

On the other hand, if you're using the connection-tracking firewall features ("Connection tracking"), the firewall is no longer symmetric. You should connect ETHER-1 (*eth1*) to the PC or laptop, and ETHER-0 (*eth0*) to the router.

After connecting the Ethernet cables, power up the OpenBlockS. Your PC won't be able to send or receive any packets until the OpenBlockS is fully up and running, but that should only take a minute or two. When it's done booting you should be able to surf the Web and ping other hosts. You can also try pinging the OpenBlockS itself, if you happen to know its address. If something seems to be wrong you may need to log in on the serial port console.

If the OpenBlockS is up and running but blocking your traffic, you'll need to debug the firewall rules. Log in and run this command:

```
# iptables --list --verbose
Chain INPUT (policy ACCEPT 0 packets, 0 bytes)
 pkts bytes target  prot opt in    out source      destination

Chain FORWARD (policy ACCEPT 62 packets, 5316 bytes)
 pkts bytes target  prot opt in    out source      destination
  304 45893 ACCEPT  tcp  --  any   any anywhere    anywhere    tcp dpt:www
  354  259K ACCEPT  tcp  --  any   any anywhere    anywhere    tcp spt:www
  248 29091 ACCEPT  tcp  --  any   any anywhere    anywhere    tcp dpt:443

  210  102K ACCEPT  tcp  --  any   any anywhere    anywhere    tcp spt:443
    0     0 ACCEPT  tcp  --  any   any anywhere    anywhere    tcp dpt:ssh
    0     0 ACCEPT  tcp  --  any   any anywhere    anywhere    tcp spt:ssh
    7   448 ACCEPT  udp  --  any   any anywhere    anywhere    udp dpt:domain
    7  1648 ACCEPT  udp  --  any   any anywhere    anywhere    udp spt:domain
    0     0 ACCEPT  udp  --  any   any anywhere    anywhere    udp dpt:bootps
    0     0 ACCEPT  udp  --  any   any anywhere    anywhere    udp spt:bootps
    0     0 ACCEPT  udp  --  any   any anywhere    anywhere    udp dpt:bootpc
    0     0 ACCEPT  udp  --  any   any anywhere    anywhere    udp spt:bootpc
  268 22512 ACCEPT  icmp --  any   any anywhere    anywhere
    2   152 DROP    all  --  any   any anywhere    anywhere

Chain OUTPUT (policy ACCEPT 0 packets, 0 bytes)
 pkts bytes target  prot opt in    out source      destination
```

If you see non-zero values in the pkts and bytes columns, it means at least some packets are getting through. If the counters for the DROP rule are high, you may want to enable logging by uncommenting the LOG rule in the sample rules from the previous section and reloading the rules. When you're logged in as *root*, you'll see a message on your screen for each packet that gets dropped. This may help you understand what, if anything, is wrong with your rules. Keep in mind that the firewall should block *some* packets—thats what it's there for!

You may also want run *tcpdump* or *tethereal* (if you have it) to help debug problems. For example, run *tcpdump* on *eth0* to see packets coming from your PC:

```
# tcpdump -n -i eth0
```

Then try surfing the Web or pinging some hosts while *tcpdump* is running. If you don't see any packets at all, then something is probably wrong with the Ethernet cable. Make sure that it is a crossover, and that it is plugged in correctly.

If you get really desperate and just want to remove the firewall rules altogether, run this command:

```
# iptables --flush
```

Powering OpenBlockS via USB

For a few bucks, you can build a cable to power the OpenBlockS from a USB port. This makes the OpenBlockS quite a bit more portable since you won't have to carry around the power supply.

USB ports must provide at least 0.5 amps at 5 volts, which corresponds to 2.5 watts. Our tests indicate the OpenBlockS draws as much as 0.64 amps from a USB port, which means the host system is providing more power than is required by the specification. Chances are that yours will as well, but there is no guarantee. Note that these measurements were taken when using a CF card for storage. We doubt that most USB ports provide enough power for a laptop hard drive.

You'll need to be careful when other USB devices are connected to the host computer. In fact, the 0.5 amp requirement is per-controller, rather than per-port. In other words, the available power is shared between all USB devices connected to a single controller. With too many devices on one controller, you may not have enough power to go around. Also, keep in mind that self-powered USB hubs generally do not provide as much power, so if you decide to use a USB hub, verify that it will supply enough power.

If you think the host computer cannot supply enough power for the OpenBlockS from a single controller, you can use a "double USB cable" to combine the power from two controllers. That should, in theory, double the amount of current available to the OpenBlockS. These double USB cables are often included with external laptop hard drive enclosures, but we don't see them being sold separately. Of course, with a soldering iron and a little creativity you can create your own.

Building the cable is relatively easy and requires a little bit of soldering. Start with a normal USB cable and cut off the end that does not plug into the computer. Strip off the protective coating, and you should find four wires. Hopefully one will be red and another black. These are, most likely, the positive and negative power wires. If you're not sure, grab a multimeter and test the wires with the cable plugged into a USB port, and with the computer powered up. You've found the right pair when the multimeter reads +5.0 volts or so. Figure 7-10 shows the pin assignments for a standard USB type-A male connector.

Expose the bare wires and connect them to a DC power plug just like the one from the OpenBlockS power supply. The one that we purchased has an outer diameter of 4.0 mm and an inner diameter of 1.7 mm. If you don't have a local electronics parts store, search the Web for "DC power plug 1.7mm 4.0mm." We recommend buying at least two in case you botch the first one. Be sure to check the power supply label for the plug polarity.

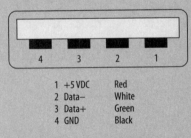

1	+5 VDC	Red
2	Data−	White
3	Data+	Green
4	GND	Black

Figure 7-10. Pinouts for USB Type A male connector.

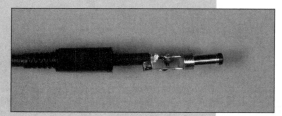

Figure 7-11. USB power cable after soldering the red and black wires to the DC power plug.

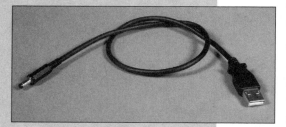

Figure 7-12. Completed USB power cable.

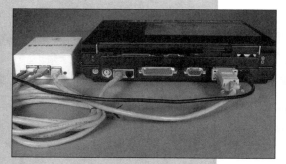

Figure 7-13. Finished project with USB power, Ethernet crossover to laptop, and upstream Internet connection.

Ours has positive on the center of the plug and negative on the outside. Yours should be the same. Figure 7-11 shows the cable just after soldering the wires to the plug. Figure 7-12 shows the completed cable.

USB cables come in different thicknesses. If you find a DC power plug like the one we used, a thick USB cable may not fit through the power plug's sheath. If you can find a thinner USB cable, however, it should fit just fine. The drawback to using a thinner USB cable is that the wires are very thin and weak. You might have a harder time stripping and soldering the thin wires, and the plug is more fragile until you can secure the sheath.

When your USB power cable is ready, try it out. If you have a multimeter, take a moment to test the continuity of your new cable. If you have any doubts about your soldering skills, use the continuity tester to make sure that the red and black wires are not in contact with each other. If it looks good, open a serial connection to the console and plug in the power cable. Since the USB cable carries a nontrivial amount of electric current, be prepared to unplug either end quickly if something doesn't seem right. You should see console output almost immediately, just as you did with the normal power supply. Figure 7-13 shows how the finished unit looks.

Extra Credit

Here are a few additional ideas that you might want to try out on your OpenBlockS, whether or not you use it for a bridging firewall.

Ethereal

Ethereal is a nice alternative to *tcpdump* for snooping on network traffic. It knows about more protocols and, therefore, is able to provide more detailed information. However, it's also a larger package and more difficult to compile. We recommend installing Ethereal only if you have a 256 MB or larger CF card, or a laptop hard drive (see "Using a Laptop Hard Drive," later in this section).

Another feature of Ethereal is its graphical user interface, which uses the GTK toolkit. Since our little box doesn't have any X Windows libraries (or other programs), we can't take advantage of the GUI. Fortunately, the *./configure* script is smart enough to detect the missing libraries and compile only the text-based version.

If you are using a CF card, you'll want to extract the source code on the NFS server, then switch to the OpenBlockS, mount the NFS share, and compile the source. The shell prompts in the following examples indicate where each command should be executed from. If you have a laptop hard drive, you can extract there and skip the NFS and chroot steps. Our instructions assume you're using NFS, just in case.

Ethereal depends on the *glib* library, which in turn requires something called *pkg-config*. You can get it from **pkgconfig.freedesktop.org**:

```
nfs# cd /disk/openblocks/comp-chroot/tmp
nfs# wget http://pkgconfig.freedesktop.org/releases/pkg-config-0.19.tar.gz
nfs# tar xzvf pkg-config-0.19.tar.gz

obs# chroot /nfs/comp-chroot /bin/sh
obs-chroot# cd /tmp/pkg-config-0.19
obs-chroot# ./configure && make && make install
```

Next, install *glib*, which is distributed with GTK. You can find it on the GTK FTP server at **ftp://ftp.gtk.org/pub/gtk/**. We recommend using the latest stable *glib* version, which at this time is 2.4.8:

```
nfs# tar xzf glib-2.4.8.tar.gz
```

Then, on the OpenBlockS:

```
obs-chroot# cd /tmp/glib-2.4.8
obs-chroot# ./configure && make && make install
```

If you haven't already installed *libpcap*, as described in "Installing tcpdump," earlier in this chapter, you'll need to do that before compiling Ethereal. You'll also need to make the operating system aware of the recently installed libraries before compiling Ethereal. Otherwise, you may get some linking errors during the next step. To make Linux rescan the shared library directories, simply execute the ldconfig command:

```
obs-chroot# ldconfig
```

Now you can compile Ethereal. Download it from **http://www.ethereal.com** if you haven't already done so. After extracting the source code on the NFS server, use these commands to compile it on the OpenBlockS:

```
obs-chroot# cd /tmp/ethereal-0.10.12
obs-chroot# ./configure && make
```

Note that the *configure* script should realize that you don't have any X-Windows libraries installed, or the GTK+ library in particular. It should still configure and compile the text-only version of Ethereal, named *tethereal*. As you'll see, compilation proceeds slowly. You'll also probably see that it fails at a particular point when the linker (*ld*) runs out of memory:

```
collect2: ld terminated with signal 15 [Terminated]
```

We tried various linker options, such as --no-keep-memory, but they didn't help. In the end, the only thing that allowed us to get past this step was to create a swapfile for Linux. We found that a 30 MB swapfile was sufficient. If you don't have 30 MB free on your filesystem, you probably shouldn't try to compile Ethereal anyway, since it takes around 66 MB when installed.

Note that swapping to a CF card is a pretty bad idea in general, because flash memory has a limited number of read/write cycles it can support. You should probably only do so in an emergency, such as this one. Here are the commands for creating a swapfile:

```
obs# dd if=/dev/zero of=/swapfile bs=1M count=30
obs# mkswap /swapfile
obs# swapon /swapfile
```

With that, compilation proceeds without running out of memory, and we can finally install Ethereal:

```
obs-chroot# make && make install
```

Again, use *rsync* to copy the recently installed files from the *comp-chroot* directories to the CF card:

```
obs-chroot# exit
obs# rsync -av /nfs/comp-chroot/usr/local /usr
```

Don't forget to remove the swapfile when you're done compiling:

```
obs[164]# swapoff /swapfile
obs[165]# rm /swapfile
```

Then, run *tethereal* and see how it works and looks:

```
obs# /usr/local/bin/tethereal
device br0 entered promiscuous mode
Capturing on br0
  0.000000  10.0.0.21 -> 10.0.0.3    SSH Encrypted response packet
len=48
  0.010029  10.0.0.21 -> 10.0.0.3    SSH Encrypted response packet
len=48
  0.010771   10.0.0.3 -> 10.0.0.21  TCP 4272 > ssh [ACK] Seq=0 Ack=96
Win=58352 Len=0
  0.019840  10.0.0.21 -> 10.0.0.3    SSH Encrypted response packet
len=48
  0.029939  10.0.0.21 -> 10.0.0.3    SSH Encrypted response packet
len=48
  0.030656   10.0.0.3 -> 10.0.0.21  TCP 4272 > ssh [ACK] Seq=0 Ack=192
Win=58352 Len=0
  0.050106  10.0.0.21 -> 10.0.0.3    SSH Encrypted response packet
len=48
  0.059844  10.0.0.21 -> 10.0.0.3    SSH Encrypted response packet
len=48
  0.060582   10.0.0.3 -> 10.0.0.21  TCP 4272 > ssh [ACK] Seq=0 Ack=288
Win=58352 Len=0
  0.070932  10.0.0.21 -> 10.0.0.3    SSH Encrypted response packet
len=64
  0.079849  10.0.0.21 -> 10.0.0.3    SSH Encrypted response packet
len=48
  0.080585   10.0.0.3 -> 10.0.0.21  TCP 4272 > ssh [ACK] Seq=0 Ack=400
Win=58352 Len=0
```

Updating the Internal Flash

You already know how to update the internal flash with the *flashcfg* utility. The OpenBlockS BIOS also has a special mode where it attempts to update the flash image using DHCP and TFTP. This may be particularly useful if the internal flash memory somehow becomes corrupted, or *flashcfg* doesn't work. To enable this mode you need to crack open the case and change a DIP-switch setting. Of course, the system should be powered off while doing that. Remove the four side screws first and then remove the top cover. Next, remove the four screws that keep the CF card adapter in place. Slide the adapter out of its snug-fitting 44-pin IDE connector. With the adapter out of the way, you can see the small DIP switch with two switches located near the coin-sized battery. Set switch #2 to ON, as shown in Figure 7-14.

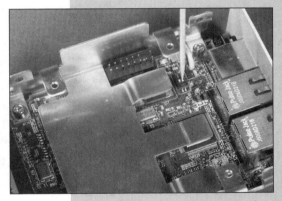

Figure 7-14. Setting DIP switch #2 to ON inside the OpenBlockS.

With switch #2 set, the OpenBlockS will make DHCP requests on ETHER-0 before loading the flash image. If the DHCP requests fail, it will proceed to load the flash image anyway. Since DHCP and/or TFTP might not work correctly the first time, you may need to repeatedly power-cycle the OpenBlockS by disconnecting the power.

The first step is to configure a DHCP server on a working Unix system. We used the one developed by ISC and put this in */etc/dhcpd.conf*:

```
subnet 10.0.0.0 netmask 255.255.255.0 {
  range dynamic-bootp 10.0.0.11 10.0.0.20;
  option broadcast-address 10.0.0.255;
  filename "zImage.initrd.treeboot";
}
```

Note that *zImage.initrd.treeboot* is the name of the file that OpenBlockS will download (via TFTP) and store onto the internal flash memory. The directory where that file exists is specified on the *tfptd* command line, which is normally started by *inetd*. For example, here is the line for *tfptd* in our */etc/inetd.conf*:

```
tftp dgram udp wait root /usr/libexec/tftpd tftpd -s /tftpboot
```

Thus, you should either copy *zImage.initrd.treeboot* to */tftpboot* or change the TFTP directory in */etc/inetd.conf*.

With *dhcpd* running and *tftpd* enabled in */etc/inetd.conf*, you're ready to boot the OpenBlockS and watch what happens. You should see it get an IP address and issue a TFTP request for the given file. Chances are, however, that it won't work the first time. If your OpenBlockS is like ours, it doesn't answer ARP requests in this mode. We had to manually add an ARP entry on the other system before it worked. We found the IP and Ethernet addresses by running dhcpd with the -d option:

```
nfs# dhcpd -d
...
DHCPOFFER on 10.0.0.18 to 00:80:6d:51:02:cd via fxp0
DHCPDISCOVER from 00:80:6d:51:02:cd via fxp0
```

Then, we manually added the necessary ARP table entry:

```
nfs# arp -s 10.0.0.18 00:80:6d:51:02:cd
```

Other problems that you may encounter include seeing errors like "permission denied" or "file not found." In these cases, double-check your directory names, file names, and permissions on both. Also check your firewall rules (if any) and run *tcpdump* or *ethereal* if necessary.

If everything goes well, you'll see something like this on the OpenBlockS console:

```
 -- FLASH BOOT Update --
Sending bootp request ...
Loading file "blah.img" ...
Sending tftp boot request ...
Transfer Complete ...
Loaded successfully ...
FLASH UPDATE Success
```

Note that it may take a little time between before the last line appears—be patient.

After the flash has been updated, power down, change DIP switch #2 back to OFF and reboot. Make sure that it correctly loads the new image before you replace everything and close up the case.

Using a Laptop Hard Drive

Another neat thing about the OpenBlockS is that it can use a laptop hard drive, like the one in Figure 7-15, instead of the Compact Flash card. You might want to install a hard drive if you have one lying around, or if you need a lot more disk space for some reason. Note that the hard drive consumes much more power than the CF card. You should not use the USB power cable in conjunction with the hard drive. Use the normal power supply instead.

Figure 7-15. A laptop (2.5-inch) hard drive.

Installing the hard drive is a simple procedure. Begin by halting the system and disconnecting the power. Remove the top of the OpenBlockS case, then remove the four screws that secure the green CF adapter board to the aluminum frame. Gently disconnect the adapter board from the 44-pin connector and remove it.

Your OpenBlockS kit should include a small, flexible grey square that appears to be some kind of plastic material, as shown in Figure 7-16. The diagrams on the Japanese documentation show that the square should be placed underneath the hard drive. We can only assume it's some kind of insulator or perhaps helps dissipate heat from the hard drive to the case. The grey square just sits loosely on top of the aluminum frame. It may move around a little bit, but won't go anywhere once the drive is installed on top of it.

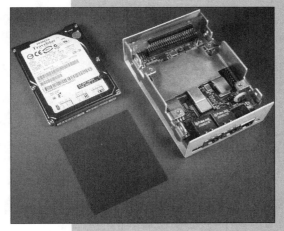

Figure 7-16. Preparing to insert a hard drive in the OpenBlockS.

Install the hard drive, as shown in Figure 7-17, by setting it in place and then sliding it forward into the 44-pin connector. You may need to apply pressure to the connector so it doesn't get pushed too far forward. Once the drive is in place, you can secure it to the aluminum frame with the four screws from the CF adapter board. Note that the screws go into the side of the hard drive, rather than the bottom.

After installing the hard drive, you can use it exactly as you used the CF card, except now you have much more disk space! You'll need to partition the drive with *fdisk* and initialize the filesystem with *mke2fs*. We highly recommend that you create at least two partitions on the hard drive: one for swapping and one or more for filesystems.

Figure 7-17. Inserting the laptop hard drive.

Trying NetBSD

With a little effort you can get NetBSD, the world's most portable operating system, to run on the OpenBlockS. The hardest part is finding a binary release that you can download and install. After a little searching, we found one at **http://tokuda.ddo.jp/NetBSD/**. The good stuff was in a subdirectory named *20050924/evbppc/binary/sets*. We downloaded the following files:

```
-rw-r--r--   1 wessels   wessels   23670263 Sep 25 22:26 base.tgz
-rw-r--r--   1 wessels   wessels     168699 Sep 25 22:26 etc.tgz
-rw-r--r--   1 wessels   wessels    3076057 Sep 25 22:25 kern-
OPENBLOCKS266.tgz
-rw-r--r--   1 wessels   wessels    8347733 Sep 25 22:27 man.tgz
```

The first step is to put the NetBSD kernel onto the OpenBlockS flash. The *kern-OPENBLOCKS266.tgz* archive contains two files: *netbsd* and *netbsd.img*. The *.img* version should be written to the internal flash memory. If the OpenBlockS is already running SSD/Linux, you can use the *flashcfg* utility. Otherwise, use the procedure described in "Updating the Internal Flash," earlier in this section. If you try to boot NetBSD right after flashing, you'll see that it sort of works, but it stops and prompts you for a root device. At this point we suggest that you set up an NFS and DHCP server. Here is a sample configuration for the ISC DHCP server:

```
host openblocks {
    hardware ethernet 00:0a:85:01:95:62;
    fixed-address 10.0.0.28;
    next-server 10.0.0.21;
    option host-name "obs";
    option routers 10.0.0.3;
    option root-path "/disk/netbsd/ROOT";
}
```

Note that the *next-server* option specifies the NFS server's IP address. You can probably omit it if the DHCP server and NFS server are the same system.

Next, create the */disk/netbsd/ROOT* directory on the NFS server and fill it up with the *base*, *etc*, and *man* sets that you downloaded:

```
nfs# mkdir /disk/netbsd/ROOT
nfs# cd /disk/netbsd/ROOT
nfs# tar xzfp /tmp/base.tgz
nfs# tar xzfp /tmp/etc.tgz
nfs# tar xzfp /tmp/man.tgz
```

When the NFS and DHCP servers are ready, boot the NetBSD kernel and enter the following values when prompted:

```
root device: emac0
dump device: (Hit Enter)
file system (default generic): nfs
root on emac0
nfs_boot: trying DHCP/BOOTP
nfs_boot: DHCP next-server: 10.0.0.21
nfs_boot: my_name=obs
```

Another option is to populate the CF card from an existing NetBSD system, if you have one. This works best if the existing system has the same architecture (PowerPC), but you may be able to make it work from a different system and some creativity with a cross-compiler.

```
nfs_boot: my_addr=10.0.0.28
nfs_boot: my_mask=255.255.255.0
nfs_boot: gateway=10.0.0.3
root on 10.0.0.21:/disk2/netbsd/ROOT
root time: 0x434d7a15
inittodr: Clock has lost 13068 day(s) - CHECK AND RESET THE DATE.
warning: no /dev/console
init path (default /sbin/init): (Hit Enter)
init: copying out path `/sbin/init' 11
init: Creating mfs /dev (408 blocks, 1024 inodes)
```

NetBSD has a neat trick: if *dev/console* does not exist, it creates a memory filesystem for *dev* and runs MAKEDEV all there. This, unfortunately, failed on our OpenBlockS because the *dev* filesystem ran out of inodes:

```
uid 0, pid 1902, command mknod, on /dev: out of inodes
mknod: cgd0o: No space left on device
[...repeats...]
```

You may see a lot of these error messages, but they stop eventually. Then you'll be prompted to enter single-user mode:

```
Enter pathname of shell or RETURN for /bin/sh: (Hit Enter)
Terminal type? [unknown] xterm
```

Use the following commands to put a NetBSD filesystem on the Compact Flash card:

```
obs# fdisk -f /dev/wd0
wd0: no disk label

Disk: /dev/wd0c
NetBSD disklabel disk geometry:
cylinders: 980, heads: 8, sectors/track: 32 (256 sectors/cylinder)
total sectors: 250880

BIOS disk geometry:
cylinders: 980, heads: 8, sectors/track: 32 (256 sectors/cylinder)
total sectors: 250880

Partition table:
0: FreeBSD or 386BSD or old NetBSD (sysid 165)
    start 32, size 250848 (122 MB, Cyls 0-980), Active
1: <UNUSED>
2: <UNUSED>
3: <UNUSED>

obs# disklabel -e -I wd0
obs# disklabel -r wd0
# wd0c:
type: ESDI
disk: SanDisk SDCFB-12
...

3 partitions:
#        size    offset     fstype [fsize bsize cpg/sgs]
  a:   250880         0     4.2BSD     0     0     0
  c:   250880         0     unused     0     0

obs# newfs /dev/rwd0a
```

Next, mount the NFS directory (again) and extract the *base* and *etc* sets onto the CF card:

```
obs# mkdir/nfs
obs# mount 10.0.0.21:/disk2/netbsd /nfs

obs# mount /dev /wd0a /mnt
obs# cd /mnt
obs# tar xzfp /nfs /base.tgz
obs# tar xzfp /nfs /etc.tgz
obs# umount /nfs
```

You'll need to make */dev* entries on the CF card:

```
obs# cd /mnt/dev
obs# sh MAKEDEV std wd0 bpf
```

Note that we didn't make all devices to preserve disk space and inodes on the CF card. You may need to go back and create more devices later.

You also need to create the */etc/fstab* file:

```
obs# cat > /mnt/etc/fstab
/dev/wd0a/ffsrw 0 1
procfs/proc    procfs   rw      0 0
^D
obs# mkdir /mnt/proc
```

Finally, set a root password so that you can log in after the system boots from the CF card:

```
obs# chroot /mnt /bin/sh
obs-chroot# passwd root
New Password:
Retype New Password:
obs-chroot# exit
```

Now you should be able to reboot the system:

```
obs# reboot
```

This time, when the kernel prompts you, give these answers instead:

```
root device: wd0
dump device (default wd0b): none
file system (default generic): (Hit Enter)
root on wd0a
mountroot: trying lfs...
mountroot: trying ffs...
root file system type: ffs
init path (default /sbin/init): (Hit Enter)
```

At some point you'll see this message:

```
/etc/rc.conf is not configured.  Multiuser boot aborted.
Enter pathname of shell or RETURN for /bin/sh:
```

Enter single-user mode, make the disk writable, and edit /etc/rc.conf. Change the rc_configured setting to YES:

```
obs# mount -o rw /
obs# vi /etc/rc.conf

rc_configured=YES
```

Now you can either type exit to continue to multi-user mode, or reboot to reboot again. After rebooting, you should be able to log in as *root* and play around with NetBSD!

Note that NetBSD does not have a *flashcfg* utility. If you want to switch back to SSD/Linux, you'll need to use the flash-updating procedure described in "Updating the Internal Flash," earlier in this section.

Cheap Wi-Fi SSH Client 8

Time

a weekend

Difficulty

moderate

What You Need

- ZipIt Wireless Messenger
- PC running Windows, Linux, or BSD

In this project, we have a little fun with the ZipIt Wireless Messenger from Aeronix. This $99 handheld device is sold as a way for kids to send instant messages without tying up the family PC. The ZipIt runs Linux and a custom instant messenger application. We'll show you how to load another Linux distribution so you can run the standard Unix utilities, including SSH. We'll also show you how to cross-compile and load your own programs onto the ZipIt.

As we went to press, the manufacturers of the ZipIT released a software upgrade (version 2.xx) that makes it impossible to use the software update procedure described in this chapter. If you buy a ZipIt and it happens to have the old software (version 1.xx), you have only one chance to load Linux as described here. Once the ZipIt's software is updated to version 2.xx, the only way to load Linux is by attempting the "3 wire mod" described at http://aibohack.com/zipit/serial.htm.

Introducing the ZipIt Wireless Messenger

The Zipit Wireless Messenger is a small handheld computer with a keyboard and LCD screen and built-in Wi-Fi. It is sold by K-Byte (a.k.a. Aeronix) as a device that kids can use to "instant message" their friends without tying up the family computer. It's about the same size as a men's wallet (see Figure 8-1), and looks a lot like the Nintendo Game Boy Advance SP.

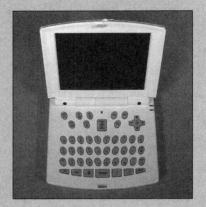

Figure 8-2. The ZipIt opened up for use.

Figure 8-3. A closeup view of the keyboard.

Figure 8-4. The ZipIt Wireless Messenger with its charger.

Figure 8-5. The ZipIt's controls and connectors.

The ZipIt supports the instant messenger protocols from AOL, Yahoo!, and MSN. Future software updates will allow the ZipIt to play streaming audio through the small speaker or headphone jack. It comes in a number of different colors. We bought a white one, shown in Figure 8-2. The ZipIt homepage is **http://zipitwireless.com**.

Inside, the ZipIt uses an ARM-based processor made by Cirrus Logic. It has 16 MB SDRAM and the software (or firmware) is stored on 2 MB of flash memory. The Wi-Fi chip is made be Agere Systems, and the sound processor by Wolfson Micro.

The keyboard, shown in Figure 8-3, is comparable in size to a BlackBerry. You won't be able to use many fingers at once, which means typing will be a little slow. Depending on how you hold the ZipIt, you may find it easier to just type with your thumbs. The keyboard has Alt, Shift, Control, and even Arrow keys. It does not have a separate row for digits 0–9. For those you must use the Alt key, which can be frustrating. Another annoyance is that the Enter and Backspace keys are not quite where you would usually expect to find them.

The LCD screen is 320 pixels wide and 240 pixels high, which is also known as Quarter VGA or QVGA. Each pixel has 4 bits, or 16 shades of grey. This is a relatively common screen size for PDAs and mobile phones. As we'll see later, the text-mode font uses 8x8 pixel characters, which results in a 40x30 character screen. Unfortunately, there is no backlighting for the LCD. You cannot really use the ZipIt in low light.

The ZipIt uses an internal rechargeable battery and comes with a small A/C adapter, shown in Figure 8-4. The battery seems to provide three or more hours of operating time, comparable to some laptops. The ZipIt Instant Messenger application puts the device to sleep if the lid is closed, which makes the battery last even longer.

We mentioned that the ZipIt has a sound processor. A small speaker is located on the bottom. It also has a headphone jack on the back side, as shown in Figure 8-5. In that same figure you can also see the on/off switch, two status lights, and the power adapter jack.

Zipit's Wireless Messenger application runs on Linux, although most people would never know it. Aeronix documents their use of Linux at **http://www. zipitwireless.com/linux.html**. Thanks to this and the work of a few smart folks, you can load your own Linux software images onto the ZipIt.

Updating the ZipIt Firmware

We'll be talking about two different firmware images. The first, called BURN3, is not much different than the original firmware from Aeronix. One important difference, however, is that you get a Linux login prompt instead of the ZipIt messenger application. Since the BURN3 firmware still includes the (large) messenger application, the flash memory does not have room for many other Linux utilities. However, it does include a program that makes it easier to update the flash memory, which you can use to load the second firmware image.

The other firmware image is called OpenZipIt. By removing the ZipIt messenger application, OpenZipIt makes room for more Linux utilities. You'll find an SSH client and server, an IRC client, a number of MP3 utilities, as well as most of the BusyBox programs. BusyBox is discussed elsewhere in Chapters 6 and 9.

We found the instructions for updating the firmware at **http://aibohack.com/ zipit/reflash.htm** and **http://www.elinux.org/wiki/ZipItWiFiFlash**. You may want to check those sites for additional or updated information.

How It Works

One feature of the ZipIt instant messenger application is that it checks for software updates each time it runs. We can exploit this feature to load a new firmware image. Here's an overview of the ZipIt's software update procedure:

1. It issues a DNS request for **www.zipitwireless.net**.

2. It sends an HTTP request to **www.zipitwireless.net**. The requested URL includes a hexadecimal number that identifies your ZipIt. The response contains three lines: the version number of the latest firmware, a URL corresponding to the current firmware image, and a checksum.

3. If the version number is newer, the ZipIt makes an HTTP request for the new firmware.

4. If the firmware download is successful and matches the checksum, it is written to the flash memory. Following that the ZipIt reboots itself.

The key to loading nonstandard firmware onto the ZipIt is intercepting the DNS query. Then you can force the ZipIt to send the HTTP request to your own server. In the next two sections we provide step-by-step instructions for loading new firmware. One method uses a program called *zrs* written by "AiboPet," which runs under Microsoft Windows. The other uses BIND and Apache on a Unix box. Select the one that you are more comfortable with.

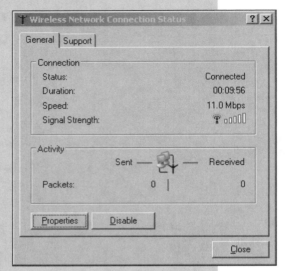

Figure 8-6. The Wireless Network Connection Status dialog box.

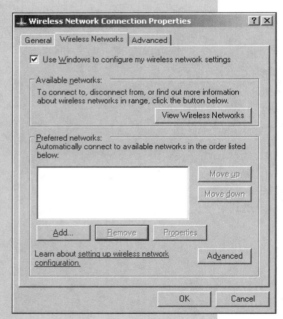

Figure 8-7. The Wireless Networks tab of the Wireless Network Connection Properties dialog box.

You should always be cautious when updating the firmware on devices such as the ZipIt. If something goes wrong during the middle of the procedure, the ZipIt may be left in a nonfunctioning state. The device is most vulnerable when it is actually writing the new data to flash memory. If this operation does not complete (due to loss of power, for example), it won't be able to boot up properly. If this happens to your Zip It, you may be able to rescue it with a complicated procedure known as the "3 Wire mod." It involves soldering tiny wires onto the ZipIt's circuit board, adding an RS-232 level shifter (see "Building a Console Cable" in Chapter 6), and uploading a new kernel over a serial port. See **http://aibohack.com/zipit/serial.htm**, and good luck!

ZRS on Windows

In order to use this approach you need a Windows box with a wireless network interface. If you don't have a Wi-Fi interface for the computer, you can use an access point connected directly to the computer's Ethernet interface instead. In other words, connect the access point's WAN port to the PC, instead of to your cable/DSL modem. Just make sure that the access point does not answer DHCP and/or DNS requests itself.

The most important step in this procedure is to make the ZipIt use the Windows box as its DNS server. The ZipIt should find a wireless network, but not get an IP address from DHCP. Then you'll see a dialog box where you can manually enter the ZipIt's IP address and DNS server. This procedure works best when there are no other Wi-Fi networks nearby. Otherwise, the ZipIt may get an address from one of them and you won't be able to manually set the IP addresses.

Here's the step-by-step process for updating the firmware with Windows:

1. Download **http://aibohack.com/zipit/zipit_reflash_ kit03.zip** and save it to the *TEMP* directory on your computer. Extract the *.zip* file so that new files are created in a subdirectory named *TEMP\ZIPIT_REFLASH_KIT03*.

2. Stop the DHCP and DNS services if they are running. Go to Control Panel→Administrative Tools→Services. If you see DHCP Server and DNS Server in the list of services, check their status. If the status is Started, right click on the line and select the Stop option.

3. Go to Control Panel→Network Connections→Wireless Network Connection, as shown in Figure 8-6. Click on Properties and then click on the Wireless Network tab to see a window like the one in Figure 8-7. Remove any existing networks from the Preferred Networks list. Select Add... and create a new network named "zipnet," as shown in Figure 8-8. Set Network Authentication to Open, set "Data encryption" to Disabled, and select the ad hoc checkbox at the bottom of the window. Click on OK when you are finished.

4. Returning to the Wireless Network Connection Properties dialog box, select the General tab, shown in Figure 8-9. Highlight the Internet Protocol (TCP/IP) line; then click on Properties, and you should see a window like the one shown in Figure 8-10. Select the "Use the following IP address" option and enter the IP address (10.0.4.1) and subnet mask (255.255.255.0); then click on OK.

5. Turn on the ZipIt. It should find your "zipnet" network, but fail to get an IP address. It brings up a dialog box where you can enter the ZipIt's address and DNS server. Enter 10.0.4.2 for the ZipIt's address, 255.255.255.0 for the netmask, and 10.0.4.1 for the DNS server and gateway. Do *not* press Next yet!

6. On the Windows box, open a shell and go to the *TEMP*\ *ZIPIT_REFLASH_KIT03* directory where you unpacked *zipit_reflash_kit03.zip*. Run the following command, the output of which is shown in Figure 8-11:

   ```
   zrs burn3 10.0.4.1
   ```

7. Now press Next on the ZipIt. It should report that a software update is available and ask you for confirmation. Press Next again, and watch the ZipIt download, verify, and install the new firmware. When the update is complete, the ZipIt will reboot itself.

8. Kill the *zrs* program on the Windows box by typing Ctrl-C. You may now take down the "zipnet" network and restore the wireless network adapter to its previous settings.

BIND and Apache

In order to use this approach, you need a wireless network with a BIND nameserver that you control, *unzip* for Unix, and an HTTP server such as Apache. As with the Windows-based procedure, the most

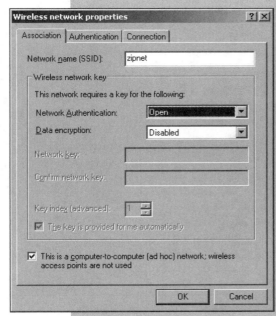

Figure 8-8. The Association tab of the Wireless Network Properties dialog box.

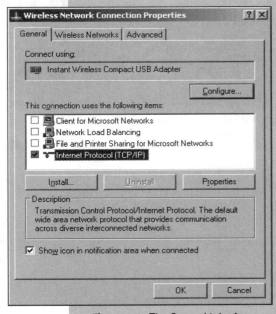

Figure 8-9. The General tab of the Wireless Network Connection Properties dialog box.

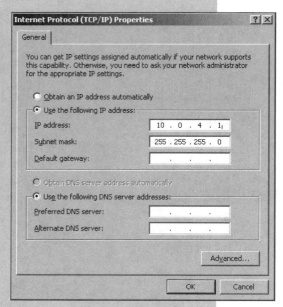

Figure 8-10. Assigning an IP address to your wireless network adapter

Figure 8-11. Running the ZRS command

important step is getting the ZipIt to send its DNS queries to your server. Here are the step-by-step instructions:

1. On the DNS server, edit BIND's *named.conf* file, which is often found in the */etc/namedb* directory, and add the following lines:

```
zone "zipitwireless.net" {
 type master;
 file "/tmp/zipitwireless.net";
};
```

2. Create the */tmp/zipitwireless.net* zone file and add these lines:

```
$TTL 86400
$ORIGIN zipitwireless.net.
@       IN      SOA     your.host.name  dns.your.host.name (
                        1 3600 900 608400 86400 )
        IN      NS      your.host.name.
www     IN      A       192.168.0.1
```

Replace *your.host.name* and *192.168.0.1* with the name and address of your server.

3. Restart your nameserver and test the new configuration:

```
# kill -HUP `cat /var/run/named.pid`
# dig @127.0.0.1 www.zipitwireless.net
...
;; ANSWER SECTION:
www.zipitwireless.net.  1D IN CNAME     zipitwireless.net.
zipitwireless.net.      1D IN A         192.168.0.1
```

4. On your HTTP server, make a user named *zippy*, and create its home directory and a *public_html* directory:

```
httpd# adduser zippy
httpd# mkdir ~zippy
httpd# mkdir ~zippy/public_html
```

5. The ZipIt will first make an HTTP request for */~zippy/NNNNN.txt*. Since we don't really know what *NNNN* will be, we use an Apache trick to map all such files to a known filename. Add this line to *httpd.conf*:

```
AliasMatch ^/~zippy/.*\.txt /home/zippy/public_html/current.txt
```

Don't forget to restart Apache after changing the configuration file. For example:

```
httpd# /etc/init.d/apache2.sh restart
```

6. Download **http://aibohack.com/zipit/zipit_reflash_kit03.zip** and save it to your */tmp* directory.

7. We need two files from the *zipit_reflash_kit03.zip* archive. One is *burn3.txt*, and the other is *burn3.bin*. Copy these to zippy's *public_html* directory:

```
httpd# cp /tmp/burn3.txt /tmp/burn3.bin .
httpd# cat burn3.txt
1.99
http://wherever/burn3.bin
E9FD47F7CE97390B2447DFE096F86479
```

Edit *burn3.txt* and change the URL line to this:

```
http://www.zipitwireless.net/~zippy/burn3.bin
```

8. Make *current.txt* a symbolic link to *burn3.txt*:

```
# ln -s burn3.txt current.txt
```

9. Test the whole setup by requesting the following URL, either with a command line client such as *wget*, or with your favorite web browser:

```
# wget http://www.zipitwireless.net/~zippy/XXXXXX.txt
```

You should see:

```
1.99
http://www.zipitwireless.net/~zippy/burn3.bin
E9FD47F7CE97390B2447DFE096F86479
```

10. You may want to run some debugging commands before starting the update procedure. You can use *tcpdump* on the DNS server like this:

```
# tcpdump -n -s 1500 -v port domain
```

We also recommend that you watch the Apache access log with a command like this:

```
httpd# tail -f /var/log/apache2/access_log
```

11. Turn on the ZipIt. Watch the screen to make sure that it selects your Wi-Fi network (instead of your neighbor's). Within a short time, you should see a screen that says "An update for the the ZipIt(tm) Wireless Messenger is available." Press Next again and watch the ZipIt download, verify, and install the new firmware. When the update is complete, the ZipIt will reboot itself.

12. Do not forget to remove the **zipitwireless.net** zone from your *named. conf* file. If you do not, you'll be very confused later on if you try to download something from the real site but keep getting error messages coming from your own server.

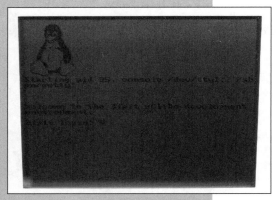

Figure 8-12. The Linux login prompt.

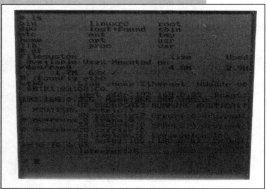

Figure 8-13. Running ifconfig.

Playing with the BURN3 Firmware

When you turn on the ZipIt after loading the BURN3 firmware, you should see Tux the penguin peeking over the top of the ZipIt logo and a message that says "Hacked by ZipItPet." After a short time, you should also see a login prompt, as shown in Figure 8-12. Type **root** and press Enter. There is no password, so you should get a shell prompt right away.

Try out a few Unix commands, such as *ls*, *ps*, *df*, and *df*. Thanks to BusyBox, you should find a lot of standard Unix utilities on the ZipIt. However, a person can have only so much fun running programs like *pwd*, *mv*, and *echo*.

One of the first things you'll notice is that the screen is only 40 characters wide. This means you'll get a messy display from programs, such as *ifconfig*, that assume the screen is at least 80 characters wide. See Figure 8-13 for an example. Another annoyance is the penguin logo stays at the top of the screen, which makes the effective display area smaller than necessary. If you press Alt-P2, you'll get a login prompt on the second virtual console, which does not have the logo. Alt-P1 takes you back to the first.

Using the keyboard is relatively straightforward, although frustrating at times. Entering IP addresses is a pain since you have to hold down the Alt key for each number, but not for the period separating them. The Next key sends a Tab character, which is useful for command-line completion. The arrow keypad works just like the arrows on your full-size keyboard. Press the ... key to get the Escape character, and press Alt-... to get a pipe character ("|").

About the most exciting thing you can do from this firmware is associate with a wireless access point, get an IP address, and ping another computer. The Wi-Fi interface usually associates with the strongest network by default. You can use *iwconfig* to see which network, if any, is currently associated:

```
# iwconfig eth0
eth0      IEEE 802.11b  ESSID:"plugh" Nickname:"Linux"
          Frequency:2.427 GHz  Access Point: 00:30:AB:0A:E3:2B
          Bit Rate=11.534 Mb/s

          ...
```

Use this command if you need to make the ZipIt associate with a particular Wi-Fi network:

```
# iwconfig eth0 essid OtherNet
```

If your Wi-Fi network uses WEP (Wired Equivalent Privacy), you can set the key with this command:

```
# iwconfig eth0 key XXXX-XXXX-XXXX-XXXX
```

Once the wireless network is set up, you can probably get an IP address via DHCP:

```
# udhcpc eth0
udhcpc (v0.9.9-pre) started
Sending discover...
Sending select for 172.16.0.242
Lease of 172.16.0.242 obtained, lease time 3600
```

Now that your ZipIt has an IP address, you can ping something:

```
# ping 172.16.0.1
PING 172.16.0.1 (172.16.0.1) 56 bytes of data.
64 bytes from 172.16.0.1: icmp_seq=1 ttl=64 time=9.0 ms
64 bytes from 172.16.0.1: icmp_seq=2 ttl=64 time=8.1 ms
64 bytes from 172.16.0.1: icmp_seq=3 ttl=64 time=7.4 ms
64 bytes from 172.16.0.1: icmp_seq=4 ttl=64 time=6.7 ms
64 bytes from 172.16.0.1: icmp_seq=5 ttl=64 time=5.1 ms
```

Note that the filesystem is actually a RAM disk. The compressed filesystem image is stored on the flash memory. The RAM disk is created each time the system boots, but changes are not written back to the flash memory. If you edit a file, such as */etc/network/interfaces*, the changes will be lost when you turn off the ZipIt.

When you're done using the ZipIt, simply turn it off. Indeed, this is your only option since there is no halt or shutdown command. Since it uses a RAM disk, you don't need to worry about corrupting the filesystem.

Running the Original ZipIt Application

If you'd like to use the ZipIt's instant messenger application, simply type **zrun**. You should then see the familiar screens as the ZipIt searches for wireless networks and connects to your instant messenger accounts.

Note that there is no way to exit the instant messenger application and return to the Linux shell. The only way to get back to the shell is to power-cycle the ZipIt. Furthermore, if you turn the ZipIt on again within a short amount of time, you'll probably find the instant messenger application is still running. Turning off the device with that application running puts it into sleep mode. We found that the ZipIt must remain off for a minute or two to fully power-cycle it.

If you want to revert back to the manufacturer's firmware, follow the instructions in "Reverting to the Original Firmware". Otherwise, if you want to have even more Linux fun with the ZipIt, install the OpenZipIt firmware as described in the next section.

Loading OpenZipIt

OpenZipIt is a firmware image that doesn't have the ZipIt messenger application. Instead, it includes some additional Linux libraries and utilities. The most interesting new application is the Dropbear SSH client and server. OpenZipIt also includes a *curses*-based IRC client called *weechat*. The other utilities are related to playing MP3 files and controlling the sound system.

Note that you must have the BURN3 firmware loaded before you can install the OpenZipIt firmware. The procedure for loading OpenZipIt is to mount an NFS filesystem and then use the *zflash* utility to copy new files to the ZipIt's flash memory.

The first step is to configure a Linux or BSD system as an NFS server. (See the Appendix for those instructions.) In the following instructions, we assume that your exported directory is named */exported/dir*.

When the NFS server is ready, download and unpack **http://www.aibohack. com/zipit/zipit_tool_extras.zip**. Copy the two files named *zflash* and *loader.bin* to your export directory:

```
nfs# cd /tmp
nfs# unzip /tmp/zipit_tool_extras.zip
nfs# ls -l NFS_REFLASH
total 42
-rw-rw-rw-  1 wessels  wessels   3376 Apr  8 16:22 loader.bin
drwxrwxrwx  2 wessels  wessels    512 Apr  8 15:58 src_loader
drwxrwxrwx  2 wessels  wessels    512 Apr  8 16:03 src_zflash
-rw-rw-rw-  1 wessels  wessels  35152 Apr  8 16:22 zflash
nfs# cp NFS_REFLASH/loader.bin NFS_REFLASH/zflash /exported/dir
nfs# chmod 755 /exported/dir/zflash
```

Next, download *zimage.dat* and *ramdisk.gz* from **http://groups.yahoo.com/ group/zipitwireless/files/OpenZipit/**. You'll need a Yahoo! account to access these files. Copy or save them to the exported directory as well:

```
nfs# cp zimage.dat ramdisk.gz /exported/dir
```

Everything is now in place to load the new firmware. But first, we have a little time-saving tip: typing long commands on the ZipIt can be frustrating. We recommend that you make a little shell script in */exported/dir* named *go.sh* containing the following command line:

```
./zflash loader.bin zimage.dat ramdisk.gz
```

Turn on your ZipIt (with the BURN3 firmware) and log in as *root*. Execute the necessary commands to get an IP address and make sure you can ping your NFS server:

```
zipit# udhcpc eth0
zipit# ping 172.16.0.4
```

Then, mount the NFS filesystem with this command:

```
zipit# mount -r -o nolock -o intr 172.16.0.4:/exported/dir /mnt
zipit# cd /mnt
zipit# ls
go.sh       loader.bin    ramdisk.gz    zflash      zimage.dat
zipit# sh go.sh
```

The zflash program performs some sanity checks on the files that you give it. If you've done everything correctly, it asks if you really want to overwrite the flash memory:

```
WARNING: this is a dangerous operation
------------------------------------------
 if power is disconnected during the
 process, the device won't work again
 if the data files provided are flawed
 the device may never boot again
Repairing the device requires soldering
 Danger level = DANGEROUS

(to proceed type "Yes")

Proceed? Yes

DANGEROUS OPERATION BEGUN
 DO NOT UNPLUG POWER/BATTERY

Erasing FlashROM...Erased!
Writing FlashROM...Wrote!
Verify FlashROM...Verified!
All done
(please reset the device)
```

When it is done, turn off the power, wait a few seconds, and then turn it back on. When it reboots you should have a screen with Tux the Penguin and a login prompt.

Playing with OpenZipIt

Logging in and setting up the network is the same as with the BURN3 firmware. Log in as *root* with no password. Use *iwconfig* and *udhcpc* to configure the network.

Remote Access with SSH

SSH is probably the most useful application on your new firmware. It allows you to log in remotely to your other systems. If you can stand using the small screen, you can now carry around the small ZipIt instead of your bulky laptop. As long as you can log into a shell account somewhere, you can run text-mode applications remotely to your heart's content: *lynx* or *links* for surfing the Web, *centericq* for AIM/MSN/ICQ, and of course *frotz* for your interactive fiction needs. OpenZipIt uses the Dropbear SSH client and server (**http://matt.ucc.asn.au/dropbear/dropbear.html**). If you normally use OpenSSH on your Linux and/or BSD boxes, you should find that Dropbear works almost exactly the same:

```
zipit# ssh -l wessels 172.16.0.4
Host '172.16.0.4' is not in the trusted hosts file.
(fingerprint 77:ae:a8:21:25:7c:ef:77:87:b9:46:0f:36:88:73:81)
Do you want to continue connecting? (y/n) y
Password:
```

If you plan to use *curses*-based applications, such as *vi* and *top*, remotely, you probably want to make sure that the remote host knows about your limited screen size. You can use *stty* to print the screen size:

```
remote% stty -a
speed 9600 baud; 30 rows; 40 columns
....
```

If you get a different answer, you can force the correct screen size, also with *stty*:

```
remote% stty rows 30 cols 40
```

Streaming Audio

In theory the ZipIt hardware and OpenZipIt software should allow you to play streaming MP3 audio files. In practice it doesn't quite work perfectly yet, at least not for us. Nonetheless, its kind of fun to experiment with.

The first step is to load a few kernel modules that enable the sound drivers:

```
zipit# insmod wm8751l
zipit# insmod ep7212_audiodma
zipit# insmod zipitaudio
```

The developer of OpenZipIt left a shell script named *usr/bin/go2* that contains those commands. You can avoid typing the long `insmod` commands and just run go2 instead.

You'll also need a streaming audio server running on another machine. We chose to use a simple server called AMPLE (**http://ample.sourceforge.net/**). Shoutcast is another obvious choice.

The OpenZipIt streaming audio client is called *freebase*. Start it with a URL that refers to your server. For example:

```
zipit# freebase http://172.16.0.4:1234/
```

You should hear music coming out of the ZipIt's small speaker. The sound is much better if you use the headphone output. However, you'll probably hear the music cut out unless the MP3 file is 64 Kb/sec or less.

You can control the audio output volume with a program called *aumix*. To use it, however, you must also specify the mixer device name, which is nonstandard:

```
zipit# aumix -d /dev/zipm -I
```

Setting the Time

OpenZipit also includes an NTP client program, named *ntpclient*. You can use this simple utility to set the device's date and time:

```
zipit# ntpclient 172.16.0.1
```

Extra Credit

Now that you're enjoying Linux on the ZipIt, here are some tips and ideas for future improvements.

Modifying the RAM disk

You may want to modify certain configuration files on the RAM disk. You may also want to add new programs or other files to the disk image. Here's the basic procedure:

```
nfs# gunzip ramdisk.gz
nfs# mount ramdisk /mnt -t ext2 -o loop=/dev/loop0
nfs# ls /mnt
bin   etc   lib       lost+found  opt   root  tmp  var
dev   home  linuxrc   mnt         proc  sbin  usr
```

Now you can edit and add files under the */mnt* partition. When you're done, unmount it and compress it again:

```
nfs# umount /mnt
nfs# gzip -9 ramdisk
```

Now you can store the updated *ramdisk.gz* image on the ZipIt with the *zflash* procedure described in "Loading OpenZipIt," earlier in this chapter. You can add new files as long as *ramdisk.gz* stays under 1.4 MB.

Reverting Back to the BURN3 Firmware

You can use the *zflash* procedure (described in "Loading OpenZipIt") to put the BURN3 firmware back onto your ZipIt. You'll need to download **http://www.aibohack.com/zipit/zipit_parts_burn3.zip**. This is the same BURN3 firmware image, except it is separated into three files suitable for use with *zflash*.

Reverting to the Original Firmware

If you want to go all the way back to the original ZipIt firmware, you can download it from the **www.zipitwireless.net** web site and use either of the techniques described in the previous sections "ZRS on Windows" or "BIND and Apache."

First, check the "Release history" section of **http://elinux.org/wiki/ZipItTechDetails** for the current software release. You'll see a table of version numbers, filenames, and checksums. Download the latest firmware image. For example:

```
# wget http://www.zipitwireless.net/~zippy/bootrom.S73HS001.bin
```

Then, create a corresponding *.txt* file that refers to the firmware filename and has the correct checksum:

```
# cat > bootrom122.txt <<EOF
1.99
http://www.zipitwireless.net/~zippy/bootrom.S73HS001.bin
9146A4C0D370EB0524838E7B06AED343
EOF
```

You should now be able to perform the update using either your own DNS and Apache servers ("BIND and Apache") or with the *zrs* utility on Windows ("ZRS on Windows").

Cross Compiling

If you're willing to work at it, you can compile your own programs to run on the ZipIt. Of course, you can't just compile and run any old program. A particular program may not compile if it tries to use libraries or hardware features that do not exist for the ZipIt. Check out the cross-compiling instructions at **http://elinux.org/wiki/ZipItCompile** if you'd like to give it a try.

Bluetooth LED Sign   9

Time

———————————————

3-4 days

Difficulty

———————————————

difficult

In this chapter we'll show you how to use a gumstix "waysmall" computer to control an LED moving sign. These are the signs that you see displaying scrolling messages in bars, restaurants, airports, and so on. The sign we're using has a serial port and a relatively open control protocol. The waysmall computer has two serial ports and a Bluetooth interface. It receives messages for the sign via Bluetooth and then issues appropriate formatting and control commands over a serial port to the sign.

If you're having a hard time seeing why we think this is a cool project, here are some ideas:

- Use it in a NOC environment to know when critical systems or services go down.

- Build your own news or stock ticker.

- Display text messages received from IM or IRC.

- Allow people to entertain themselves by posting messages from their mobile phones.

- Display the artist and title of a song being played on your digital jukebox.

- Remind you when the next bus or train is coming.

What You Need

- **Gumstix basix platform board with Bluetooth**

- **Gumstix waysmall STUART expansion board**

- **Multi Media Card (optional)**

- **(2) Mini-DIN-8 to DB9 null-modem serial cables**

- **Scrolling LED sign with serial port, such as Pro-Lite Tru-Color II**

- **RJ11 plug**

- **RJ11 plug crimper**

- **PC running Linux with GCC installed**

- **Bluetooth-enabled PC, phone, or PDA**

If you just want to control the sign from a computer, you don't really need the gumstix. All you need is a serial port and some code. However, using Bluetooth opens up more possibilities, such as sending messages from PDAs and mobiles phones, and easily allowing more than one person (or computer) to display a message.

The inspiration for this project goes back to a *Linux Journal* article published in 1999 in Issue 62 (**http://www.linuxjournal.com/article/2823**). The author of that article, Walt Stoneburner, also maintains a number of web pages about various LED signs (**http://wls.wwco.com/ledsigns/**). Walt's original work was done with the Pro-Lite PL-M2014R sign, with which he seems to have a love/hate relationship. He also mentions BetaBrite signs as another inexpensive alternative. In fact, both Pro-Lite and BetaBrite appear to use the same communication protocol.

We decided to use a Pro-Lite sign also, largely because someone has written a Perl module that implements the control protocol. We purchased a Pro-Lite sign through eBay, not really knowing if it would work with this module. In fact it works very well. It turned out to be a PL-M2014RV6, which is printed only on the back of the sign. Neither the user manual nor box gives any hint as to the model number of the sign. This leads us to believe that Pro-Lite probably does not make any other similar signs that are not compatible with the same control protocol.

Figure 9-1. Front side of the gumstix board.

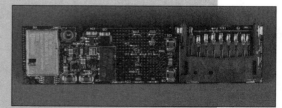

Figure 9-2. Back side of the gumstix board, showing Bluetooth and MMC connectors.

Introducing the gumstix

The gumstix is an extremely small general-purpose computer system by today's standards. It is based on Intel's XScale processor, which is really an ARM CPU. The gumstix is similar to the kind of hardware that you'd find inside a cell phone, PDA, or GPS. Not surprisingly, the gumstix is about the same size and shape as a stick of gum, as shown in Figures 9-1 and 9-2.

The gumstix comes in either 200 or 400 MHz models. The original boards have 4 MB flash memory and 64 MB RAM. Newer "xm" models feature 16 MB flash memory. A version of Linux (currently kernel 2.6.11) and the BusyBox suite of applications are pre-installed.

The gumstix comes with a number of daughterboard options. Technically, "gumstix" refers only to the CPU board itself. When paired with a daughter board and a case, the gumstix becomes a "waysmall" computer. We'll use the terms interchangeably in this book.

For this project we've chosen the waysmall STUART daughterboard, which includes two serial ports and a USB device interface; it also allows you to use Bluetooth in addition to the two serial ports (earlier offerings were wired up in such a way that the second serial port and the Bluetooth port used the same UART). Figure 9-3 shows the two boards side by side. Note that the "waysmall original board" also has two serial ports, but you cannot use the second port and the Bluetooth interface at the same time.

The waysmall STUART board allows us to use them together. A number of other daughter boards are available from the manufacturer, including some with audio, Compact Flash, and even Ethernet.

The gumstix board also includes a Multi Media Card (MMC) slot. Here you can add more storage if the on-board flash memory (4 or 16 MB) is not enough. You might want to get an MMC card for the gumstix, if only because it is a convenient way to transfer files. Note that even though Secure Digital (SD) memory cards look exactly like MMC cards, they are not quite the same thing (see **http://en.wikipedia.org/wiki/Secure_Digital**). Both MMC and SD seem to work well from Linux. However, if you want to access the card from the gumstix boot monitor, perhaps to copy a new software image, you'd better stick with MMC.

Assembling the System

When you receive your gumstix kit you'll need to assemble the following pieces:

- The gumstix processor board
- The waysmall STUART daughter board (part number BRD00003)
- The waysmall case
- The Bluetooth antenna (included with the processor board)

Snapping the two boards together is simple. Align the boards on top of each other so that the white, rectangular connectors are together. Press the boards together until you hear a "snap." Figure 9-4 shows how they look when connected and with an MMC card inserted into the slot. At this point you can actually start tinkering with the gumstix if you like. But you might as well take the time to fit it into its little case.

Figure 9-3. The gumstix and waysmall daughter board.

Figure 9-4. The gumstix and waysmall boards connected, with SD memory card inserted.

What's a STUART

The gumstix's PXA processor has four different UARTs, or Universal Asynchronous Receiver Transmitters. They are named FFUART, STUART, BTUART, and HWUART. The first serial port is connected to FFUART. The waysmall STUART board connects the STUART to the second serial port. That means that you cannot use both Bluetooth and the second serial port with the original waysmall board. See http://www.gumstix.org/tikiwiki/tiki-view_faq.php?faqId=13.

Figure 9-5. We need to cut a notch in the waysmall case for the Bluetooth antenna.

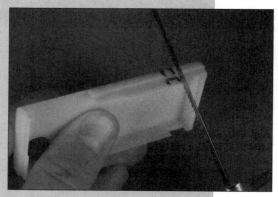

Figure 9-6. Cutting the case with a coping saw.

Figure 9-7. The Bluetooth antenna installed.

The two boards should fit snugly inside the white plastic waysmall case. Figure 9-5 shows our case, which unfortunately didn't come with a cutout for the Bluetooth antenna, so we made our own. It looks like the gumstix site does sell a version of the case with a hole for the antenna. Either we ordered the wrong one or they only offered it after we bought ours. Since the case is made of plastic, it is easy to cut out a notch. We marked the top of the case with two lines on each side of the antenna and used a small coping saw to cut out the notch, as shown in Figure 9-6. The result is shown in Figure 9-7.

Exploring the gumstix

To start playing with the gumstix, connect the serial port cable between the gumstix and your PC, and use a terminal program such as *kermit*, *screen*, or HyperTerminal to set up a serial console and then apply power. In Figure 9-8 you see a pair of round mini-din connectors, which are serial ports. The one that is closest to the center is ttyS0, or the console port. The other one is ttyS2. The gumstix serial port is configured for 115,200 bps and 8N1.

The power connector is located on the side of the case. As soon as you apply power, you should see the following output on the console:

```
U-Boot 1.1.1 (Oct  3 2004 - 18:38:12)

*** Welcome to Gumstix ***

U-Boot code: A3F00000 -> A3F1B01C  BSS: -> A3F4CB54
RAM Configuration:
Bank #0: a0000000 64 MB
erase_region_count = 32 erase_region_size = 131072
Flash:  4 MB
Hit any key to stop autoboot:  0
### JFFS2 loading 'boot/uImage' to 0xa2000000
Scanning JFFS2 FS: .... done.
### JFFS2 load complete: 809898 bytes loaded to 0xa2000000
## Booting image at a2000000 ...
   Image Name:   uImage
   Image Type:   ARM Linux Kernel Image (gzip compressed)
   Data Size:    809834 Bytes = 790.9 kB
Load Address: a0008000
Entry Point:  a0008000
Verifying Checksum ... OK
Uncompressing Kernel Image ... OK

Starting kernel ...
```

Then you'll see a more-or-less typical Linux kernel boot sequence. At the end is a login prompt:

```
Welcome to the Gumstix Linux Distribution!

gumstix login:
```

Enter **root** at the login prompt and **gumstix** for the password. Then you should have a no-frills shell prompt from which you can run commands such as *ps*, *ls*, and *df*. Note that most of these commands are a part of the BusyBox collection, which we also talked about in Chapter 6.

Take some time to explore the system and find out what's there and what's not. For example, the gumstix has *vi*, but not *less*. It has an SSH server (Dropbear) and an HTTP server (Boa). It has *ifconfig*, *ping*, and other networking utilities, but no true Ethernet interfaces.

Figure 9-8. Connecting the waysmall computer to a laptop.

You can get Ethernet on other gumstix expansion boards, just not on the one we are using (waysmall STUART).

Be sure to take a moment to marvel at how much functionality the gumstix has on its tiny, 4MB filesystem:

```
# df -h
Filesystem              Size    Used Available Use% Mounted on
/dev/mtdblock2          3.8M    3.4M    388.0k  90% /
```

Customizing the System

Admittedly, there is not much to customize, but you might want to:

- Change the root password.
- Add a non-root user.
- Change the hostname, via */etc/hostname*.
- Change the time zone, via */etc/TZ*.

In the next section, we'll show you how to add software packages to the gumstix.

Building Software for the gumstix

The gumstix folks provide a nifty *buildroot environment*. This is a directory structure that you can copy to an existing Linux box. It provides a cross-compiler so you can build new binaries for the gumstix. You'll need the cross compiler later when we write some code for sending messages to the sign.

The buildroot environment is available through a Subversion source code control server. To get it, you first need to install a Subversion client on your other Linux box. For example, to install the Subversion client on Gentoo, try this:

```
# USE="-berkdb" emerge -av subversion
```

With Subversion installed, use this command to check out the gumstix buildroot environment:

```
# svn co http://svn.gumstix.com/gumstix-buildroot/trunk gumstix-buildroot
```

You may notice that the checked-out repository is not very big (about 15 MB). That's because it doesn't actually contain all the files that you need to create the environment. It mostly contains scripts, *Makefiles*, and empty directories. These scripts and *Makefiles* download various source files, such as a C library, C/C++ compiler, and the Linux kernel, from various other locations. To finish the installation:

```
# cd gumstix-buildroot
# make
```

Unless something is seriously wrong, *make* should run to completion without errors. The end result is a J2FFS filesystem image, which will be named *root_fs_arm_nofpu*.

The buildroot environment includes some extra software packages that are not built by default. For example, we were frustrated with the BusyBox */bin/ sh* and wanted to use *bash* instead. Getting *bash* compiled for the gumstix is as easy as adding this line to the top-level *Makefile*:

```
TARGETS+=bash
```

Then run *make* again. You can search the *Makefile* for other commented-out TARGETS lines to see what other software is available. You can also list the **.mk* files in the *make* directory.

After you've built new software, how should you copy it to the gumstix? If you have a program like *minicom*, you can use the *Zmodem* file-transfer protocol to upload it. Another option is to use a MMC card, if you have one. Unfortunately you cannot (or should not) remove the MMC card while the system is running. A third option is to connect the gumstix's USB port to another computer and use *usbnet* (see **http://www.gumstix.org/tikiwiki/tiki-index.php?page=tutorial**) to copy the files over. Finally, another way is to install the new J2FFS filesystem image on the gumstix flash. Although that procedure is overkill if you have just one or two files to copy, we'll describe it anyway, in case you want to upgrade all of the gumstix software later.

These instructions for installing a new filesystem image come from the *gumstix. org* web site. Be sure to check there occasionally for more recent instructions.

The gumstix boot monitor, called *u-boot*, supports uploading new file-system images with the Kermit transfer protocol. We'll use the Kermit terminal emulation program on Linux to do this:

```
% kermit
C-Kermit 8.0.209, 17 Mar 2003, for Linux
 Copyright (C) 1985, 2003,
  Trustees of Columbia University in the City of New York.
Type ? or HELP for help.
C-Kermit> set port /dev/tts/0
C-Kermit> set speed 115200
/dev/tts/0, 115200 bps
C-Kermit> set carrier-watch off
C-Kermit> connect
Connecting to /dev/tts/0, speed 115200
```

Power up your gumstix and interrupt the boot procedure by pressing any key within three seconds:

```
U-Boot 1.1.1 (Oct  3 2004 - 18:38:12)

*** Welcome to Gumstix ***

U-Boot code: A3F00000 -> A3F1B01C  BSS: -> A3F4CB54
RAM Configuration:
Bank #0: a0000000 64 MB
erase_region_count = 32 erase_region_size = 131072
Flash:  4 MB
Hit any key to stop autoboot:  0
GUM>
```

From here, issue the following command to tell the gumstix you are uploading a file:

```
GUM> loadb a2000000
```

Then escape back to the Kermit prompt by typing **Control-\ C** (or whatever it told you the escape sequence is). At the Kermit prompt, issue the following commands to send the file:

```
C-Kermit> robust
C-Kermit> send /tmp/root_fs_arm_nofpu
```

Kermit displays the upload progress, which should take a few minutes. When it's done, you'll see the C-Kermit prompt again. Connect back to the serial port, and you'll see a status message from the gumstix about the upload:

```
C-Kermit> connect
Connecting to /dev/tts/0, speed 115200
 Escape character: Ctrl-\ (ASCII 28, FS): enabled
Type the escape character followed by C to get back,
or followed by ? to see other options.
----------------------------------------------------
## Total Size      = 0x003b2da4 = 3878308 Bytes
## Start Addr      = 0xA2000000
```

Then, issue the following commands to install the new filesystem image on the gumstix flash. Note, if you have a 16 MB "xm" model, use **era 1:2-127** instead:

```
GUM> echo ${filesize}
3B2DA4
GUM> era 1:2-31
Erase Flash Sectors 2-31 in Bank # 1
.......................... done
GUM> cp.b a2000000 40000 ${filesize}
Copy to Flash... done
GUM>
```

When it's done, reboot the gumstix:

```
GUM> reset
resetting ...

U-Boot 1.1.1 (Oct  3 2004 - 18:38:12)

*** Welcome to Gumstix ***

U-Boot code: A3F00000 -> A3F1B01C  BSS: -> A3F4CB54
RAM Configuration:
Bank #0: a0000000 64 MB
erase_region_count = 32 erase_region_size = 131072
Flash:  4 MB
Hit any key to stop autoboot:  0
### JFFS2 loading 'boot/uImage' to 0xa2000000
Scanning JFFS2 FS: ....... done.
### JFFS2 load complete: 710820 bytes loaded to 0xa2000000
## Booting image at a2000000 ...
   Image Name:   uImage
   Image Type:   ARM Linux Kernel Image (uncompressed)
   Data Size:    710756 Bytes = 694.1 kB
   Load Address: a0008000

   Entry Point:  a0008000
   Verifying Checksum ... OK
```

Learning About Bluetooth

One of the most exciting things about the gumstix is its built-in Bluetooth interface. Bluetooth is sometimes called "Personal Area Networking," which is to say that it has a range of about 10 feet. One of the most common uses for Bluetooth today is for mobile phone headsets and synchronizing PDAs.

Bluetooth devices support a number of "profiles" designed to facilitate interoperation. For example, there's a headset profile, a fax profile, a serial port profile, a file transfer profile, and many more. We'll be using the Serial Port (SP) profile, which creates a virtual serial port over a Bluetooth connection.

The gumstix boots with Bluetooth enabled, so we don't need to worry about configuring the kernel or drivers. For example, you should see something like this when the kernel boots:

```
Bluetooth: Core ver 2.7
NET: Registered protocol family 31
Bluetooth: HCI device and connection manager initialized
Bluetooth: HCI socket layer initialized
Bluetooth: HCI UART driver ver 2.1
Bluetooth: HCI H4 protocol initialized
Bluetooth: L2CAP ver 2.6
Bluetooth: L2CAP socket layer initialized
Bluetooth: BNEP (Ethernet Emulation) ver 1.2
Bluetooth: BNEP filters: protocol multicast
Bluetooth: RFCOMM ver 1.3
Bluetooth: RFCOMM socket layer initialized
Bluetooth: RFCOMM TTY layer initialized
```

Those messages indicate Bluetooth support in the kernel. One of the system *rc* scripts, */etc/init.d/S30bluetooth*, is responsible for configuring devices and starting various daemon processes. It is executed automatically each time the system boots. You can also run it manually to start and stop the Bluetooth-related daemons:

```
# /etc/init.d/S30bluetooth stop
Stopping Bluetooth subsystem: pand dund rfcomm hidd sdpd hcid /dev/
ttyS3.
```

To start them again, run:

```
# /etc/init.d/S30bluetooth start
Set (GPIO,out,clear) via /proc/gpio/GPIO7
Set (GPIO,out,set) via /proc/gpio/GPIO7
Starting Bluetooth subsystem: /dev/ttyS3 hcid sdpd rfcomm pand.
```

pand is the Personal Area Network daemon. It provides TCP/IP over Bluetooth. As cool as it sounds, you won't need it for this project. You can disable *pand* by editing */etc/default/bluetooth*. Find the PAND_ENABLE variable and set it to false.

HCI stands for Host Controller Interface. *hcitool* and *hciconfig* are tools that you'll use to configure Bluetooth on the gumstix. Use this command to see the address of the local interface:

```
# hcitool dev
        hci0    00:80:37:1C:3A:FF
```

You may want to add this address to your */etc/bluetooth/hosts* file:

```
# echo 00:80:37:1C:3A:FF gumstix > /etc/bluetooth/hosts
```

Also run *hciconfig*, which should remind you of *ifconfig*:

```
# hciconfig hci0 up
# hciconfig -a
hci0:   Type: UART
        BD Address: 00:80:37:1C:3A:FF ACL MTU: 672:8  SCO MTU: 64:0
        UP RUNNING PSCAN ISCAN INQUIRY
```

```
RX bytes:900 acl:0 sco:0 events:99 errors:0
TX bytes:838 acl:0 sco:0 commands:48 errors:0
Features: 0xff 0xfb 0x01 0x00 0x00 0x00 0x00 0x00
Packet type: DM1 DM3 DM5 DH1 DH3 DH5 HV1 HV2 HV3
Link policy: RSWITCH HOLD SNIFF PARK
Link mode: SLAVE ACCEPT
Name: 'Gumstix (0)'
Class: 0x820116
Service Classes: Networking, Information
Device Class: Computer, Palm
HCI Ver: 1.1 (0x1) HCI Rev: 0x8105 LMP Ver: 1.1 (0x1) LMP
Subver: 0x8d40
Manufacturer: Ericsson Technology Licensing (0)
```

We initially had a lot of difficulty with Bluetooth on the gumstix. It was not communicating very well with other Bluetooth devices. At first, we suspected interference from our nearby 802.11 network. But eventually we found some good suggestions in the *gumstix-users* mailing list archive. The trick was to change the setting for HCIATTACH_SPEED in *etc/default/bluetooth*:

```
HCIATTACH_SPEED=230400
```

Most Bluetooth interfaces for PCs have a USB interface. On the gumstix, however, Bluetooth uses a Universal Asynchronous Receiver/Transmitter (UART), which is essentially a serial port. *hciattach* is the program that attaches the Bluetooth device to the UART. HCIATTACH_SPEED is the speed at which these two devices should communicate. The default setting of 921600 is too high, especially for our 200 MHz model gumstix. By lowering this setting, all of our Bluetooth communications problems disappeared. These speed problems may have been fixed in the recent gumstix software releases. However, since this application does not require high speed communication, we still recommend the 230400 setting.

The *hcid* daemon manages local Bluetooth devices and responds to certain Bluetooth queries. It has a configuration file, named */etc/bluetooth/hcid.conf*. This configuration file is where you'll set the security policy and other parameters, such as the device name. Here is our *hcid.conf*:

```
# HCId options
options {
        autoinit yes;
        security none;
        pairing none;
}

# Default settings for HCI devices
device {
        name "LED sign";
        class 0x820116;
        iscan enable; pscan enable;
        lm master,accept;
        lp rswitch,hold,sniff,park;
}
```

The security none line means that other Bluetooth devices can connect without establishing a trust relationship first. If you set it to auto instead, you'll need to place a numeric password in /etc/bluetooth/pin and give that number to Bluetooth users who are allowed to connect.

One of the most important *hcid.conf* settings is the link mode (lm), which we set to master,accept. In a Bluetooth connection, one side is the master and the other side is the slave. The device that initiates a connection assumes the role of master. This means that the gumstix becomes the slave for incoming connections. However, when the gumstix is the slave, it becomes undiscoverable by other devices. Fortunately, Bluetooth allows devices to switch roles after connecting. The link-mode setting controls how the device treats *incoming* connections. When set to master,accept this device accepts incoming connections in slave mode, but then requests to switch roles and become the master.

Testing the Bluetooth Connection

Eventually, our goal is to be able to send messages to the sign from a phone or PDA. But if you are new to Bluetooth, you'll probably have an easier time if you start playing with another Bluetooth-enabled Linux computer. To demonstrate how to get Bluetooth up and running, we'll show you how to log into the gumstix from another computer.

On your other computer, make sure that Bluetooth is up and running. If you've never done this before, you may want to refer to Chapter 7 of *Linux Unwired* (O'Reilly). When you have the Bluetooth interface up and the gumstix nearby, run this command on the other computer:

```
desktop # hcitool inq
Inquiring ...
        00:80:37:1C:3A:FF        clock offset: 0x2269    class: 0x820116
```

If you don't get any output the first time, run the command again. Note that the Bluetooth address (00:80:37:1C:3A:FF here) should match what you see in the *hciconfig* output on the gumstix. If not, then either you are running the command from the wrong computer or you have other Bluetooth devices nearby.

At this point you can try using *l2ping* to test low-level Bluetooth connectivity:

```
desktop # l2ping 00:80:37:1C:3A:FF
Ping: 00:80:37:1C:3A:FF from 00:E0:98:CC:A3:B4 (data size 20) ...
20 bytes from 00:80:37:1C:3A:FF id 200 time 37.74ms
20 bytes from 00:80:37:1C:3A:FF id 201 time 31.09ms
20 bytes from 00:80:37:1C:3A:FF id 202 time 35.18ms
20 bytes from 00:80:37:1C:3A:FF id 203 time 28.39ms
20 bytes from 00:80:37:1C:3A:FF id 204 time 30.48ms
20 bytes from 00:80:37:1C:3A:FF id 205 time 36.68ms
20 bytes from 00:80:37:1C:3A:FF id 206 time 42.81ms
```

The next step is to try to establish a "serial port" connection over Bluetooth. This uses a Bluetooth protocol called Radio Frequency Communications (RFCOMM). To begin, you must bind a remote Bluetooth address to a local pseudo-tty device. Here is the command that binds the first RFCOMM tty to the gumstix Bluetooth address:

```
desktop # rfcomm bind 0 00:80:37:1C:3A:FF
```

To print the current bindings, run *rfcomm* with no arguments:

```
desktop # rfcomm
rfcomm0: 00:80:37:1C:3A:FF channel 1 clean
```

Next, configure a serial port communications program, such as *minicom*, to open the *rfcomm* device. It might be either */dev/bluetooth/rfcomm/0* or */dev/rfcomm0*, depending on your particular Linux distribution and version. The port speed settings are unimportant for Bluetooth. After starting the communications program, press Enter a few times and you should see a login prompt:

```
Welcome to the Gumstix Linux Distribution!
```

```
gumstix login:
```

Now you can log into the gumstix over Bluetooth. If you are brave, you can even do away with the serial cable connected to *ttyS0* and just use Bluetooth instead. We don't recommend it, however.

Here are some other commands that may help you debug Bluetooth problems. When the Bluetooth connection is established, *rfcomm* shows some slightly different output:

```
desktop # rfcomm
rfcomm0: 00:80:37:1C:3A:FF channel 1 connected [tty-attached]
```

You can also see some connection information with *hcitool*:

```
desktop # hcitool con
Connections:
        < ACL 00:80:37:1C:3A:FF handle 41 state 1 lm MASTER
```

The Pro-Lite LED Sign

For this project we need a LED messaging sign that we can control through a serial port. Unfortunately, the market for these signs is not very "hacking friendly." That is, the sign makers perceive their customers as people who are not smart enough to write their own software for controlling the sign. Sign manufacturers do not openly publish the protocols used to control their signs. The LED signs are often expensive and sold as a part of a kit that includes Windows-based software or even a dedicated computer.

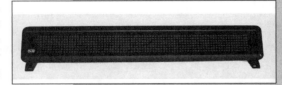

Figure 9-9. The Pro-Lite PL-M2014R LED sign.

Figure 9-9 shows what the PL-M2014R looks like. It's slightly more than two feet wide and four inches high. The power and serial port connectors are on the left side. It also comes with a remote control (not pictured). Figure 9-10 is a close-up of the sign. Here you can see the individual pixels (LEDs). The display is 7 LEDs high and 80 wide. The sign is wide enough to display about 13 characters in the normal font.

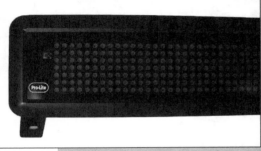

Figure 9-10. Close-up of the Pro-Lite sign showing individual pixels.

Purchasing a Pro-Lite sign can be a little tricky. Only a few online retailers offer it, and you may have to call a salesperson to place an order. We used Ebay, where a small number of Pro-Lite signs were selling for between $50 and $175.

Pro-Lite Sign Features

The PL-M2014R has 26 *pages*, named with the letters A to Z. Each page is limited to about 1,000 characters. Pages can either be displayed individually, or chained together. When displayed individually, the message in a given page is displayed over and over until the sign is instructed to do otherwise. In chained mode, pages are displayed one after the other, repeating in the same order each time.

The PL-M2014R boasts 26 different "colors." In fact, it has five different colors (red, orange, yellow, lime, green), 3 brightness levels (dim, normal, bright), and a number of color combinations (rainbow, green on red, etc). See Table 9-1 (page 257) for the list of available colors.

The sign also has 8 different "fonts" or character sizes. In addition to the normal font, it has bold, italic, and flashing. These can be combined to create fonts such as "flashing bold italic." See Table 9-2 (page 258) for the full list.

The sign also has 26 different "effects." Most of these determine how messages appear or disappear. For example, you can have messages enter from the left, top, or bottom, or just appear all at once. Also included among the possible effects are commands to pause the scrolling display and to show the date and time. See Table 9-3 (page 259) for the full list of effects.

The Pro-Lite has a trivia mode and comes with a number of pre-loaded questions and answers. In trivia mode it displays a normal page, then question, then another normal page, and finally the answer. You can delete all the trivia data to have more memory for your own messages. You can also program your own trivia questions and answers.

If you just need the sign to display messages that don't change very often, you can use the infrared remote control. However, for our purposes, we'll need to use the sign's serial port to send instructions from the gumstix.

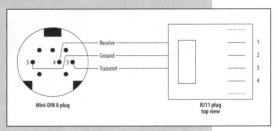

Figure 9-11. Diagram of the serial cable between gumstix and the sign.

The Serial Port

The Pro-Lite sign should come with a serial cable. It has a DB9 connector on one end and an RJ11 plug on the other. The gumstix uses a round 8-pin Mini-DIN connector, so this cable won't work. You might be able to find a DB9-to-Mini-DIN-8 adapter, but we think it's not too difficult to make a custom cable. One easy way is to buy a pre-made cable with the Mini-DIN connector, then cut off the other end and crimp an RJ11 plug in its place.

The serial cable needs only three wires: receive data, transmit data, and signal ground. On the mini-din connector these are pins 3 (Transmit), 4 (Ground), and 5 (Receive). These should be connected to pins 1, 2, and 3 of the RJ11 plug as shown in Figure 9-11. Note that we're assuming the RJ11 plug has 4 pins, such that 2 and 3 are in the center, but some might actually have 6. If you have a 6-pin plug, then add one to the RJ11 pin assignments.

The PL-M2014R's serial port defaults to 9,600 bps, which is the highest speed that it supports.

Using the gumstix's second serial port on the waysmall STUART board requires a little bit of voodoo. We have to tell the gumstix processor to connect the second serial port to the PXA's STUART. Put the following lines into /etc/init.d/S60ttyS2 and make the file executable:

```
#!/bin/sh
#
# Configure /dev/ttyS2
#

if test "$1" = "start" ; then
        echo "Configuring /dev/ttyS2:"
        modprobe proc_gpio
        echo "AF2 in" > /proc/gpio/GPIO46
        echo "AF1 out" > /proc/gpio/GPIO47
fi
```

Then either reboot or run the script manually:

```
# /etc/init.d/S60ttyS2 start
Configuring /dev/ttyS2:
Set (AF2,in,set) via /proc/gpio/GPIO46
Set (AF1,out,set) via /proc/gpio/GPIO47
```

Testing the Sign's Serial Port

After building the cable, you should test it out to make sure that everything is connected and working properly. Here's how you can send some simple test messages to the sign from the shell:

```
# T=/dev/ttyS2
# stty -F $T speed 9600 cs8 \
 -parenb -cstopb cread clocal \
 -crtscts -ignpar -echo nl1 cr3
# stty -F $T opost -ocrnl onlcr

# cat $T >/dev/null &
# echo '<ID01>' > $T
# echo '<ID01><PA>testing 1 2 3 ... ' > $T
# echo '<ID01><RPA>' > $T
```

The stty commands configure certain serial port parameters, such as the speed, flow-control, and other settings. The cat command is necessary to read characters coming back from the sign. The echo commands send data to the sign.

Each sign command begins with the token <ID01>. This is the identifier for sign #1, in case you have multiple signs chained together. The first command that we send is empty and is there just to wake up the sign in case we haven't talked to it for a while. The second command sends some text to the sign. <PA> refers to page A of the sign's memory. The third command, <RPA>, means "run page A."

Here's another neat little trick. You can use the following command to display the current date and time:

```
# date '+<ID01><PA>%c ' > $T
```

As you continue playing with the sign, you'll probably discover some of its annoying quirks. In particular, updates to the currently displayed page take effect immediately. In other words, a long message gets cut off as soon as you send a new one. Normally, this won't be a problem. But it does become difficult to use the sign as a frequently updated display. To see what we mean, try this:

```
# while true; do date '+<ID01><PA>%c ' > $T ; sleep 1 ; done
```

Putting It All Together

By now you should have Bluetooth working. That is, you can log in to the gumstix over Bluetooth from another computer or perhaps a PDA. You should also be able to send messages to the LED sign over the serial port. In this section, we'll explain how to glue these two together.

Bluetooth Configuration

One of the neat things about Bluetooth is you can run a number of different services on the same interface using *channels*. We'll actually run a number of "virtual serial ports" over the Bluetooth connection. This allows multiple PDAs/phones/computers to be connected at the same time. It also means that we can reserve one channel for logging into the gumstix and the other channels for talking to the sign. By default the gumstix runs *getty* on channel 1. We need to set up the other channels using *rfcomm*.

Earlier we showed you how to use `rfcomm bind` on another computer to bind a local RFCOMM device to a remote Bluetooth address. But on the gumstix we don't know the addresses of the devices that will connect. We want to accept RFCOMM connections from anyone. In this case we use `rfcomm listen` instead. It waits for an RFCOMM connection on a given channel and then sets up the necessary binding. Our *getty* process uses *rfcomm0* and channel 1. Use this command to accept incoming connections on *rfcomm1* and channel 2:

```
gumstix # /usr/sbin/rfcomm -r listen 1 2
```

`rfcomm listen` waits for a remote connection, stays running as long as the other side is connected, and then exits when the connection is closed. Therefore, we need a way to start another `rfcomm listen` for the next incoming connection. You can use a *while* loop in a shell script or, even better, do so by adding these lines to */etc/inittab*:

```
null::respawn:/usr/sbin/rfcomm -r listen 1 2
null::respawn:/usr/sbin/rfcomm -r listen 2 3
null::respawn:/usr/sbin/rfcomm -r listen 3 4
null::respawn:/usr/sbin/rfcomm -r listen 4 5
null::respawn:/usr/sbin/rfcomm -r listen 5 6
```

Reboot or type **init -q** to have *init* re-read its configuration file and start these processes.

By default, the gumstix only has four RFCOMM device entries in */dev*. The preceding example goes up to *rfcomm5*, so we'll need to add at least two more. One way to do it is by editing *sources/device_table.txt* in the *gumstix-buildroot* source tree. Then, of course, build and install a new filesystem image as described in "Building Software for the gumstix," earlier in this chapter. An easier way is to execute a few `mknod` commands manually. Even though */dev/* is a memory filesystem, the device entries should persist between reboots. To add four new RFCOMM devices, run:

```
/bin/mknod /dev/rfcomm4 c 216 4
/bin/mknod /dev/rfcomm5 c 216 5
/bin/mknod /dev/rfcomm6 c 216 6
/bin/mknod /dev/rfcomm7 c 216 7
```

Next, we need to talk about Bluetooth's Service Discovery Protocol (SDP). This protocol allows one Bluetooth device to ask another about the services it provides. For example, to see the services offered by your gumstix, you can type:

```
gumstix # sdptool browse ff:ff:ff:00:00:00
```

Services are not automatically advertised. Even though we have some *rfcomm* listeners, they won't be announced via SDP until we explicitly add them. The syntax is:

```
gumstix # /usr/bin/sdptool add --channel=2 SP
```

Note that SP refers to Bluetooth's Serial Port profile. It is essentially a virtual serial port running over the Bluetooth connection.

You may have noticed that the gumstix advertises an SP on RFCOMM channel 1 by default. This channel is used by *getty* so we can log in to the gumstix over Bluetooth. We think it is a good idea to leave *getty* running, but you probably don't want it announced by SDP because, as we'll see later, certain Bluetooth applications will try connecting to the first SP channel they find. They should connect to the LED sign process, rather than *getty*. So we need to delete this channel from the SDP configuration. We recommend adding the following lines to */etc/init.d/S31bluetooth*:

```
# delete the entry for channel 1, which connects to our getty
# assume its id is always 0x10000
/usr/bin/sdptool del 0x10000

/usr/bin/sdptool add --channel=2 SP
/usr/bin/sdptool add --channel=3 SP
/usr/bin/sdptool add --channel=4 SP
/usr/bin/sdptool add --channel=5 SP
/usr/bin/sdptool add --channel=6 SP
```

If you want to get really fancy, you can also use *sdptool* to add descriptions for each SP channel:

```
/usr/bin/sdptool setattr 0x010001 0x100 "LED Sign Chan 1"
/usr/bin/sdptool setattr 0x010002 0x100 "LED Sign Chan 2"
/usr/bin/sdptool setattr 0x010003 0x100 "LED Sign Chan 3"
/usr/bin/sdptool setattr 0x010004 0x100 "LED Sign Chan 4"
/usr/bin/sdptool setattr 0x010005 0x100 "LED Sign Chan 5"
```

Getting Messages from Bluetooth to the Sign

The next step in our little project is to write some code that reads messages from the RFCOMM devices, adds some formatting instructions, and then writes them to the Pro-Lite sign. Example 9-1 shows one way to accomplish this in C. We call this program *rfcomm-to-sign*.

Example 9-1. The rfcommm-to-sign.c program

```c
#include <stdio.h>
#include <unistd.h>
#include <stdlib.h>
#include <string.h>
#include <fcntl.h>
#include <err.h>
#include <assert.h>
#include <termios.h>
#include <syslog.h>
#include <errno.h>
#include <sys/file.h>

#define INPUT_BUF_LEN 1024
#define LOCK_PATH "/tmp/sign.lck"

int
get_sign_lock(void)
{

 int fd = open(LOCK_PATH, O_RDONLY|O_CREAT);
 if (fd < 0)
  err(1, LOCK_PATH);
 if (flock(fd, LOCK_EX) < 0)
  err(1, LOCK_PATH);
 return fd;
}

int
open_sign(char *dev)
{
 struct termios T;
 int fd = open(dev, O_RDWR);
 if (fd < 0)
  err(1, dev);
 syslog(LOG_DEBUG, "sign opened");
 if (tcgetattr(fd, &T) < 0)
  err(1, "tcgetattr");
 cfsetspeed(&T, B9600);
 T.c_cflag = CS8 | CREAD | CLOCAL;
 T.c_iflag = 0;
 T.c_oflag = 0;
 T.c_lflag = 0;
 T.c_cc[VMIN] = 0;
 T.c_cc[VTIME] = 0;
 if (tcsetattr(fd, TCSANOW, &T) < 0)
  err(1, "tcgetattr");
 return fd;
}
```

```c
int
open_rfcomm(char *dev)
{
 int fd;
 for (;;) {
  if ((fd = open(dev, O_RDWR)) >= 0)
   break;
  if (ENODEV != errno)
   err(1, dev);
  sleep(3);
 }
 syslog(LOG_DEBUG, "%s opened", dev);
 return fd;
}

int
read_rfcomm(int fd, char **line)
{
 static char inbuf[INPUT_BUF_LEN];
 char c;
 int l = 0;
 while ((read(fd, &c, 1) > 0) && l < INPUT_BUF_LEN) {
  if (c == 0xd || c == 0xa || c == 0x0) {
   if (l)
    break;
   else
    continue;
  }
  inbuf[l++] = c;
 }
 inbuf[l] = 0;
 syslog(LOG_DEBUG, "read {%s}", inbuf);
 *line = &inbuf[0];
 return l;
}

int
write_sign(int fd, char *buf, int len)
{
 int i;
 char junk[10];
 for (i = 0; i < len; i++) {
  if (write(fd, buf+i, 1) < 0) {
   syslog(LOG_ERR, "write_sign: %s", strerror(errno));
   break;
  }
  read(fd, junk, 10);
  usleep(5000);
 }
 return i;
}

int
write_sign_str(int fd, char *buf)
{
 int len = 0;
 syslog(LOG_NOTICE, "writing {%s} to FD %d", buf, fd);
```

```
  len = write_sign(fd, buf, strlen(buf));
  len += write_sign(fd, "\r\n", 2);
  return len;
}

int
write_message(int fd, char *buf, int len, char *page, char *nextpage)
{
  int nblen = len + 50;
  char *newbuf = malloc(nblen);
  write_sign_str(fd, "<ID01>");
  snprintf(newbuf, nblen, "<ID01><P%s>%s<FZ><%s>", page, buf, nextpage);

  write_sign_str(fd, newbuf);
  free(newbuf);
  return 0;
}

void
validate_page(char *page)
{
  if (strlen(page) > 1 || *page < 'A' || *page > 'Z')
   errx(1, "Page should be a single character A-Z");
}

int
main(int argc, char *argv[])
{
  int rfcomm;
  char *buf = NULL;
  char *rfcomm_dev = NULL;
  char *sign_dev = NULL;
  char *page = NULL;
  char *nextpage = NULL;

  if (argc != 5) {
   fprintf(stderr,
     "usage: rfcomm-to-sign rfcommdev signdev page nextpage\n");
   exit(1);
  }
  openlog("rfcomm-to-sign", 0, LOG_DAEMON);
  rfcomm_dev = argv[1];
  sign_dev = argv[2];
  page = argv[3];
  nextpage = argv[4];
  validate_page(page);
  validate_page(nextpage);

  rfcomm = open_rfcomm(rfcomm_dev);
  for (;;) {
   int len;
   int lock;
   int sign;
   write(rfcomm, "ready>\r\n", 7);
   if ((len = read_rfcomm(rfcomm, &buf)) < 0)
    break;
   lock = get_sign_lock();
   sign = open_sign(sign_dev);
```

```
    write_message(sign, buf, len, page, nextpage);
    close(sign);
    close(lock);
  }
  return 0;
}
```

Here's how *rfcomm-to-sign* works. It takes four command-line arguments: an RFCOMM device pathname, the serial port pathname for the sign, and two sign page names (A–Z). The first page refers to where the message will be stored, while the second will be the name of the page to display after this one.

The program begins by opening the RFCOMM device. The open() call will fail until another device establishes a connection on the corresponding channel, so the program loops until the open() call succeeds. Then it reads characters from the RFCOMM device. When it reads an end-of-line character, it writes the message to the sign. Since the sign serial port may be shared by numerous processes (i.e., other RFCOMM channels), the program uses file locking to make sure that it has exclusive access to the serial port while writing.

Note that you can't compile source code on the gumstix itself. You'll need to cross-compile it on another Linux box using buildroot tools, described in "Building Software for the gumstix," earlier in this chapter. Assuming the source code file is named *rfcomm-to-sign.c*, you can compile it like this (adjusting the pathnames as necessary):

```
desktop # XGCC=/some/where/gumstix-buildroot/build_arm_nofpu/staging_
dir/bin/arm-linux-uclibc-gcc
desktop # $XGCC -Wall -o rfcomm-to-sign rfcomm-to-sign.c
```

Copy the binary to the gumstix using Zmodem, Kermit, or with the MMC card. You need to run the program for every RFCOMM channel that you want to use. Assuming you've saved the binary as */usr/bin/rfcomm-to-sign*, add these lines to */etc/inittab*:

```
null::respawn:/usr/bin/rfcomm-to-sign /dev/rfcomm1 /dev/ttyS2 A B
null::respawn:/usr/bin/rfcomm-to-sign /dev/rfcomm2 /dev/ttyS2 B C
null::respawn:/usr/bin/rfcomm-to-sign /dev/rfcomm3 /dev/ttyS2 C D
null::respawn:/usr/bin/rfcomm-to-sign /dev/rfcomm4 /dev/ttyS2 D E
null::respawn:/usr/bin/rfcomm-to-sign /dev/rfcomm5 /dev/ttyS2 E A
```

As usual, execute init -q to have *init* start these processes without rebooting.

Note that *rfcomm-to-sign* uses *syslogd* for most errors and debugging. Check */var/log/messages* for errors and notifications the first few times you run the program. Also keep in mind that */var/log/messages* is on a memory filesystem and is lost each time you reboot. If you have problems, run the program from a shell window and see what happens when you send a message to the sign through Bluetooth.

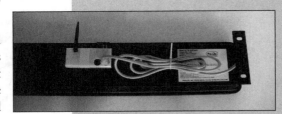

Figure 9-12. Mounting the gumstix to the back of the Pro-Lite sign.

Figure 9-13. Launching BtSerial.

Figure 9-14. Device names shown by BtSerial.

Figure 9-15. BtSerial's diagnostic messages.

Mounting the gumstix on the Sign

Most likely you'll want to put the sign up on display for others to see. If so, you can take a few minutes and attach the gumstix to the back of the sign, as shown in Figure 9-12. With a few sticky pads and cable ties, you can hide everything, including the serial cable. You'll probably want to leave the Bluetooth antenna sticking up (or down) a little bit for better reception.

Sending Messages to the Sign

Finally we have everything in place to send a message to the sign from a Bluetooth-enabled device. This section describes a few ways to do just that!

From PalmOS

If you have a Palm PDA or a phone that runs PalmOS, you can install the free BtSerial Pro application from **http://www.whizoo.com/apps/btserial.php**. As the name implies, it is a Bluetooth serial port communication program.

After launching BtSerialPro, you'll see the screen shown in Figure 9-13. Click on Open to locate nearby Bluetooth devices. BtSerialPro opens up another little window and displays a list of device names, as shown in Figure 9-14. We gave our gumstix the name "LED sign" (in */etc/bluetooth/ hcid.conf*). Click on Connect to establish the Bluetooth connection.

When BtSerialPro establishes a Bluetooth connection, you should see the diagnostic messages shown in Figure 9-15. It will say "RFCOMM connection up!" and tell you about the maximum packet size. The ready> prompt comes from our *rfcomm-to-sign* program and provides further evidence that the communication is working properly.

Now you can enter some text to send to the sign. Either use the Grafitti area or bring up the keyboard and enter a message. Figure 9-16 shows where we typed "go cougs!" on the Send line. After clicking on the Send button, BtSerialPro writes the message over the RFCOMM channel to the sign. Then our program sends another ready> prompt, indicating it is ready for another message.

From KDE

KDE, the K Desktop Environment, has pretty good support for Bluetooth. If you've installed the KDE Bluetooth utilities, you'll see a little blue "K" (similar to the Bluetooth "B") in your KDE panel. If you need help installing the KDE Bluetooth software, visit **http://kde-bluetooth.sourceforge.net/**. On Gentoo Linux we installed *net-wireless/kdebluetooth* from Portage.

Clicking on the KDE Bluetooth icon brings up Konqueror (the KDE web/file browser) with **bluetooth:/** in the location box (Figure 9-17). The main window shows two icons: one for the LED sign and another for the local Bluetooth device. The icons are chosen based on the class reported by each device.

Click on the LED sign icon and you'll see something like the window shown in Figure 9-18. Now you are browsing the services available on the gumstix. Although you can click on the Public Browse Group Root and SDP Server icons, they don't really lead to anywhere interesting since KDE doesn't know how to display the data it receives. The useful icons are the ones that look like serial port cables. They show up as "Sign Page 1," etc. for us because we added those descriptions to our */etc/init.d/S31bluetooth* file.

Click on one of the serial port icons to establish an RFCOMM connection. KDE should then bring up the Bluetooth Serial Chat window, as shown in Figure 9-19. Here you'll see the ready> prompt from *rfcomm-to-sign*. Type some text into the bottom box and click on Send. In our example we're hoping that someone receives our request for a pizza.

From a Linux Shell

Sending messages to the sign from the Linux shell is almost as easy as just *echo*ing or *cat*ing text to the RFCOMM device file. However, it depends on how you do it. But before we get to that, we have to talk a little about *stty*.

The stty command controls certain terminal device characteristics, such as data rate, flow control, end-of-line processing, and more. Before using shell commands to read from and write to RFCOMM devices, you should make sure they have reasonable *stty* settings. In particular, echo must be disabled. Otherwise characters read from the gumstix-side of the connection will be echoed back to the gumstix, creating an endless loop. You should also ensure that the read characteristic is enabled. You can set both of these with one command:

```
desktop # stty -echo cread < /dev/bluetooth/rfcomm/1
```

Fortunately, the *stty* settings are "sticky," so you should only need to set them once before using an RFCOMM device.

Now, if you want to interactively write messages to the sign, simply run:

```
desktop # cat > /dev/bluetooth/rfcomm/3
```

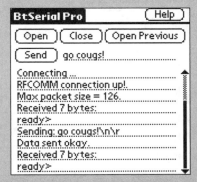

Figure 9-16. Sending a message.

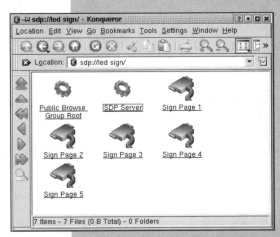

Figure 9-17. Browsing Bluetooth in KDE.

Figure 9-18. Browsing Bluetooth services.

Figure 9-19. KDE Bluetooth chat.

Then type your messages, one line at a time. The RFCOMM connection stays up as long as *cat* stays running. You can type as many messages as you like, but with our one-page-per-RFCOMM-device design, each additional message overwrites the previous one.

Generating messages using echo from a shell script is a little trickier. The problem is that the RFCOMM device must stay open long enough for the gumstix to open the RFCOMM device on its side and then read from it. This command, for example, probably won't work:

```
desktop # echo "this does not work" > /dev/bluetooth/rfcomm/2
```

The reason is that the device gets closed right after the message is written. The RFCOMM connection does not stay up long enough for our *rfcomm-to-sign* program to return from its short sleep() and successfully open the device.

An easy way to solve this problem is to add a sleep call after the echo and run both commands from a subshell, like this:

```
desktop # (echo "this works better" ; sleep 5) > /dev/bluetooth/
rfcomm/2
```

Our *rfcomm-to-sign* program uses a three-second sleep between attempts to open the RFCOMM device, so five seconds here should be sufficient. You may want to write a little shell script that hides some of the ugliness. For example:

```
#!/bin/sh
set -e
RNUM=$1 ; shift
stty -echo
exec > /dev/bluetooth/rfcomm/$RNUM
cat
sleep 5
```

Then you can use it like this:

```
desktop # echo "this works better" | ./ledsign.sh 1
```

Another way is to use a slightly more complicated shell script that also reads from the RFCOMM device. If we can make it read the ready> prompt before writing the message, we can be sure that the message is actually received by *rfcomm-to-sign*. Here is one way to do it:

```
#!/bin/sh
set -e
RNUM=$1; shift
read MSG
exec < /dev/bluetooth/rfcomm/$RNUM
exec > /dev/bluetooth/rfcomm/$RNUM
stty -echo cread
read prompt
echo "$MSG"
read prompt
```

The script first reads the message from *stdin*. Then it reassigns *stdin* and *stdout* to the RFCOMM device. It reads the prompt from *rfcomm-to-sign*, writes the message, and then waits for the next prompt. We also added the necessary *stty* settings for good measure. Here's how you would use it:

```
desktop # date | ./ledsign.sh 4
```

One drawback to the second version is that it might get stuck on one of the read prompt calls. Since there is no timeout, the script will block until interrupted. If you are sending messages to the sign automatically (versus interactively), you may want to use the sleep() approach instead.

Pro-Lite Control Protocol

As we mentioned earlier, you can use different colors, fonts, and effects with the Pro-Lite sign by inserting special codes in your message. For example, to display a message in red, you could send:

```
<CB>50% Off Today Only
```

The following tables show the control codes for the sign's colors, fonts, effects, and a few miscellaneous things.

Colors

Table 9-1 lists the 26 color codes supported by the Pro-Lite sign. Note that the sign really only has five colors: red, orange, yellow, lime, and green. The yellow and lime colors are almost the same. One of the colors, called Rainbow, uses all five colors at once.

In addition to the five colors, the sign also has three different brightness levels. Some of the color codes use shadows and different background colors as well. Some of these look okay, and some look hideous. You should try them out for yourself to see which ones you like.

Table 9-1. The Pro-Lite's color codes

Code	Color
<CA>	Dim red
<CB>	Red
<CC>	Bright red
<CD>	Orange
<CE>	Bright orange
<CF>	Light yellow
<CG>	Yellow
<CH>	Bright yellow
<CI>	Lime
<CJ>	Dim lime

Code	Color
<CK>	Bright lime
<CL>	Bright green
<CM>	Green
<CN>	Dim green
<CO>	Yellow/green/red
<CP>	Rainbow
<CQ>	Red/green 3-D
<CR>	Red/yellow 3-D
<CS>	Green/red 3-D
<CT>	Green/yellow 3-D
<CU>	Green on red
<CV>	Red on green
<CW>	Orange on green
<CX>	Lime on red
<CY>	Green on red 3-D
<CZ>	Red on green 3-D

Fonts

Table 9-2 lists the Pro-Lite's font codes. Note that these all start with the letter "S," probably because the Pro-Lite documentation also refers to these as size codes.

The font choices are pretty simple: normal, bold, italic, and bold plus italic. Any of those can be made to flash as well, for a total of 8 font codes. The bold font looks okay, but italic is a little too hard to read. The bold plus italic font displays about half as many characters on the sign as the normal font.

Table 9-2. The Pro-Lite's font codes

Code	Font
<SA>	Normal
<SB>	Bold
<SC>	Italic
<SD>	Bold italic
<SE>	Flashing normal
<SF>	Flashing bold
<SG>	Flashing italic
<SH>	Flashing bold italic

Effects

Table 9-3 lists the 26 different effects. As you use the sign more and more, you'll probably want to take advantage of these effects to break up the monotony of a simple scrolling display.

Table 9-3. The Pro-Lite's effect codes

Code	Effect
<FA>	AUTO (L)
<FB>	OPEN (L)
<FC>	COVER (L)
<FD>	DATE
<FE>	CYCLING (L)
<FF>	CLOSE LEFT (T)
<FG>	CLOSE RIGHT (T)
<FH>	CLOSE CENTER (T)
<FI>	SCROLL UP (L)
<FJ>	SCROLL DOWN (L)
<FK>	OVERLAP (L)
<FL>	STACKING (L)
<FM>	COMIC 1 (L)
<FN>	COMIC 2 (L)
<FO>	BEEP
<FP>	PAUSE (T)
<FQ>	APPEAR (L)
<FR>	RANDOM (L)
<FS>	SHIFT (L)
<FT>	TIME
<FU>	MAGIC (L)
<FV>	THANK YOU
<FW>	WELCOME
<FX>	SLOW SPEED
<FY>	NORMAL SPEED
<FZ><x>	CHAIN to page x (T)

Some of these effects are meant to be used at the beginning of a message. They affect the way that the message appears on the display. Such effects are marked with (L) in the table. For example, the OPEN effect erases the display and then causes the message to appear one column at a time from both ends leading toward the center. The COVER effect is similar, except that the display is not erased first. The AUTO effect introduces the message with a randomly chosen effect and color each time. The RANDOM effect, on the other hand, introduces the message by turning on one pixel at a time in a random order. MAGIC is similar to AUTO, except that it only affects the color.

The effects marked with (T) are meant to be used at the end of a message. They affect the way that the message disappears. For example, CLOSE LEFT erases the message one row at a time from right to left. You may find the PAUSE effect to be very useful. It freezes the display for one second. The Pro-Lite documentation says that this is a trailing effect, but you can use it in the middle of a message too.

Two effects are named DATE and TIME. These display the date and time based on the sign's internal clock. Apparently these effects use hardcoded colors that you cannot change. See the next section for the command that sets the sign's clock.

The CHAIN effect is somewhat special because it must be followed by another code representing the next page to display. For example, <FZ><C> tells the sign to display page "C" next.

Note that some of the codes have different effects in older versions of the Pro-Lite protocol. For example, Walt Stoneburner's site describes an earlier version of the sign software where DATE and TIME were together in a single effect.

Miscellaneous

Table 9-4 lists a few miscellaneous protocol commands. We use the first one (<Px>) in *rfcomm-to-sign.c* to program each page. The second one (<RPx>) instructs the sign to run (or display) the specified page immediately.

Table 9-4. Miscellaneous protocol commands

Code	Description
<Px>	Program page *x*
<RPx>	Run (display) page *x*
<TYYYYMMDDWhhmmssX>	Set the time

The code for setting the time is a little bit different than the others. Most of the commands must be preceded by a sign identifier, such as <ID01>. The time-setting command, however, must not. That means that you can't use *rfcomm-to-sign* to set the time since the program inserts the ID string before each command.

In the command string given in Table 9-4, the T represents an actual "T" (for time). All other letters must be replaced by numbers. *YYYYMMDD* represents the year, month, and day. W represents the day of the week (1–7). *hhmmss* represents the hour, minute, and seconds. X is either 0 (for AM/PM mode) or 1 (for 24-hour mode).

Make sure that the gumstix clock is set correctly before using the following commands to set the sign's clock. (We've noticed that the gumstix' clock is reset when it reboots.) Since you can't use *rfcomm-to-sign* to set the clock, you can use this trick instead:

```
# T=/dev/ttyS2
# stty -F $T speed 9600 cs8 -parenb -cstopb cread clocal \
        -crtscts -ignpar -echo nl1 cr3 opost -ocrnl onlcr
# cat $T >/dev/null &
# date '+<T%Y%m%d%u%H%M%S0>' > $T
# kill %1
```

Extra Credit

If you've followed all the steps in this chapter, you have a pretty neat Bluetooth-enabled, Linux-powered LED sign. Here are some ideas for making the project even better.

Using OBEX Transfers

We've shown you how to transfer data from a handheld device to the gumstix using Bluetooth's serial port emulation. While this seems to work okay, it is not the only option. If your phone/PDA doesn't have an application that supports the Bluetooth serial port (SP) profile, you can use the Object Exchange (OBEX) protocol instead.

OBEX is, essentially, a file transfer protocol. Bluetooth devices use OBEX to send images, vCards (i.e., address book entries), calendar data, and other types of files. OBEX was originally developed for use with infrared (IrDA) interfaces, but has been adopted by Bluetooth as well.

Your gumstix should already have everything you need to accept files via OBEX. In particular, make sure that the OBEX Push Daemon, */usr/sbin/opd*, is present. If not, you'll need to go to the gumstix buildroot environment as described in "Building Software for the gumstix," earlier in this chapter, and build a new filesystem. Make sure that openobex has been added to the TARGETS variable in the top-level *Makefile*:

```
# For Bluetooth
TARGETS+=bluez-utils openobex
```

If you changed the *Makefile*, build a new root filesystem and upload it to the gumstix flash memory. Recall that by updating the flash memory, any files that you have added or edited will be lost. If you have an MMC or SD card, you may want to make a copy of these files before updating the flash memory:

OBEX Versus SP

If you have the option to use either OBEX or SP, you may prefer to use OBEX for long or repeated messages. You can save a long message as a note or memo and then send it many times. SP mode, on the other hand, is better for usage that resembles a conversation. Once the serial port session has been established, you can quickly send multiple messages.

- */etc/default/bluetooth*
- */etc/bluetooth/hosts*
- */etc/bluetooth/hcid.conf*
- */etc/init.d/S60ttyS2*
- */etc/inittab*
- */etc/init.d/S31bluetooth*

You'll need to make an important change to */etc/bluetooth/hcid.conf*. One of the settings there is the device class. Bit #20 (0x100000 hex) in the class value should be turned on to indicate OBEX support. The default value is 0x820116, so you can change it to 0x920116:

```
# Local device class
class 0x920116;
```

Reboot or restart the Bluetooth daemons after editing *hcid.conf*. Then, after verifying that *opd* is installed, add these lines to */etc/init.d/S31bluetooth*:

```
test -d /tmp/obex || mkdir /tmp/obex
/usr/sbin/opd --mode OBEX --channel 10 --path /tmp/obex --sdp --daemon
```

Files sent to the gumstix will appear in the */tmp/obex* directory. The --sdp option instructs *opd* to automatically advertise the OBEX service via the Service Discovery Protocol. You may want to run *opd* manually a few times before running it from *S31bluetooth*. Use the same command line, but without the --daemon option.

When *opd* is running, make sure that OBEX appears in the list of Bluetooth services:

```
# sdptool browse ff:ff:ff:00:00:00
...
Service Name: OBEX Object Push
Service RecHandle: 0x10006
Service Class ID List:
  "OBEX Object Push" (0x1105)
Protocol Descriptor List:
  "L2CAP" (0x0100)
  "RFCOMM" (0x0003)
    Channel: 10
  "OBEX" (0x0008)
Profile Descriptor List:
  "OBEX Object Push" (0x1105)
    Version: 0x0100
```

Now you are ready to attempt a file transfer from your phone or PDA. If you have a PDA running PalmOS, go to the Memo Pad and create a new memo. While still viewing the memo, press the Menu button. You should see a Send Memo option. Select it and then find your gumstix in the device list. Click on OK. If everything works, you should have a new file in the */tmp/obex* directory.

Bluetooth-enabled mobile phone users may have to work a little harder to use OBEX transfer. If your phone has a way to store notes or memos, it probably also has an option to send them via Bluetooth. Otherwise, you can try sending an address book entry to the gumstix. It should show up on the other side as a vCard. If you plan to use this technique to get messages to the LED sign, you'll need to write some code to strip out the vCard tags and other formatting.

If you're having a hard time getting OBEX to work, kill the *opd* daemon process and run it from the command line. You should see output like this during a successful transfer:

```
                    obex_event: 1  6( EV_UNKNOWN)  0(   CMD_CONNECT)   0
Unknown event 6 !
                    obex_event: 1  1( EV_REQHINT)  0(   CMD_CONNECT)   0
                    obex_event: 1  2(     EV_REQ)  0(   CMD_CONNECT)   0
opd[338]: OBEX connect from 00:07:E0:00:1F:F8
                    obex_event: 1  3( EV_REQDONE)  0(   CMD_CONNECT)   0
                    obex_event: 1  1( EV_REQHINT)  2(       CMD_PUT)   0
                    obex_event: 1  0(EV_PROGRESS)  2(       CMD_PUT)   0
                    obex_event: 1  0(EV_PROGRESS)  2(       CMD_PUT)   0
                    obex_event: 1  2(     EV_REQ)  2(       CMD_PUT)   0
HEADER_LENGTH = 15
Handle_OBEX_CMD_PUT() Skipped header 05
HEADER_TYPE = 'text/plain' #11
00: 74 65 78 74 2f 70 6c 61 69 6e 00              text/plain.
Handle_OBEX_CMD_PUT() Skipped header c0
Filename = /tmp/obex/memo via.txt
Wrote /tmp/obex/memo via.txt (15 bytes)
                    obex_event: 1  3( EV_REQDONE)  2(       CMD_PUT)   0
                    obex_event: 1  1( EV_REQHINT)  1(CMD_DISCONNECT)   0
                    obex_event: 1  2(     EV_REQ)  1(CMD_DISCONNECT)   0
opd[338]: OBEX disconnect from 00:07:E0:00:1F:F8
                    obex_event: 1  3( EV_REQDONE)  1(CMD_DISCONNECT)   0
                    obex_event: 1  4( EV_LINKERR)  0(   CMD_CONNECT)   0
opd[338]: lost link to 00:07:E0:00:1F:F8
```

Once OBEX is working to the point where files appear in the */tmp/obex* directory, you'll need to write some scripts that send the message to the sign. The following shell script should help get you started:

```
#!/bin/sh
# scan-obex.sh: periodically scan the OBEX dropoff
# directory and send incoming messages to the sign

cd /tmp/obex
test -d /tmp/trash || mkdir /tmp/trash
```

```
while true ; do
        sleep 1
        for k in * ; do
                test "$k" = "*" && continue
                echo "found file: $k"
                msg=`cat "$k"  | tr '\r' ' ' | tr '\n' ' '`
                msg=`echo $msg`
                echo "sending message: $msg"
                /usr/local/bin/to-sign.sh A $msg
                mv "$k" /tmp/trash

                sleep 30
        done
done
```

Note that the *to-obex.sh* script assumes that files might contain whitespace characters. It also changes newlines and carriage returns in the message to spaces. It calls another script, named *to-sign.sh*, to actually send the message to the sign:

```
#!/bin/sh
# to-sign.sh: write a message to the LED sign tty

T=/dev/ttyS2
PAGE=$1; shift
MSG="$*"

stty -F $T speed 9600 cs8 -parenb -cstopb -cread clocal crtscts \
        -ignpar -echo nl1 cr3
stty -F $T  opost -ocrnl onlcr
cat $T >/dev/null &
echo "<ID01>" >$T
echo "<ID01><P${PAGE}>        $MSG<FP>" >$T
echo '<ID01><RP${PAGE}>' >$T
```

Remove Special Characters from Received Messages

Most of the Pro-Lite control codes do useful things like change colors and add special effects. However, it probably won't take a really curious person very long to find a number of ways to hack the sign. For example, a simple command can delete all pages from memory.

To protect against this, you may have to block certain Pro-Lite commands. You could just block all commands by disallowing the < and > characters, for example. But that seems like overkill since many of the commands are useful.

Filtering Offensive Messages

If you plan to use the sign in a public setting where anyone can post a message, you can be sure that someone will write an offensive message just to see if they can. You may be forced to add some filtering to the code. For example, a simple method for detecting profanity is to compare words in messages with those in a "bad words" file.

One Less Power Supply

It would be nice to have only one power cord running from the wall to the sign. The Pro-Lite uses a 9V power supply, while the gumstix uses 5V. With a handful of parts and a little soldering, you should be able to build a gizmo that takes 9V from the sign's supply and provides 5V to the gumstix. It might be as simple as an LM7805 voltage regulator plus a heat sink.

Prepending the Device Name to Messages

If you use the sign in a public setting, it may be nice to automatically insert the Bluetooth device name into every message. This adds some accountability and makes the message display similar to a chat room.

Each time *rfcomm-to-sign* gets a new RFCOMM connection it can run `rfcomm show` to get the address of the device connected on its channel. Then it can run `hcitool name x:x:x:x:x:x` to get the connected device's name.

If prepending device names is too awkward, you may want to at least consider giving each page a different color. At the very least this allows viewers to tell when one message ends and another begins. Of course, if messages include color codes, such as <CB>, the sender can override the default color for a page, anyway.

Aging Messages from the Sign

Depending on your particular use of the sign, it may make sense to put a time limit on how long a particular message will be displayed. The sign doesn't have any built-in features to support this, so you'll need to implement it in software on the gumstix.

One approach is to modify *rfcomm-to-sign* so that it keeps track of how long it has been trying to open the RFCOMM device. After some amount of time, say 10 minutes, it can send a message to the sign to erase the corresponding page. If you are using the page-chaining technique, you don't want to actually erase the page, but instead send an empty message followed by an instruction to jump to the appropriate page.

A Bluetooth device cannot be connected to more than seven other devices at once. However, each device can use multiple RFCOMM channels and some devices may be disconnected when idle.

Scaling the Software

Our design has a one-to-one mapping of RFCOMM channels to sign pages. Although our examples use only five channels and pages, you could easily extend this to all 26 of the Pro-Lite's pages.

The drawback is that each page requires two processes running from */etc/ inittab*: the `rfcomm listen` process, and *rfcomm-to-sign*. At some point this may become a significant burden for the lil' gumstix.

One way to reduce the number of processes is by modifying *rfcomm-to-sign* so that a single process manages all channels and pages. This makes the program more complicated since it will need to use nonblocking I/O and `select()`. On the upside, however, a single process makes certain sign-related tasks easier. For example, you can chain pages together based on the number of active messages or change the order in which they are displayed.

With a single *rfcomm-to-sign* process, you can also do away with the one-channel-per-page limitation. Instead, messages might be displayed in the order they are received, regardless of who sends them.

You can, in theory, have up to 60 RFCOMM channels. However, since each channel requires a separate `rfcomm listen` process, this may not be realistic. If you really need that many, you'll probably want have a look at the *rfcomm* source code and see if you can write a new program that manages multiple listeners, or perhaps build it directly into a program like *rfcomm-to-sign*.

Running an NFS Server

A couple of the projects in this book utilize a Network File System (NFS) server. This appendix provides basic instructions for setting up an NFS server on an existing Linux or FreeBSD box.

About NFS

NFS is, as the name implies, a protocol for accessing remote filesystems over a network. The NFS server *exports* one or more filesystems. NFS clients *mount* exported filesystems and then access their files normally.

If you have an existing Linux or BSD box, you should be able to turn it into an NFS server without much trouble. NFS features must be enabled in your kernel, and usually are by default. If you've disabled NFS in your kernel, you'll need to either load a kernel module or build a new kernel. In addition, a properly configured NFS server has a number of daemon processes, including *nfsd* (or *rpc.nfsd*), *mountd* (or *rpc.mountd*), *portmap rpc.statd*, and *rpc.lockd*. NFS clients do not require any daemon processes.

The Exports File

The */etc/exports* file lists filesystems that are to be exported (i.e., made available) via NFS. The file format is a little bit complicated, but the basic format is:

```
/filesystem [-options] [addrs]
```

Each line specifies a *filesystem* that should be exported with certain *options*. If *addrs* is given, then only those clients are allowed to mount the *filesystem*.

Here is one of the simplest *exports* files possible:

```
/usr
```

That file makes the */usr* directory available to everyone that can reach your NFS server. You might be able to get by with something that simple. In some cases, however, you'll need an option or two. Here are a few useful options:

-ro

> Specifies that the directory should be read-only. Unless you add the -ro option, NFS clients are allowed to write to the exported directory, subject to standard Unix permissions of course.

-maproot=root

> By default, remote access from the *root* user is treated as though the remote userid is *nobody*. This prevents abuse by remote superusers, but can be annoying when you are doing useful work as *root*. Add the option -maproot=root to allow *root* to read and write files with full root privileges. This gives total control to anyone with root privileges on a remote machine, so try to avoid using this option if you can.

-alldirs

> By default, NFS clients must mount the same directory that is exported. For example, if the server exports */usr*, the client cannot mount */usr/ local*. To remove this restriction, use the -alldirs option.

Starting NFS Services

What follows are basic instructions for starting NFS without rebooting your system. Unless you are already using NFS for another reason, we do not recommend that you permanently enable NFS. Instead, start and stop it as necessary to reduce your exposure to potential security issues.

Linux

First, you'll need to make sure that the *nfs-utils* package is installed on your system. RedHat users and other RPM-enabled systems should locate a recent *nfs-utils* RPM and install it. For Debian Linux:

```
# apt-get install nfs-kernel-server
```

For Gentoo Linux:

```
# emerge nfs-utils
```

Once *nfs-utils* is installed, you should be able to start the NFS daemon processes by running these two *init.d* scripts:

```
# /etc/init.d/portmap start
# /etc/init.d/nfs start
```

You may want to refer to the Linux NFS-HOWTO, which can be found at **http://nfs.sourceforge.net/nfs-howto/**.

FreeBSD

On FreeBSD you can start all of the NFS-related services with this simple command:

```
# /etc/rc.d/nfsd onestart
```

Note that by using *onestart*, you can start the services without enabling them in */etc/rc.conf*.

showmount

After starting the NFS server processes, test your exports file with this command:

```
# showmount -e
Exports list on localhost:
/usr                               Everyone
```

If you don't see any filesystems exported, check the format of the */etc/exports* file and try again. Don't forget to restart the server after modifying the file. On most systems you can also just send a HUP signal to the *mountd* process.

Mounting

An NFS client mounts the remote filesystem with the mount command. The remote filesystem is specified as an IP address, followed by colon, and then the remote directory. For example:

```
# mount 172.16.1.1:/usr /mnt
```

Small Form Factor PCs

Four hot new DIY books from the makers behind MAKE and Maker Faire!

Eccentric Cubicle

Who says cubicles need to be dreary? Eccentric Genius creator Kaden Harris introduces a highly entertaining parallel universe of surreal office-based projects — from desktop guillotines and crossbows to mood-enhancing effects and music makers — that are sure to pique the curiosity of even your most jaded office comrades.

$29.99

Making Things Talk

New open-source platforms with simple I/O boards and development environments translate to affordable options for makers on a budget. This book is packed with projects that show what you need to know and do to get your creations talking to each other, connecting to the web, and forming networks of smart devices.

$29.99

The Best of Make

MAKE has become one of the most celebrated new magazines to hit the newsstands If you're just catching on to the MAKE phenomenon and wonder what you've missed, this book contains the best DIY projects from the magazine's first ten volumes — a sure-fire collection of fun and challenging activities.

Find out why MAKE has attracted a passionate following of tech and DIY enthusiasts worldwide. With The Best of MAKE, you'll share the curiosity, zeal, and energy of Makers — the citizen scientists, circuit benders, homemakers, students, automotive enthusiasts, roboticists, software developers, musicians, hackers, hobbyists, and crafters — through this unique and inspiring assortment of DIY projects chosen by the magazine's editors.

$34.99

Put together by popular demand, The Best of MAKE is the perfect gift for any maker. Do you or someone you know have a passion for the magic of tinkering, hacking, and creation? Do you enjoy finding imaginative and unexpected uses for the technology and materials in your life? Then get on board with The Best of MAKE.

Illustrated Guide to Astronomical Wonders

Authors Robert Bruce Thompson and Barbara Fritchman Thompson show how serious astronomy is now within the grasp of anyone. An indispensable guide to the equipment you need and how and where to find hundreds of spectacular objects in the deep sky — double and multiple stars as well as spectacular star clusters, nebulae, and galaxies.

$29.99

Spend more than $40 on books
and get 40% off!
Order today in the Maker Store:
store.makezine.com

Enter Promo Code SFF40
Offer good for MAKE and HACKS book purchases at Maker Store

Make: Books

Make:
technology on your time

"The kind of magazine that would impress MacGyver."
—*San Francisco Chronicle*

In the pages of MAKE magazine, we'll teach you how to:

- Snap your own aerial pictures using a kite built from Popsicle sticks, a disposable camera, and a timer made of Silly Putty

- Design your own board game

- Make a two-cylinder Stirling Engine with aluminum cans

- Zoom from tree to tree on a backyard zip line

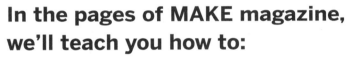

» You'll learn all this and more when you subscribe today at makezine.com/subscribe

» Or share MAKE with others — give a gift at makezine.com/gift

» Get one issue FREE with promo code T8SFF

If you can imagine it, you can MAKE it. » makezine.com